DATE DUE

man's glassy essence

ADVANCES IN SEMIOTICS

General Editor, Thomas A. Sebeok

man's glassy essence

Explorations in Semiotic Anthropology

MILTON SINGER

> . . . man, proud man,
> Drest in a little brief authority,
> Most ignorant of what he's most assur'd,
> His glassy essence, like an angry ape,
> Plays such fantastic tricks before high heaven
> As make the angels weep.
>
> —Shakespeare,
> Measure for Measure
> Act II, Scene 2

INDIANA UNIVERSITY PRESS • BLOOMINGTON

Manufactured in the United States of America

Library of Congress Cataloging in Publication Data

Singer, Milton B.
Man's glassy essence.

(Advances in semiotics)
Bibliography: p.
Includes index.
1. Ethnology—Philosophy.   2. Symbolism.
3. Semiotics.   I. Title.   II. Series.
GN452.5.S56   1984   306'.01   83-48108
ISBN 0-253-33675-9
1 2 3 4 5 88 87 86 85 84

contents

PREFACE

In 1962 at a conference on kinesics, proxemics, and paralinguistics at Indiana University, Margaret Mead suggested that the term "semiotics" be adopted to designate the study of "patterned communication in all modalities" (Sebeok et al. 1964). Judging from the number of books and articles that have since been published on the "semiotics of"—architecture, the circus, literature, music, painting—her suggestion met a widely felt need for naming a new field of research. "Semiotics," however, had to compete with another term, "semiology," which had been proposed by Saussure as a new science to study "the life of signs at the heart of social life," and suggested by Lévi-Strauss in 1960 as a proper field of study for anthropology, at least that part of it not already preempted by linguistics.

Until quite recently "semiotics" and "semiology" have been used almost interchangeably to designate the study of signs (see Random House Dictionary, 1979). Since the two terms, however, derive from different intellectual and practical traditions, and in their modern form are associated with different theories of signs—for example, Peirce's *semiotic* and Saussure's *semiologie*—it is useful to compare and contrast the two theories from the perspective of problems of meaning and communication within social and cultural anthropology (Jakobson 1975; Sebeok 1976; Singer 1978; Boon 1979). The subtitle of this book reflects a decision to apply Peirce's theory of signs, *semiotic*, to anthropology. The anthropological value of that decision will need to be judged by its fruits in the chapters that follow. The story of how I came to opt for Peirce over Saussure may illuminate the nature of the options and the consequences for a semiotic anthropology. This preface sketches the biographical events that led to the "semiotics" commitment and to the writing of each chapter. The introduction describes the decision as a dialogical response to some of the controversies generated by Lévi-Strauss's structural and semiological anthropology, especially in the 1960s and 1970s.

In 1968, when the *nouvelle vague* in anthropology from France was still running strong, I described in a departmental memorandum on research and teaching plans my intention to devote time to the new field of "Philosophical Anthropology":

During the next decade, 1968–1978, I plan to continue my research and teaching interests in India and the comparative study of civilizations. However, I shall devote more time to the field of "philosophical anthropology," by which I mean the description and analysis of the value systems and belief systems of particular cultures, of changes in these systems, and of their relations to social structure, environment, and personality. This is a newly emerging field in anthropology and has recently attracted wide interest because of the work of Claude Lévi-Strauss in the structural analysis of myths and the application of the linguistic methods of componential analysis to folk classifications of kin, colors, diseases, plants and animals, and to other domains of culture.

Neither the name, subject matter, methods, nor theory of this field has yet been fixed, although its rapid development is being fed by linguistics, philosophy, psychology, and comparative religion, as well as by the more established branches of anthropology. In my own work, I intend to draw on my specialized training in symbolic logic, the philosophy of science, and social psychology for help with the formulation of a general theory of cultural symbol systems.

How "philosophical anthropology" became "semiotic anthropology" and led to the writing of *Man's Glassy Essence* will now be briefly described.

After joining with Fred Eggan and other colleagues (including Firth, Srinivas, and Fortes) in a series of seminars (1969–73) to review the history of Radcliffe-Brown's career in different countries, I wrote in 1973 the original draft of "A Neglected Source of Structuralism: Radcliffe-Brown, Russell and Whitehead." Because of the controversy aroused by this paper and because my views have not essentially changed since, I have published the original version together with a postscript written in 1982, which describes some of the historical documentation, chiefly the testimony of Radcliffe-Brown's students and colleagues, for the argument that Russell and Whitehead were significant sources for Radcliffe-Brown's structuralism and philosophy of science, and probably indirect sources for Lévi-Strauss as well (Singer 1984).

The research, writing, and discussion of "A Neglected Source of Structuralism" convinced me that both French structuralism and British structural functionalism lacked an adequate theory of symbolism. It also convinced me that Peirce seemed to offer the most comprehensive and profound theory of signs *(semiotic)* capable of dealing with the relations of signs to subjects and objects in social and cultural contexts without the need to add, or to subtract, *ad hoc* epistemological and ontological assumptions in order to validate the "reality," social and psychological, of cultural symbol systems.

A seminar I planned for the autumn of 1973 was called "Structuralism and Semiotics." The appropriate contrast, I realized by 1974, was not

"Structuralism and Semiotics" but "Semiology and Semiotics," a contrast between Saussure's and Peirce's general theory of signs. In deference to Peirce's strictures on the "ethics of terminology," I changed the name of the new research field in 1974 to "semiotic anthropology" and dropped the designation "philosophical anthropology," since the ambiguity of the latter generated confusion with an older field in philosophy so named.

In 1974 and 1975 my course in culture theory organized the syllabus of readings and topics in terms of a contrast between Peircean and Saussurean approaches to a theory of signs, and I presented an ideal-typical analysis of the contrast and its implications for some of the problems of meaning and communication in anthropology.

In 1976 I restated this analysis in a public lecture at Thomas Sebeok's Research Center for Language and Semiotic Studies in Bloomington, Indiana. The lecture was originally titled "Culture Theory Tilts to Semiotics," but after its cordial reception from the Sebeoks and other colleagues and students, I was emboldened to call it "For a Semiotic Anthropology" (Umiker-Sebeok 1977; Singer 1978; chap. 2).

The Bloomington lecture and visit marked an important turning point in my "tilt to semiotics." In addition to speaking publicly on "semiotic anthropology" to a sympathetic audience of leading scholars in the field of semiotic research, I also had an opportunity to discuss with Indiana University Press arrangements for publishing a book to be called *Man's Glassy Essence: Explorations in Semiotic Anthropology*. A stop at the Peirce Edition Project at Indiana University–Purdue University in Indianapolis gave me the pleasure of meeting its chief editor, Max Fisch, as well as some of his coeditors, and the opportunity to inspect the vast corpus of Peirce manuscripts from which the new critical edition was being compiled.

An invitation from the American Anthropological Association to deliver their 1978 Distinguished Lecture in Los Angeles created the public occasion on which to introduce "semiotic anthropology" and Peirce to a professional audience of anthropologists. I used the occasion to show how the idea of a phenomenological self sometimes recommended to anthropology by Redfield, Hallowell, Opler, and Geertz, among others, could be constructed from Peirce's fragmentary suggestions for a semiotics of the self (Singer 1980; chap. 3).

At a 1979 conference on "New Approaches to the Self" sponsored by the Center for Psychosocial Studies in Chicago and organized by Benjamin Lee, I presented a sequel to the chapter on "Signs of the Self," in which I argued that Peirce's semiotic and phenomenological conception of the self could be separated from his physiological and physical theories. That paper traced the social and pragmatic character of a semiotic self from Peirce to Royce, James, Baldwin, Cooley, Mead, Redfield, Geertz, and Warner in a continuing semiotic tradition of symbolic interactionism, locating personal and social identity in the use of personal pronouns in dialogue (Singer 1982; chap. 4).

Applications of semiotic anthropology to some ethnographic materials and observations are illustrated in chapters 5 and 6, "Emblems of Identity" and "On the Semiotics of Indian Identity." The "Emblems" chapter was first presented in a shorter version in the 1980 series of annual lectures in honor of Harry Hoijer, organized by Professor Jacques Maquet and the Department of Anthropology at the University of California at Los Angeles (Singer 1982a). The idea for the chapter grew out of revisits to and observations in Lloyd Warner's "Yankee City," which began in 1974. I was pleasantly surprised to find that Warner's neglected monograph, *The Living and the Dead, a Study of the Symbolic Life of Americans,* included not only a study of "cultural performances" (Memorial Day and Tercentenary celebrations) similar to my Madras studies, but also a theory of symbolism that was genuinely semiotic.

Warner's training under Lowie and Kroeber in Berkeley, his fieldwork in Australia under Radcliffe-Brown's supervision, and his teaching career at Harvard and Chicago no doubt account for his publishing a pioneer monograph in semiotic anthroplogy as early as 1959. But his brilliant idea of reversing Durkheim's emblem analogy for Australian aboriginal totemism ("the totem is the flag of the clan" to "the flag is the totem of Yankee City") generated an analysis of emblems as symbol systems that needs only Peirce's semiotics of indexicality to give "Yankee City"'s emblems a local habitation, a name, and an identity.

Recognition of how Warner successfully combined a theory of identity emblems with the description of cultural performances in "Yankee City" suggested a semiotic approach to the problem of Indian identity, which I had previously tried to interpret as a purely cultural construction. Peirce's semiotic and social theory of the self offered a method for interpreting my observations on Indian identity, at least that of Sanskritized Indians, in terms of an idealized Indian self expressed and observed in action *(karma),* feeling *(bhakti),* and thought *(jnana)* (Singer 1981; chap. 6). The "Semiotics of Indian Identity" also reveals some unexpected similarities to the semiotics of American identity and a method for comparing the world views and cosmologies of India and the United States in their true inwardness.

If this preface gives the impression that semiotic anthropology developed inexorably from a blueprint drawn in 1968, that is an illusion. There was no detailed blueprint; there was much improvisation, and there were all sorts of happenings and conversations with colleagues to stimulate specific directions of exploration. If I have emphasized some of the continuities in a developing field, that was perhaps more to sketch the semiotic reconstruction of an idealized history than to give a realistic description of how a new field develops. Redfield's conclusion to his 1956 Huxley Lecture about the future of anthropology as a study of natural social and cultural systems applies as well to these explorations in semiotic anthropology: "We do not enact a science. It grows. If one declares that anthropology is to be done in such and such a way, then soon thereafter it will be done differently, yet not entirely differently, for if the first conception of method is rigorous and relevant to fact, the later development will grow out of it" (Redfield 1962:139).

ACKNOWLEDGMENTS

Except for the introductory chapter, which was the last to be written, the order of the chapters follows the order in which they were originally drafted. The special occasions for which they were written are described in the preface. To the indidivuals and institutions who provided the opportunities for public lectures and their publication I am deeply grateful. For support of the research and travel on which the book is based, a general acknowledgment must also be made to the National Institutes of Mental Health, Small Grants Section, 1977, Division of Extramural Research Programs; to the Rockefeller Foundation for a Humanities Fellowship in 1978–79; and to the Lichtstern Research Fund of the Department of Anthropology at the University of Chicago. Kathryn Barnes, administrative assistant in the department, and her staff promptly and cheerfully took responsibility for the typing and reproduction of the manuscript.

I would also like to acknowledge a more specific debt of gratitude to a collegial circle of readers who took an active interest in the book from its inception, gave the project personal support, and, not least, read and commented on the first drafts of chapters and, sometimes, on second and third drafts as well. This circle included Fred Eggan, Max Fisch, Paul Friedrich, Clifford Geertz, David Mandelbaum, Thomas A. Sebeok, Michael Silverstein, Melford Spiro, and M. N. Srinivas. My wife, Helen, also merits special thanks for time, attention, and insights given, as with previous work.

The valuable help of a wider circle of readers who have read and commented on a single chapter has been specifically acknowledged in previously published portions of the chapters.

I have tried to take some account of readers' comments, including those comments that came in after the abbreviated versions of chapters were published. I would particularly note those of A. Aiyappan, Dilip Basu, James Boon, S. Chandrasekhar, Edward Dimock, Edwin Gerow, Elizabeth Jacoby, Bimal Matilal, Loki Pandey, Frits Staal, Manly Thompson, Hervé Varenne, Bernard Weissbourd, A. Wiercinski, Aram Yengoyan, and Victor Yngve.

Chapter 6 is dedicated to the memory of my Sanskritist colleague J. A. B. van Buitenen. Beyond specific acknowledgments to his writings, I should like to record my sense of gratitude to him for the liberating vision he had of Sanskrit as a window on a living culture and civilization. His generous contributions in books, translations, lectures, and personal discussion to the cooperative program in Southern Asian Studies at the University of Chicago brought his grand vision home to us in speech and prose that was as down-to-earth and commonsensical as it was profound in scholarship. His monumental project to translate all of the *Mahabharata* remains unfinished, but he finished enough of it to convince us that it is a great epic and, as he liked to say, an encyclopedia of Indian civilization.

I would like to think that the semiotics of Indian identity offers an approach to the comparative study of world views that would have pleased both Robert Redfield, who first sent me to India for his project on intercultural understanding, and the late Dr. V. Raghavan, illustrious Sanskritist and my cultural guide on our first visit to Madras. That neither lived to discuss and explore this approach to our shared goal is a matter of deep regret.

Permission to include previously published and abbreviated versions of chapters in this book has been kindly granted by Indiana University Press for "For a Semiotic Anthropology," in Thomas A. Sebeok, ed., *Sight, Sound and Sense*, 1978; American Anthropological Association for "Signs of the Self," in *American Anthropologist* 82: 485–507, 1980; Plenum Publishers for "Personal and Social Identity in Dialogue," in Benjamin Lee, ed., *Psychosocial Theories of the Self*, 1982; and Schenkman Publishers for "On the Semiotics of Indian Identity," in the *American Journal of Semiotics* I:85–126, 1981, edited by Thomas and Irene Winner.

The appearance of this book in Indiana University Press's series on Advances in Semiotics is due to the imaginative initiative of its editor, Thomas Sebeok.

In transliterating Sanskrit words without the use of diacritics, I have followed the practice of Dr. V. Raghavan, in his UNESCO *Anthology of Sanskrit Literature* (Raghavan 1956).

Douglas Goodfriend helped me during the summer of 1977 to record interviews and take photographs described in chapter 5. I am grateful to Bette-Jane Crigger for preparing the index.

man's glassy essence

1

Introduction: Search for a Theory of Cultural Symbolism

THE SEMIOTICS OF IDENTITY

Scholars do not all agree in their interpretation of Isabella's speech about man's "glassy essence" in *Measure for Measure*. Some have suggested that "glassy" usually means "brittle" in Shakespeare, although it is difficult in this particular context to interpret a "brittle essence." A more common suggestion is that "glassy" means "mirrorlike" or "reflecting," and a philosopher has recently discussed this interpretation of Shakespeare's lines around the notion that man is a mirror of nature (Rorty 1979; Grabes 1975).

It would take a thorough study of Shakespeare's references to man's essence to decide which of the several suggested readings of "glassy" is most Shakespearean. And not only his references to man's essence in general but also the references to the nature of different kinds of men—in the speeches of Shylock, Othello and Iago, Richard III, King Lear, Prospero and Caliban. Isabella's plea to Angelo for mercy has obvious parallels to Portia's plea in *The Merchant of Venice*. Perhaps that is as good a starting point as any for an inquiry into Shakespeare's references to man's "glassy essence"—the quality of mercy.

In this book, however, I am not so much interested in what Isabella or Shakespeare meant by "man's glassy essence" as in what Peirce meant by it. He quotes the two lines "most ignorant of what he's most assur'd, his glassy essence" several times in his writings, especially in contexts where he discusses the nature of man. One of the earliest and most explicit of these contexts is his Lowell Lecture XI of 1866, in which he gives a short general answer to the question "What is man?": "He is a symbol" (Peirce 1982:494).[1]

Although Peirce was an amateur Shakespeare scholar, I do not think he intended his short answer that man is a symbol to imply that the essence of man was to be a mirror or that it was brittle. To develop fully the implications of Peirce's short answer would require a careful analysis of his theory of signs and symbols, in the Lowell Lectures as in his later writings, a task beyond the scope of the present book and best left to Peirce specialists. Peirce's semiotic conception of human nature, however, does have important implications for modern anthropological theory, and it is some of these that the following chapters explore.

If we suppose, at least as a hypothesis, that man is essentially a symbol, what follows for a theory of culture, society, human nature, personality, and the self? The answer depends not only on the logical consequences of Peirce's definitions of "symbol" and "semiotic" but also on the empirical character of the problems in these domains to which the definitions are thought to be relevant. Peirce's dictum, "my language is the sum total of my self," for example, is an intriguing suggestion, but how does one go about trying to verify it empirically? It is, moreover, the kind of generalization that might be interpreted to apply to a particular individual, a family, a social class, an occupational group, a nation, and other kinds of groups. Peirce was quite aware of the systematic ambiguity of such concepts as *identity* and *self-identity*, and in his discussions of them not only recognized the need for explicit empirical differentiations but appealed as well to available empirical observations made by himself and other observers. A number of his empirical examples are described in the following chapters, especially in chapters 2 and 3. One example, not mentioned in these chapters, is that of "a child who uses three words only, *name, story, matter*. He says *name* when he wishes to know the name of a person or thing; *story* when he wishes to hear a narrative or description; and *matter* . . . when he wishes to be acquainted with the cause of anything" (Peirce 1982:501). Peirce comments that it is "a wonderful thing that the child's individuality should have been shown so strongly, at that age, in selecting these three words out of all the equally common ones which he had heard about him. Already he has made his list of categories, which is the principal part of any philosophy" (ibid.).

Presumably, Peirce is citing the sayings of a three-year-old quoted in *Harper's* magazine. He also speculates on how the one three-year-old whose speech concentrates on the words *name, story*, and *matter* develops a "philosophy": "Constantly, in using these words, this philosophy becomes more and more impressed upon him until, when he arrives at maturity of intellect, he may be able to show that it is a profound and legitimate classification. Tell me a man's *name*, his *story*, and his *matter* or character; and I know all there is to know of him" (ibid.:502–503).

One wonders, after Peirce points out that the child's philosophy "furnishes an emendation upon the mighty Aristotle" (by adding the *name* to Aristotle's the *what* [the story] and the *why* [the cause]) whether it is Peirce's own mental development that is being described as well as that of a child about whom he read in *Harper's* magazine. In any case, since it is the idiosyncratic aspect of the child's character and philosophy that is being described, it follows that the child's "language" and self differ from the "languages" and selves of other children in his family, class, nation, and world. Peirce left no doubt, however, that he intended his equation of "language" and "self" to apply to the wider social groupings. And he occasionally suggested linguistic characterizations of them, as in his 1863 characterization of his own era in the United States as "idistical" (ibid.:113).

To say, therefore, that man's glassy essence consists in his being a symbol implies more than that he is a window that frames a vision of the world or a mirror that reflects the cosmos. It implies, in addition, that the distinctive core of human personality is to function as a symbol—to denote objects, to signify properties and relations of objects, and to create and interpret signs in conversations with oneself and with others. For Peirce, this "core" or "seed" of personality expresses a "philosophy—a way of regarding things; not a philosophy of the head alone—but one which pervades the whole man" (Peirce 1982:501).

In this sense, each self has a distinctive and "outreaching identity," an "essence and a meaning subtile as may be" that is "the true and exact expression of the fact of sympathy, fellow-feeling—together with all unselfish interests,—and all that makes us feel that he has an absolute worth" (ibid.:498).

Peirce's semiotic conception of the self and personality as an "outreaching identity" and of human nature as a "glassy essence" of feelings, efforts, and cognitions underlies the following effort to develop a semiotic anthropology. American pragmatism's historical development of a theory of self-identity as formed from, constituted by, and expressive of conversation, a conversation of gestures, games, and play, as well as of pronouns and other words, is traced to Peirce's semiotic conceptions in "Personal and Social Identity in Dialogue." The modern anthropological extension of this theory to a "conversation of cultures" and a "dialogue of civilization" by Boas, Sapir, Redfield, Warner, Friedrich, Silverstein, and Geertz, among others, brings the pragmatic and symbolic interactionist approach to the problem of national and international identities.

That an American identity can be symbolically and historically traced in the emblems, words, and cultural performances of a small New England city was first demonstrated in Warner's "Yankee City" study. The updating of that study in chapter 5 not only confirms the continued viability of Warner's pioneer semiotic approach but also suggests how a "Yankee" identity has been changing as "ethnics" and "newcomers" become "old-timers" after two generations of local residence and are invited to participate in the restoration and reenactment of the old emblems of identity.

The semiotics of Indian identity may be far more complex a problem than the semiotics of American identity because India has a far older civilization; a greater diversity of languages, religions, castes, and ethnic groups; and a population almost four times greater than that of the United States. Yet the problem is a manageable one for study and reflection, as Nehru has shown in his book *The Discovery of India.* There are, moreover, some unexpected parallels between Indian identity and American identity, for example, in the conception of human nature as consisting of feelings, actions, and knowledge, and in the theory of signs and symbols itself. These parallels raise the question whether, in spite of the differences in national emblems and words, and of all the other differences, American conceptions of national and personal identity have been influenced by Indian thought. That is a possibility which Peirce himself raises and considers plausible for the sources of New England transcendentalism and of his own philosophy. It is, in any case, a possibility congenial to a dialogue of civilizations for which the ancient Upanishadic words "you are *that*" *(tat tvam asi)* are still relevant, especially if these words are interpreted, as Nehru interprets them, as an expression of a "metaphysical democracy" that finds the self in everything and everything in the self.

SEMIOTICS AND SEMIOLOGY

The brief historical sketch in chapter 2 of how the earlier global notions of culture and society were transformed by the 1950s into concepts of complementary cultural systems and social systems not only helps account for the emerging efforts of anthropologists in the 1960s and 1970s to analyze cultures as symbolic systems; it is also intended to clarify some of the options in theories of symbolism that had crystallized by the mid-1970s. The comparison and contrast between Saussurean *semiology* and the Peircean *semiotics* in chapter 2 is intended as an ideal-typical construction of prominent trends in the interpretation of these two theories of signs, not a detailed description of Saussure's and Peirce's respective historical theories or the theories of particular followers. The construction can be used to interpret past developments as well as to guide future ones.

It is, of course, possible to construct a Saussure/Peirce dictionary that reduces the apparent differences between them and yet to find other differences that provide significant diacritics for distinguishing Lévi-Strauss's structuralism from Geertz's pragmatism (Boon 1979, 1983). The differences between Lévi-Strauss and Geertz show a family resemblance to those between Lévi-Strauss and Radcliffe-Brown, or between Lévi-Strauss and Malinowski, or between Lévi-Strauss and Victor Turner, or between Dumont and Srinivas.

The family resemblance that runs through these differences seems to me to be of the sort that can be interpreted by the Saussure-Peirce contrast, namely, that between a dyadic sign-relation, in which sound images (the signifiers) acquire their "meanings" or "concepts" (the signified) from a conventionalized linguistic code *(langue)*, and a triadic sign-relation, in which the sign denotes an object, signifies a property or relation of that object, and interprets another sign in an endless interchange between utterers and interpreters of the signs. The Peircean sign-relation includes as one constituent conventional associations of linguistic signs with concepts, but it also includes as essential constituents iconic signs, which resemble their objects, indexical signs, which name or point to their objects, and a community of interpreters, which establishes and continues to maintain and develop a particular system of signs and interpretations.

Saussure did not deny the existence of names, objects, or "natural" signs or "symbols." He insisted that "the linguistic sign does not unite a name and a thing but a concept and a sound image" (1966:65–66) and that "natural data have no place in linguistics" (ibid:80). The problem of how linguistic signs are related to natural objects, social institutions, national culture, geography, race, etc., belongs to "external linguistics." "My definition of language presupposes the exclusion of everything that is outside its organism or system—in a word, of everything known as 'external linguistics'" (ibid.:20–23).

The point at which Saussure excludes from his definition of language as a system, and from his definition of a linguistic sign, the relations of language to natural objects, social institutions, culture, geography, and the rest is precisely where the Peircean semiotics differs—by including the relations of signs to objects, people, and social institutions *within* the definition of signs and symbol systems. In Saussure's definition of "semiology," there is a broader conception of signs more closely approximating Peirce's semiotics, but it was Saussure's specific definition of the linguistic sign and of the *internal* system that became influential in linguistics and anthropology.

The contrast between a Saussurean theory of signs, or *semiology*, and a Peircean theory of signs, or *semiotics*, it has been suggested, presents two different directions for the study of symbols in anthropology. A popular general characterization of the contrasting directions describes the Saussurean option as structuralist, cognitive, and humanistic, and the Peircean option as functionalist, utilitarian, and naturalist. A first approximation, this characterization turns out to be inaccurate. A more accurate general characterization, at least as a preliminary hypothesis, would be to describe the *semiological* anthropologist as interested in the description and analysis of cultural symbol systems—totemism, myths, rituals, ceremonies, kinship terms—as cognitive systems, abstracted from their ethnographic context of social relations and individual action and feeling. The *semiotic* anthropologist, on the other hand, may be interested in the study of the same symbol systems but would like to anchor that study in an ethnographic context of interpersonal relations and individual emotions and activity. Whether this kind of contrast in anthropological approaches represents a mutually exclusive binary opposition or a complementarity of approaches that can be consolidated in a unified conceptual synthesis is a question that will be answered after we briefly consider the relations of structuralism to functionalism and symbolism in the theoretical orientations of some French, British, Indian, and American social and cultural anthropologists.

STRUCTURALISM AND SYMBOLISM

Followers and critics of Lévi-Strauss sometimes speak as if his structural anthropology included a comprehensive theory of all symbolic phenomena. The relationship between structuralism and symbolism is more opaque than such a claim implies. Boon's interesting study *From Symbolism to Structuralism: Lévi-Strauss in a Literary Tradition* (1972) is persuasive on the close affinity between structuralism and the symbolism of such writers as Mallarmé, Baudelaire, Rimbaud, and Proust. The demonstration of the affinity, however, depends on Boon's finding that the symbolists' "correspondences" were also structuralist à la Lévi-Strauss, and not on his discovery of the converse, that structuralism is a form of symbolism. This is perhaps a primary sense in which structuralism includes a theory of symbolism—namely that structural concepts and methods can be applied to an analysis of symbolic phenomena—totemism, myths, ritual, and the like (for example, Leach 1967). Otherwise, there is nothing intrinsically symbolical about structural anthropology. Lévi-Strauss himself seems to have recognized this, for when he explicitly refers to a general theory of signs, he cites Saussure's "semiology," Peirce's definition of "sign," or the everyday sense of "translating meanings" from one language to another (Lévi-Strauss 1976: 9–11).

Lévi-Strauss gives a semiotic definition of anthropology in his Inaugural Address at the Collège de France: "Men communicate by means of symbols and signs. For anthropology, which is a conversation of man with man, all things are symbol and sign which act as intermediaries between two subjects" (Lévi-Strauss 1976:10). He does not explain how such a conception of anthropology follows from his notion of structure, nor does he show how things that act as intermediaries between two subjects become symbols and signs without introducing special assumptions about the nature of things, signs, and subjects.

A stone axe, he writes, can be a sign if in "a given context, and for the observer capable of understanding its use, it stands for the different implement which another society would use for the same purpose" (Lévi-Strauss 1976:11). This conclusion requires, among other assumptions, Peirce's definition of a "sign" as something that stands for something to someone, a configurational analysis of techniques as culture patterns, and a comparative analysis of the functional equivalence of different techniques in different cultures.

In his famous effort to consolidate social anthropology, economics, and linguistics into a unified structure of communication, Lévi-Strauss recognized that persons and goods and services were not the same as utterances, i.e., signs and symbols (Lévi-Strauss 1963a:297), but he tried to give the structure a semiotic character by arguing that persons are speakers of language, and that goods and services require symbols or signs in order to be successfully exchanged when the exchange system reaches "a certain degree of complexity" (ibid.).

The special assumptions Lévi-Strauss adds to his structuralism in order to give it a semiotic character are not in themselves implausible or undesirable. One might argue that they are necessary if structuralism is to deal adequately with anthropological problems of signification and communication. In fact, structural anthropology would be incapable of dealing with these problems as long as structural analysis was confined only to an analysis of the *relations* between cultural phenomena and did not interest itself in the symbolic nature of the phenomena. Lévi-Strauss sometimes cites an unnamed mathematician who told him that a mathematical analysis (of marriage rules, for example) would be interested not in the different forms of marriage but only in the relations between them. If followed strictly, such an interpretation of structure and structural analysis would denude cultural and social phenomena of any independently existing subjects, objects, or causal relations among them. In this interpretation, anthropology becomes a search for formal relations and structures and their topological transformations within different domains of culture and across different cultures (ibid.: 311–15).

Some followers and critics of Lévi-Strauss's structuralism at times attribute to him a purely formal application of the mathematical concept of "structure," thereby laying structural anthropology open to charges of formalism, lack of ethnographic verifiability, and absence of causal explanatory power—in short, to a denial that it has become the "concrete science" of structure and symbol that it aspires to be (see especially Mounin, Maquet, Diamond, Krader, and Adams, in Rossi 1974).

Such charges, occasionally provoked by an isolated statement or two, are in general based on misunderstandings, as Lévi-Strauss himself has often explained.[2] He is certainly not a formalist, and there is very little mathematical and logical formalism in his work. The rare attempt to frame an algebraic formula or something like the abstract analysis of a mathematician should not prevent us from recognizing that Lévi-Strauss practices the informal and "concrete logic" that he attributes to the "savage mind"—that is, "delineating structures in order to effect correspondences among sensory systems and only (if ever) finally determining their logic" (Boon 1972:208).

Far from abstracting structure from ethnographic context, Lévi-Strauss's structural analyses show an almost obsessive concern with the ethnographic details of the cultural phenomena (whether marriage rules or myths) that he is analyzing. He may be the astronomer of the social sciences, but he does not hesitate to use the microscope on specific studies.

The impression that structural anthropology practices an abstract formalism careless of ethnographic facts arises from the fact that some of Lévi-Strauss's theoretical and programmatic statements define the requirements of a structural model in terms of game theory. His description of social anthropology as a semiological science that studies systems of signs and symbols "regulated by internal laws of implication and exclusion," and "transformable . . . into the language of another system with the help of substitutions" (Lévi-Strauss 1976:18–19) reinforces the impression.

Such statements when read in isolation certainly sound like a program for constructing an *abstract algebra* or *formal calculus* of cultural symbol systems. Yet to see it so would be an erroneous interpretation, for in practice Lévi-Strauss and other structural anthropologists are very much interested in the *meanings* of the symbol systems, both the conscious meanings expounded by native informants and the unconscious meanings revealed by the anthropologist's comparisons of structural transformations and indirect perceptions; for example, that the semantic function of the opossum in North and South American myths is to signify stench (Lévi-Strauss 1970:1977).

Whatever the merits and demerits of particular criticisms of structural anthropology on the grounds of poor ethnography, there can be no doubt that Lévi-Strauss's vision of culture as a game of signs and symbols played according to a hidden logic of combinatory rules includes both a procedure for discovering that logic as well as a requirement of empirical validity for the inspired guesses at mathematical pattern. That the logic sought is a concrete logic of sensory qualities embedded in "the total social fact" assures us, nonetheless, that while some structuralist models may not exist within "the order of fact" when first constructed, they may eventually be verified, or falsified, by the application of empirical, naturalistic, and functional criteria of validation.

FUNCTIONALISM AND SYMBOLISM: MALINOWSKI

The functionalists and structural-functionalists did not escape the necessity of introducing into their anthropological theorizing some special assumptions and concepts about the nature of signs and symbols. Even Malinowski, with his populist and pragmatic emphasis on the primitives' ordinary use of words in concrete contexts of social interaction as the arbiter of their meaning, tried to combine that emphasis with a semantic theory based on Ogden and Richards's semantic triangle, in his pioneering essay, "The Problem of Meaning in Primitive Languages" (Malinowski 1946 [1923]).

In the 1923 essay Malinowski finds a similarity between his theory of meaning and Ogden and Richards's "new science of symbolism" and even identifies their contextual definition of reference in a "sign-situation" with his own "context of situation" theory of meaning. He also recognizes a kinship with the independent studies of aphasia by Henry Head and the linguistic studies of A. H. Gardiner. The philosophical studies of symbols and mathematical data "so brilliantly carried on in Cambridge" by Russell and Whitehead are credited with having given "a most important impetus" to the science of language (Ogden and Richards 1946:298).

In his 1935 volume on *The Language of Magic and Gardening*, Malinowski is more emphatic in distinguishing his "context of situation" theory not only from traditional philology but also from the definition of language found in Sapir's *Language:* "a method of communicating ideas, emotions and desires by means of a system of voluntarily produced symbols." In fact, the only work he cites with a point of view akin to his own is the "excellent monograph" by Grace A. De Laguna, *Speech, Its Function and Development* (1927), wherein she "follows the lines indicated by John Dewey in *Experience and Nature* (1925) and G. H. Mead in numerous articles, and expounds a general theory of language from a moderate behavioristic point of view" (Malinowski 1965 [1935]:59–60n.).

The British linguist J. R. Firth, who knew Malinowski and his work and is sympathetic to his approach, gives the following concise description and evaluation of Malinowski's ethnographic analysis of language in the Ogden and Richards essay as well as in several monographs on the Trobriands:

> Ranging himself with the primitive man's pragmatic outlook and regarding language as a mode of action rather than as a counter-sign of thought (1923, pp. 459, 479), Malinowski selected for notice only such features of

his languages as were essentially bound up with his contexts of situation in trading, fishing (1923, p. 474), gardening and similar pursuits. There, he noticed direct indications of these activities, references to the surroundings, words of command, words correlated with action (1923, p. 473), the expressions of feeling and passion bound up with behaviour, many of them stereotyped in form, such as spells, chants and narratives.

It is language material of this kind which he presents throughout his ethnographic work with little or no development of formal description as understood by linguists. The linguistic treatment of ethnographic texts, from *Argonauts of the Western Pacific* (1922) to *Coral Gardens and Their Magic* (1935), is fundamentally the same though in *Coral Gardens* we are given a "full treatment" of the "language of agriculture." (Firth 1957:105)

Firth believes that Malinowski's key concept of *context of situation* was probably derived from the linguists Philipp Wegener and Sir Richard Temple. Although Firth thinks that Malinowski "did not grasp the full theoretical implications of Wegener's hints," he himself "places a high value on Wegener's realization that the context of situation provided a valid configuration of elements comprising persons, objects, non-verbal events as well as language between which significant relations obtained, thus constituting a set of functions as a whole" (ibid.:103).

This semiotic interpretation of "context of situation" was contemporary with Peirce, since Wegener's *Situationstheorie* was published in 1885 (see chap. 4 for a modern application of Peirce). Firth places Malinowski's conception of language in the tradition of British empiricism and suggests that Wittgenstein "would probably have endorsed Malinowski's views on meaning" (ibid.:91).

In his essay on "The Epistemological Background to Malinowski's Empiricism," Leach points out that Malinowski's training in the pure sciences made him sensitive to the revolutionary scientific trends already begun at the time he entered British academic life in 1910, namely, Einstein's theory of relativity, Whitehead and Russell's non-Aristotelian logic, and Freud's psychology of the individual (Leach 1957:120–21). But the main epistemological source for Malinowski's empiricism identified by Leach is William James's pragmatism, empiricism, and individualism, a philosophy that was in vogue in 1910. Invoking a contrast drawn by Gallie between James's pragmatism and Peirce's pragmatism, Leach makes the perceptive suggestion that this contrast between the two kinds of pragmatism "surely parallels the closely analogous contrast between the Functionalism of Malinowski and the Functionalism of Durkheim, Mauss and Radcliffe-Brown" (ibid.:122; Gallie 1952).

If this parallel exists, it would suggest that Malinowski's empiricism may have been a reaction *against* the theoretical constructions of Einstein, Whitehead and Russell, and Freud. The textual evidence, in any case, is stronger for Malinowski's knowledge of James and of Dewey than it is for any direct Peircean influence on Durkheim, Mauss, and Radcliffe-Brown, although there may have been some indirect influence through Ogden and Richards. The evidence is stronger for a Russell-Whitehead influence on Radcliffe-Brown (Singer 1984).

Leach's contrast between Malinowski's and Mauss's interpretations of the *kula* seems more persuasive:

> Mauss' interpretation though not 'pragmatic' provides a most important supplement to Malinowski. Mauss, in essence, sees 'potlatch' behavior of the *kula* type as 'symbolizing' the ambivalent friendship-hostility aspects of the relationship ties which constitute the component elements in the social structure. It is an abstract interpretation which implies that Trobrianders, in carrying out their *kula* rituals, are also, in a symbolic way, 'saying things' to one another which they certainly could not put into words. (Leach 1957:133)

And this is perhaps the sense intended by Leach's parallel contrasts between James and Peirce and between Malinowski and other functionalists—that a similarity between two relations of "opposition" neither presupposes nor implies an identity of the terms opposed, that is, an identity between Malinowski and Radcliffe-Brown, or between James and Peirce. Malinowski's functionalism did not lead him to formulate a theoretical concept of social structure, perhaps because he did not care for "kinship algebra" and because, as Fortes has suggested, "he revived, in a new-fangled form, Kroeber's early view of kinship terminologies as primarily linguistic and psychological facts, not 'determined' by 'social conditions'" (Fortes in R. Firth 1957:176).

Malinowski's functionalism differs in this respect from Radcliffe-Brown's structural functionalism, a difference that is analogous to the difference in pragmatisms between James, who did not care for formal logical analysis, and Peirce, who made original contributions to the logic of relations and other branches of formal logic.

STRUCTURAL-FUNCTIONALISM AND SYMBOLISM: RADCLIFFE-BROWN

Radcliffe-Brown, although generally inclined to subordinate culture to social structure, developed a theory of symbolism based on several sources—Durkheimian analysis of myths, beliefs, and rituals as collective "symbolic representations"; Whitehead's theory of symbolism; Perry's *General Theory of Value;* and the Heraclitean and Chinese philosophy of the unity of opposites (see Singer 1984). This theory, however, remained rudimentary and largely implicit. In his 1932 preface to the second edition of *The Andaman Islanders*, for example, Radcliffe-Brown pointed out that in the chapters devoted to the "meaning" and the "function" of rites and myths, "no definitions of those terms are given. It seems desirable to supply them." The definition is brief but to the point: "Just in the sense that words have meanings, so do some other things in culture—customary gestures, ritual actions and abstentions, symbolic objects, myths . . . are expressive signs. The meaning of a word, a gesture, a rite, lies in what it expresses, and this is determined by its associations within a system of ideas, sentiments, and mental attitudes."

Granting that meanings are difficult for ethnological fieldworkers to discover, and that "there is no standardized technique for their discovery," Radcliffe-Brown concluded that it was "necessary for ethnology to provide itself with a method of determining meanings as effective and free from 'personal equation' as the methods by which a linguist determines the meanings of words and morphemes in a newly studied language" (Radcliffe-Brown 1948: IX).

The linguistic analogy is described in further detail and followed in the text of *The Andaman Islanders* (ibid.: 234–35). This is hardly a full-blown theory of cultural symbolism and hardly sufficient to persuade us that "symbolic representations" are chosen because they are "good to think," but it does indicate an early trend in Radcliffe-Brown's thought that was to culminate, in his second lecture on totemism, in a dual opposition—the opposition of friendly antagonists such as Eaglehawk and Crow, a relation of *structural opposition*, and the opposition of contrary terms, "Eaglehawk" and "Crow," a relation of *logical opposition*. That Radcliffe-Brown considered the latter relation a "symbolic representation" of the former relation of structural opposition between animal species, and between human beings, in Australian totemism as well as in other totemic societies, impressed Lévi-Strauss as an anticipation of "genuine structuralism" and his own postulate of homology between nature and culture (Lévi-Strauss 1963a:83–92).

Radcliffe-Brown illustrated the "double opposition" of two social groups with a graphic description of "sex totemism" in New South Wales:

> An Australian camp includes men of a certain local clan and their wives who, by the rule of exogamy, have come from other clans. In New South Wales there is a system of sex totemism, by which one animal species is the "brother" of the men, and another species is the "sister" of the women. Occasionally there arises within a native camp a condition of tension between the sexes. What is then likely to happen, according to the accounts of the aborigines, is that the women will go out and kill a bat, the "brother" or sex totem of the men, and leave it lying in the camp for the men to see. The men then retaliate by killing the bird which in

that tribe is the sex totem of the women. The women then utter abuse against the men and this leads to a fight with sticks (digging sticks for the women, throwing sticks for the men) between the two sex groups in which a good many bruises are inflicted. After the fight peace is restored and the tension is eliminated. The Australian aborigines have the idea that where there is a quarrel between two persons or two groups which is likely to smoulder the thing to do is for them to fight it out and then make friends. The symbolic use of the totem is very significant. This custom shows us that the idea of the opposition of groups, and the union of opposites, is not confined to exogamous societies. (Radcliffe-Brown 1958:25–26)

This example probably served Radcliffe-Brown as a concrete prototype of how a cognitive relation of "opposition" between two cultural categories ("men" and "women"), and a social relation of "structural opposition" between two kinds of persons, men and women, are mediated in a context of social interaction by the symbolic representations, or totems, of each group. As such, the description might also serve as a kind of emblem for Radcliffe-Brown's structural functionalism, to contrast with Lévi-Strauss's description of myths unconsciously thinking themselves in the human mind according to a postulate of homology between nature and culture (Singer 1984:sections 40–77).

In Radcliffe-Brown's analysis of cultural symbolism there is a mode of social interaction that mediates the presentation and interpretation of the sign (for example, the sex totem), but not in Lévi-Strauss's. This contrast derives in part from the fact that for Radcliffe-Brown the symbolism is an integral part of a *social system*, which includes a *social structure*, as the totality of interpersonal relations, and the customary *social usages* in which the structure is expressed and can be observed.

Historically, Radcliffe-Brown probably developed this general conception of a social system in continuing Rivers's debate with Kroeber on the relation of classificatory kinship terminologies to social institutions. Radcliffe-Brown insisted that the kinship nomenclatures and the categories of relationship they designated were more than "little systems of semantic logic," whose structure and history should be studied in their own right, as Kroeber suggested; for Radcliffe-Brown the kinship terms also fix and control modes of customary behavior and mutual obligations of relatives toward one another and thus help determine a kinship system as a type of social system (Eggan 1968; Kroeber 1909, 1952; Radcliffe-Brown 1952; Singer 1968). The implication of such a concept of social system for a theory of symbolism was already drawn by Radcliffe-Brown in *The Andaman Islanders;* the meaning of a word, a gesture, a rite depends not only on the associations of the symbol within a system of ideas, sentiments, and mental attitudes but also on the social cohesion and solidarity that the symbols express and help to maintain.

STRUCTURALISM AND CONFIGURATIONISM

The contrasts between Lévi-Strauss's structuralism and Malinowski's and Radcliffe-Brown's functionalism are not as sharp and exclusive as they are usually interpreted to be. Lévi-Strauss himself has blurred the contrasts by admitting that his structural analysis presupposes for its foundation Durkheim's and Mauss's empiricism and functionalism of "the total social fact" (Lévi-Strauss 1976) and that Radcliffe-Brown's second lecture on totemism contains genuine structural analysis (Lévi-Strauss 1963a). Lévi-Strauss's frequent expression of indebtedness to Boas, Lowie, Kroeber, and other American anthropologists is usually read as an acknowledgment of the accuracy and value of their detailed ethnographic and ethnological studies. This interpretation is probably correct as an indication of Lévi-Strauss's respect for empirical and historical description. There is also a less obvious kinship in theoretical orientation between Lévi-Strauss's structuralism and the American configurationism that derives from Boas. As early as 1911 Boas became interested in the processes of a "cultural dynamics" that integrated discrete cultural traits into coherent and persistent patterns. He saw such a "cultural dynamics" as a tendency that countered the diffusion of traits and trait complexes. He suggested that such a dynamic trend could be found in the unconscious patterning of language, myths and ceremonies, art designs, forms of social organization, and other domains of culture (Boas 1911). Boas applied the approach in empirical studies of linguistic categories, tales, myths, and needle-case designs to describe the patterning of tribal cultures (Stocking 1968:4–8).

Some of Boas's students extended and developed the approach in a half dozen different directions. Sapir applied it to the study of unconscious patterning of individual speech and behavior and combined it with Freudian and Jungian notions of unconscious symbolism to formulate his useful distinction between "condensation symbols" and "referential symbols" (Sapir 1949b:565). Benedict, influenced by Sapir's psychological interests and Gestalt psychology, tried to interpret the configurations of whole cultures as expressions of different psychological types of personality and values (Benedict 1934). Also continuing the interest in unconscious psychological patterning of individual behavior, Margaret Mead took the approach to Samoa (1928) and later to New Guinea (1930), where she met Reo Fortune and Gregory Bateson. The encounter with British social anthropology led Mead to a greater interest in structures of interpersonal relations in social organization and Bateson to a greater interest in the culturally standardized expression of emotions *(ethos)* and ideas *(eidos)* (Mead 1939, 1972; Bateson 1958 [1936]). Their collaboration on the study of Balinese character (Bateson and Mead 1942) not only marked a genuine merger of American cultural and British social anthropology but probably also set the pattern for the cooperative research on national character in which Bateson, Mead, Benedict, Gorer, Metraux, and other anthropologists participated in the early 1940s (Mead 1959:351–55).

One of Boas's students, Alfred Kroeber, although analyzed for one year (1917) and attempting to practice analysis for two years (1918–20), expressed reservations about the psychological interpretations of culture patterns formulated by Sapir, Benedict, and Mead (T. Kroeber 1970: 101–19). Preferring to interpret culture patterns wholly in terms of cultural symbols, values, and styles, Kroeber applied his interpretation in a massive empirical way to the stylistic growth and decline of civilizations (Kroeber 1944, 1963). One hears intermittent echoes of American configurationism in Lévi-Strauss's structural anthropology, but it is Kroeber's interpretation of kinship terminologies as little systems of semantic logic that provides the most direct link between Boas's emphasis on the unconscious patterning of linguistic categories and the structuralist interest in native cultural categories of kinship, myth, ritual, and other structured domains.

That Kroeber also provides a direct link between Boas and the ethnosemantics of Goodenough, Conklin, et al., is more widely recognized, a fact that suggests that French structuralism may be more closely affiliated with American configurationism than with British, American, or French functionalism. The interpretation of structures and patterns of culture as semantic systems unites Lévi-Strauss and the American configurationists, and also divides both from the functionalists—Durkheim, Malinowski, and Radcliffe-Brown—who interpret cultural symbol systems as pragmatic systems.

Kroeber, Evans-Pritchard, and Redfield have noted the differences in connotations between "pattern" and "structure," tracing the former to a humanistic provenience and the latter to a scientific one. Yet, as Redfield also pointed out in his Huxley Lecture on "Societies and Cultures as Natural Systems," there are significant resemblances between the configurationists and the structuralists, functional and cognitive. They all assume that they are studying systems that are not pure figments of imagination, that the systems are organized wholes that can be compared in specific respects, and that the complementarity of the social systems with the cultural systems encourages the hope for a synthesis (Redfield 1962:124–28).

FRENCH STRUCTURALISM MEETS THE OTHER STRUCTURALISM

By the early 1960s the differences between Lévi-Strauss's structuralism and Radcliffe-Brown's structural functionalism had become the agenda for spirited debates. Leach defined the issue as a difference between comparison and generalization in social anthropology. Comparison is a kind of "butterfly collecting," while true generalization requires "inspired guessing at mathematical pattern" (Leach 1961b:1–8).[3] On the other side, Fortes framed the issue in terms of the difference betwen a cryptographer trying to decipher fragmentary signs of an unknown code and the participant observer whose intensive fieldwork and intimate knowledge of the local dialect enabled him to understand the meaning of ritual, myth, and belief in the ongoing context of social life (Fortes 1966).

Geertz's definition of religion as a "symbol system" and his distinction between a "model of" and a "model for" reality suggested a way of transcending the opposition between structuralism and structural functionalism without accepting either (Geertz 1966 in 1973:93–94), almost a decade before he formulated the hermeneutics for an "intepretive anthropology" in terms of "thick description" (Geertz 1973:chap. 1).

An international seminar on African religions and ritual concluded that French structuralist and British structural functionalist approaches were not incompatible but complementary, and that both were needed. Victor Turner, a member of the seminar who pointed out the difference between the British and French approaches to ritual and symbolism, also suggested in his own paper a tripartite division of operational meaning, exegetical meaning, and positional meaning, which seemed to offer a way of combining the two approaches (Fortes and Dieterlen 1965:vii–viii, 9–15, 78–95).

Those of us who were teaching and doing research on social and cultural anthropology in the 1960s were stirred by the dramatic confrontations between structuralism's defenders and its critics. Lévi-Strauss's autobiographical *Tristes Tropiques*, individual articles such as "The Structural Study of Myth," "The Story of Asdiwal," his inaugural lecture at the Collège de France on "The Scope of Anthropology," and his reanalysis of the "totemic illusion" and the "savage mind" not only provided eagerly adopted teaching material but stirred imaginations and debate. Colorful titles of articles such as "Lévi-Strauss in the Garden of Eden" (Leach), "Some Muddles in the Models" (Schneider), and "The Cerebral Savage" (Geertz) attracted the attention of nonanthropologists as well and gave everyone the feeling that "it was all terribly interesting," as Geertz somewhat ironically described the atmosphere.

My own interests in those years (1960–68) were engaged with two trips to India and the organization of an academic program in Southern Asian studies. But India was not so remote as to escape the attentions of structuralists. Lévi-Strauss's application of the approach to the Indian caste system in his article on "The Bear and the Barber" (1963) did not attract much attention, but Yalman's "DeTocqueville in India" (1969) introduced Dumont's *Homo Hierarchicus, The Caste System and its Implications* to English-speaking readers. Dumont's work, which applied Lévi-Strauss's structural analysis to the Indian caste system, attracted wide attention from Indianists and non-Indianists alike and stimulated controversies similar to those that structuralism created in other areas (see, for example, the articles in *Contributions to Indian Sociology* [1957, 1959] by Dumont and Pocock, and Bailey on "For a Sociology of India").[4]

My research and writing on India was not greatly influenced by Lévi-Strauss's or Dumont's structuralism, although I made use of the notions of *social structure* and *cultural system*. These notions entered my work from other sources, chiefly Radcliffe-Brown, Eggan, Redfield, and M. N. Srinivas; and Peirce, Carnap, and Russell.

Redfield and Srinivas were both exposed to Radcliffe-Brown's teachings, Redfield as a colleague at Chicago in the 1930s, and Srinivas as a student at Oxford in the late 1940s. Each assimilated Radcliffe-Brown's concept of *social structure* and further elaborated his concept of *culture* in a different direction. Redfield's basic concepts in his Yucatan studies adapted Radcliffe-Brown's generalizing approach to social anthropology. *Social structure* as a network of social relations, *community* as a territorial group, and even *culture* as a set of conventional understandings expressed in act and artifact were entirely consistent with Radcliffe-Brown's structural-functionalist framework (Redfield 1941:14–15). In his later work on civilizations Redfield maintained the complementarity of *culture* and *social structure* but extended both concepts to take account of the increased scale, complexity, and historical depth of civilizations. Elaborating his earlier protosemiotic and structuralist conceptions of culture, he introduced the concept of the *structure of tradition* in a civilization, which embraced the "great tradition" cultivated by a specialized elite as well as the "little traditions" of the folk. The interaction of these two levels of cultural tradition, Redfield theorized, occurred within the context of a *societal structure* of small and large communities that organized the cultural and other specialists through their activities and social roles and structures over time in a *social organization of tradition* to produce the *historic structure* of a civilization (Redfield 1955b; Redfield and Singer 1954; Redfield 1956; Singer 1976).

Redfield intended to do fieldwork in a living civilization, to enter it "from the bottom up," in a village, but his intention was frustrated—in China by the political events of 1949 and in India by serious illness in 1955. The kind of research that attracted him was a study of world view, perhaps along the lines of Griaule's *Conversations with Ogotêmmli*, the blind

Dogon philosopher (Griaule 1965). In any case, Redfield's essay on "Art and Icon," one of his last, written for the inauguration of the Museum of Primitive Art in New York, drew on Ogotêmmli as well as on Peirce's description of contemplating an icon to conclude that,

> Whether we come to see the artifact [a wooden carving of Dogon twins] as a creative mastery of form, or see it as a sign or symbol of a traditional way of life, we are discovering, for ourselves, new territory of our common humanity. . . .
>
> In coming to understand an alien way of life, as in coming to understand an alien art, the course of personal experience is essentially the same: one looks first at an incomprehensible other; one comes to see that other as one's self in another guise. (Redfield 1962:468, 488)

When I started to apply Redfield's theories to India in 1954, I found that M. N. Srinivas's monograph on *Religion and Society among the Coorgs* (1952) helped me build a bridge between a rather abstract conceptual framework and the concrete experience of Indian society and culture. Srinivas's definitions and use of the concepts "Sanskritic Hinduism" and "Sanskritization" in the Coorg study suggested a manageable entry into the complexities of doing a field study of the structure and changes of a "great tradition" in the metropolitan center, Madras (Singer 1955; Redfield 1955b; Singer 1980b). Although I was not aware of it at the time, the relevance and congruence of the Coorg study to my own probably derived in part from the fact that Srinivas and Redfield shared Radcliffe-Brown's structural functionalism and were trying to extend it to a study of civilization. Radcliffe-Brown's *Andaman Islanders* (1922, 1932), Srinivas's *Coorgs* (1952), and numerous tribal and village field studies formed the rungs of a Redfieldian folk-urban continuum of Indic civilization on which I was able to climb to a study of Sanskritic Hinduism in Madras City. Historical and textual studies of Indic civilization were also indispensable for the ascent to the "great tradition" (see Marriott 1955 and Singer 1980b:chap. 2).

STRUCTURE, SYMBOL, AND REALITY

By the time I was putting together the volume on *Krishna: Myths, Rites and Attitudes* and the study of the Madras industrialists, I already suspected that the significant difference between French structuralism and British structuralism was not the notion of structure, or empiricism, functionalism, and naturalism. We were all structuralists and empiricists then! The significant issue seemed to be the relation of symbol systems and their structures to reality—persons, objects, and historical events. For Lévi-Strauss and Dumont, only the relations within social and cultural systems mattered, not the nature of the terms related. The terms were not substances existing independently of their relations; to assume that they were was to commit the fallacy of "substantializing" individuals and groups, objects and events (Singer 1982a:87–88).

In this view persons, objects, and events can exist independently, if at all, under two special conditions: in a cosmic chaos before systems are formed, and in the wake of disintegrating systems when they are dismantled and washed away by the tides of history. Under these conditions anthropology becomes "entropology," a study of increasing disorder (Lévi-Strauss 1970 [1964]:397).

This position seems to me to be based on Saussure's definition of a linguistic sign as a dyadic relation between signifier and signified, and on a misunderstanding of how mathematical models are related to empirical interpretations.

Saussure's doctrine that linguistic signs and their meanings are relationally defined (and exist only in differences) seems to be based on a generalization from the phoneme. Lévi-Strauss in turn generalized Saussure's structural analysis of the phoneme to nonlinguistic entities as well. Jakobson identified the problematic nature of such generalizations as early as his 1942–43 *Lectures* in New York (1978:64): "Saussure understood the purely differential and negative character of phonemes perfectly well, but instead of drawing out the implications of this for the analysis of the phoneme he overhastily generalized this characterisation and sought to apply it to all linguistic entities. He went so far as to assert that there are in language only differences with no positive terms."

In Lévi-Strauss and Dumont and other "structuralists" this generalization of Saussure's structural analysis of the phoneme was combined with the mathematical-logical concept of structure to produce the nonsequitur that structured social and cultural systems have no positive terms, only relations (Lévi-Strauss 1963a:279–80; Saussure 1966 [1915]: 120–22; Jakobson [1942–43] 1978:62–67; Dumont 1957 [1970]: 9n16; 1980: chap. 2, §21, 23).

British structuralism, on the other hand, especially in Radcliffe-Brown's version, developed a relational analysis of *social structure* without dissolving the independent reality of subjects and objects. Already immunized by Russell's critique of a substance-attribute metaphysics and Whitehead's "fallacy of misplaced concreteness," Radcliffe-Brown did not commit the fallacy of "substantialization" or assume that independently existing subjects and objects were permanent mental and bodily substances. He assumed they were events whose existence and relational structures were verifiable by direct or indirect observation. His concept of *culture*, although not as fully developed as his concept of *social structure*, did not require special epistemological and ontological assumptions to validate the existence of "phenomenal reality" as the object signified by "symbolic representations."

In spite of introducing a rather abstract concept of social structure as *general structural form*, Radcliffe-Brown balanced that conception with empirical concepts of *actually existing social relations, behavioral events, and social usages* considered as directly observable *cultural processes*. A somewhat similar strategy was adopted by some American cultural anthropologists (for example, Kroeber, Benedict, Sapir, Mead, Kluckhohn, and White); while insisting that *cultural patterns* and *cultural configurations* were not concrete cultural objects or individual behavior, they nevertheless regarded the patterns as constructed from implicit and explicit behavior and material culture.

One might argue that these parallels between British structural functionalism and American configurationism should include French structuralism—that Lévi-Strauss's abstract *models* of *social structure*, which do not exist "on the order of facts," are also balanced by concretely observable *social relations* as "total social facts." Such a three-way parallelism does exist and indicates a pervasive structuralist trend in modern social and cultural anthropology (see Singer 1968; Lévi-Strauss 1963a:59, 324–45). But French structuralism has developed a distinctive feature beyond such parallelism: it has eliminated empirical objects and empirical egos as independently existing subjects and objects of structural analysis.

In a memorable sentence Lévi-Strauss described this structuralist riddle: "I therefore claim to show not how men think in myths, but how myths operate in men's minds without their being aware of the fact" (Lévi-Strauss, 1970:12). This is not quite the riddle of the Sphinx or the statement of a mystic—"Zen-Marxist" or other—but the sober conclusion from detailed structural analysis of a large corpus of South and North American myths. Lévi-Strauss did not deny that all sorts of empirical materials—the local language, geography, history, social structure—were incorporated into the myths by a process of *bricolage*, but these materials do not determine the structure of the myths or represent the objects signified by the myths. What, then, does determine the structure of the myths, and what do they signify? Lévi-Strauss's answer is novel and surprising: assuming that the mythical structures have been delineated by ethnographic and structural analysis, he writes that what he is "concerned to clarify is not so much what there is *in* myths (without, incidentally, being in man's consciousness) as the system of axioms and postulates defining the best possible code, capable of conferring a common significance on unconscious formulations which are the works of minds, societies, and civilizations chosen from among those most remote from each other" (Lévi-Struass, 1970:12).

This grand project to crack the universal code for mankind's cultural unconscious rests on Lévi-Strauss's belief that in myth-making "the mind is left to commune with itself and no longer has to come to terms with objects," and is "reduced to imitating itself as object," thus implying "the existence of laws operating at a deeper level" (ibid.: 10).

Lévi-Strauss admits that his search for "the constraining structure of the human mind" has been rightly described by Ricoeur as "Kantism without a transcendental subject." He sees this characterization, however, not as a deficiency, but as "an inevitable consequence, on the philosophical level, of the ethnographic approach . . . chosen." Since his ambition is "to discover the conditions in which systems of truths become mutually convertible and therefore simultaneously acceptable to several different subjects, the pattern of those conditions takes on the character of an autonomous object, independent of any subject" (ibid.: 11).

The realization of this ambition is problematic, considering that the only object signified by the myths is "the human mind," that the mind is not usually left to commune with itself in myth-making, and probably not in any other activity, and that there are no acceptable procedures for discovering the constraining structures of mind independently of any subject or any object—independently, that is, of *empirical* subjects and *empirical* objects, and not only of *transcendental* subjects and objects (ibid: 332–34).[5]

At first glance, the structural functionalists and the configurationists appear to have escaped the epistemological and ontological riddles haunting structuralism. Yet considering some recent controversies raising questions about whether all material objects and even the id are "culturally constituted" as symbol systems, it must be admitted that French structuralism and symbolism have been attracting some sympathetic British social anthropologists, as well as French and American critics (Douglas 1973; Firth 1973; Leach 1976; Sperber 1974; Spiro 1979). In spite of Redfield's and Evans-Pritchard's predictions almost thirty years ago that anthropology was about to return to a historical perspective, all varieties of structuralism and configurationism continue to be haunted by the riddle of why the events of history seem to elude "the order of structure." Could the answer to the riddle be that structuralists, structural functionalists, and configurationists have been too ardent in their embrace of pattern and structure, thereby reducing events and the individual existence of persons, objects, and history to personality structures, culture patterns, and structural histories? (Evans-Pritchard 1951; Redfield 1956; Eggan 1966; Rosen 1971; Sahlins 1981, 1982; Needham 1972; Yngve 1975, 1981.)

SYNTACTICS, SEMANTICS, AND PRAGMATICS

The convergence of structural anthropology, functionalism, structural functionalism, and configurationism on the problem of the relation of symbols to structure and reality, although a bit surprising, springs from a combination of two circumstances, one negative and one positive, which these four anthropological positions share. The shared negative circumstance is that none of the positions has developed a theory of symbolism that is intrinsic to a conception of structure, function, or configuration. To repair this deficiency they have turned to philosophers and mathematicians, psychologists and linguists, not only for concepts of structure and configuration but also for a theory of symbolism that can be integrated with these concepts. A more positive circumstance simultaneously reinforced the search for a theory of symbolism, namely, that all four anthropological positions were committed to grasp the "native"'s point of view, his relation to life, to realize his vision of his world, as Malinowski phrased it (1961 [1922]:25). Since neither the concept of structure nor the concept of pattern and configuration gave *direct* access to "native" world view, cosmology, and value systems, it became necessary to develop a theory of symbols and their meanings that would provide an *indirect* access. The program for a "comparative epistemology" pioneered by Durkheim and Mauss (1903) and to some extent realized by Granet on China (1933) and Radcliffe-Brown in Australia, the Sapir-Whorf hypothesis for inferring American Indian world views from their "fashions of speaking" (Hoijer 1954), and Lévi-Strauss's aspiration to find the concrete and unconscious logic of the "savage mind" through a structural and semiological analysis of myths have been notable efforts to interpret the meanings of ritual, myth, speech, and other symbolic phenomena of other cultures in terms provided by the "natives," even if the latter do not always explain the symbols in the same manner as anthropologists (Singer 1984).

Those efforts have continued into the present, as seen in the Redfield program to compare the world views and cosmologies of living civilizations through a study of their folk cultures as well as their "great traditions" (Singer 1976), in the linguistically based projects to combine "emic" with "etic" description and analysis (Goodenough 1970, 1971), in Geertz's use of Schutz's phenomenological theory to frame his analysis of *Person, Time, and Conduct in Bali* (1966), and in Geertz's more recent proposal of a hermeneutics for an interpretive anthropology that provides access to the distinctive "inwardness" of different cultures (Geertz 1973, 1974, 1980a).

One of the major motivations for undertaking this book's explorations is the realization that the new anthropological paradigm lacks an adequate theory of symbolism and meaning. Because of its comprehensive and profound character, Charles Peirce's general theory of signs, which he called *semiotic*, is a promising candidate for the theory of symbolism apparently missing as yet from the anthropological paradigm.

In proposing to apply Peirce's theory of signs to some problems of meaning and communication in anthropology, these chapters will treat Peirce neither as a venerable ancestor nor as a living contemporary, but will see his work as a rich source of theoretical analysis, insight, and suggestion. Fortunately, scholarship on Peirce has grown so fast in recent years that it is possible to draw upon many of his original papers previously unpublished or inaccessible. New biographical information, critical editions, and critical analyses of his works are appearing almost daily (see Fisch 1981, 1982 for a summary). Under these circumstances, it is not necessary to undertake didactic expositions of Peirce's theory. He is a difficult writer and is best studied in his own words and diagrams. Here exposition and interpretation of Peirce's theory of signs have been limited to those aspects that seem immediately relevant for anthropological applications. Reader and author will depend, in any case, on Peirce scholars to correct and supplement these passages' selections and interpretations where needed.

It is also important to recognize that Peirce's theory of signs has become part of a living tradition in philosophy and to a lesser extent in linguistics, a tradition that can be drawn on for interpreting and extending Peirce himself. An illustration of this point that is highly relevant for a semiotic anthropology is Peirce's classification of semiotic into three branches: *pure grammar*, *logic* proper, and *pure rhetoric*. Obviously an echo of the medieval trivium, Peirce's classification was defined in such a way that it was easily adapted by Morris and Carnap as a modern classification of semiotic into *syntactics*, *semantics*, and *pragmatics*. As such, it has been widely discussed by some philosophers, linguists, communications engineers, and even literary critics (Peirce CP:2.227–29; Morris 1955 [1938], 1970; Carnap 1939, 1956; Jakobson 1975; Silverstein 1972, 1975, 1976; Sebeok 1976; Cherry 1966; Greenberg 1948, 1957; V. Turner 1979; Weinreich 1968; Segre 1973). The trichotomy *syntactics*, *semantics*, and *pragmatics* is not quite identical with Peirce's trichotomy of *pure grammar*, *logic* proper, and *pure rhetoric*, especially when he explains the three branches of semiotic as respective sciences of the conditions for the *meaning*, *truth*, and *fertility* of any sign used by a scientific intelligence (CP:2.227–29). That would bring the first two sciences under *semantics*, and the third perhaps under *pure rhetoric*. But Peirce also describes the task of *pure grammar* as defining and classifying the different kinds of signs and their relations to one another, which is a fair approximation for the modern *syntactics* (Fisch 1981:25–28; Kloesel 1981:127–33; Krois 1981:16–30; Peirce 1978).

An early perception of the Peircean and Saussurean options in modern linguistics and anthropology was Greenberg's (Greenberg 1964 [1948]:8): "The linguist has always been interested in *la langue*, not *la parole*, and this classic distinction in linguistics corresponds to the division of language into syntactics and semantics on the one hand, and pragmatics on the other."

More significant, perhaps, than the correspondence between Saussure's classic distinction and the modern trichotomy of syntactics, semantics, and pragmatics is the fact that the trichotomy derives from Peirce's conception of *semiotics*. Greenberg credits Morris with the first formulation of the modern trichotomy, but Morris acknowledged its source in Peirce (Morris 1970:19–20). The importance of the Peirce ancestry for the trichotomy is not simply a matter of priority; it shows that the trichotomy represents three branches of semiotics that can organize the different branches of linguistics under a unified program of theory and research. Greenberg was aware of the potential unifying value of the semiotic trichotomy and constructed a classificatory schema on its basis that makes room for social linguistics, ethnolinguistics, and psycholinguistics, as well as for the symbolism of games, religion, and art.

Drawing on Morris's definition of semiotics as a science of signs, their meanings or *designata*, and the sign users, Greenberg accepts Morris's threefold division of semiotics into syntactics, semantics, and pragmatics in terms of three different levels of abstraction. At the most abstract level, syntactics studies the relations of signs to one another without reference to the meanings or users of the signs. Semantic analysis is less abstract, since it studies the relations of signs to their meanings but not to the sign users. Pragmatic analysis is at the least abstract level, since it includes the sign users. Although the point is not always explicitly made, pragmatics presupposes syntactics and semantics, if only because Peirce's definition of a sign as an irreducible triadic relation of sign, object, and interpretant cannot be interpreted in pragmatic terms without including the relations of signs to signs, of signs to objects, and the relations as well of signs to their interpreters. On the other hand, there is a sense in which syntactics and semantics operationally presuppose pragmatics, as Greenberg observes, for the data for syntactic and semantic analysis need to be collected by observing the use and interpretation of symbol systems and their designata, as well as the sign users.

The threefold division of semiotics into syntactics, semantics, and pragmatics provides a useful framework for a general theory of symbolism, a framework that can deal with many problems in linguistics, sociolinguistics, psycholinguistics, and ethnolinguistics, as Greenberg points out. More immediately relevant is the application to some of the issues we have noted in the debates between structuralism, functionalism, structural functionalism, and configurationalism. Lévi-Strauss's structuralism, for example, practices a semantic analysis of myths, rituals, and kinship categories—not a formal, syntactic analysis, as is sometimes claimed, nor a pragmatics. The contrast with the pragmatics of Malinowski on the magic power of words or that of Radcliffe-Brown on sex totemism seems fairly clear-cut. This is not to say that Lévi-Strauss always avoids pragmatics; his essay on "The Effectiveness of Symbols" represents a lapse from

"genuine structuralism," just as Radcliffe-Brown's second lecture on totemism, according to Lévi-Strauss, represents a tilt toward it.

In any case, the tripartite classification of semiotics enables us to describe and discuss such issues without falling into the fallacy on the one
hand of "misplaced concreteness," that is, treating abstract entities ("native cultural categories," for example) that are the end products of complex
analysis and abstraction as concrete observable objects, or, on the other
hand, that of "misplaced abstractness," that is, treating particular individuals, groups, and objects as if they were abstract structures. Because of
the mutual presuppositions and implications of syntactics, semantics, and
pragmatics, it would be arbitrary to assign methodological or ontological
priorities to the structural, cultural, or social systems delimited by each
kind of analysis.

Between Peirce's threefold division of semiotics into three branches and
Morris's 1938 trichotomy of syntactics, semantics, and pragmatics lies a
history of major discoveries in mathematics and symbolic logic. This is
not the place to review that history (see Quine 1981:148–55 for a concise
summary), but a sketch of some of the larger contributions to a general
theory of symbolism will indicate that Morris was codifying previous
developments rather than launching a new theory. It may appear paradox-
ical to look for a theory of symbolism in mathematics and symbolic logic.
Mathematicians and symbolic logicians no doubt are adept in the design-
ing and use of specialized symbolisms, but they do not as a rule have a
great deal to say about the symbolism and its meaning. One aim, in fact,
of the trend toward formalization in mathematics and symbolic logic has
been to reduce the mention of and discussion about the symbols to a
minimum while regimenting their use to follow explicit and strict rules, as
if they were counters in a game. Formulations of axiom sets for arithmetic
and geometry, and of formal calculi for propositions and classes, represent
notable successes in formalizing different branches of mathematics and
logic. They do not as such represent contributions to a general theory of
mathematical and logical symbolism. Ironically, some of the contributions
to a theory of symbolism have been generated in spite of the formalization
program and in spite of Goedel's proof of its impossibility.[6] Among these
must be reckoned the explicit formulation of rules for the construction of
symbolic systems of different kinds, definitions of individual formulae and
sentences in a system, and stipulation of the conditions for the consistency
and completeness of a system. The study of the abstract structural relations between the elements of these systems, and of the transformations
that preserve specified structures, has been one of the chief motivations of
intellectual curiosity in these fields, even when empirical applications are
scarce or slow to appear.

What about the meanings of the symbols? Strict formalists would have nothing to do with them; they hold that mathematical and logical symbol systems should be constructed without reference to the meaning of the symbols; the systems should be left as uninterpreted systems. Russell's quip that in pure mathematics "we never know what we are talking about, nor whether what we are saying is true," represents an early formulation of this view. His later position was more linguistic (Russell 1980 [1940]; 1959:208–13). Quine's formulation that arithmetic, symbolic logic, and set theory developed from "a progressive sharpening and regimenting of ordinary idioms" is more pragmatic (Quine 1981:150). His notion of "disinterpretation" is a useful reminder that purely formal mathematical and logical systems are not really uninterpreted systems. Their customary interpretations have been set aside, not mentioned in the formal exposition, but are usually assumed in the informal exposition.

Hilbert's distinction between the symbolism of mathematics and the informal description of that symbolism in *metamathematics;* Carnap's generalization of that distinction to one between an *object-language*, which uses particular expressions, and a *metalanguage*, in which syntactical or semantical rules are formulated concerning the expressions in the object-language; and Tarski's and the Polish logicians' distinction between logic and *metalogic* represent variant and closely related solutions to the problem of how to talk about the symbols of formal mathematical and logical systems.[7]

These distinctions confirm Quine's insight about "the sharpening and regimenting of ordinary idioms," for to speak about a mathematical or logical system as a "language," or as a "language game," as in the later Wittgenstein, is certainly a sharpening of colloquial speech. Silverstein's extension of this strategy to "metapragmatics" in linguistics and cultural anthropology brings the sharpened idiom back home—home not only to language but also to society, culture, and personality.

CONCLUSION

The relevance and value of the trichotomy syntactics, semantics, and pragmatics for a semiotic anthropology should by now be clear—it brings together within a single theory of signs the major results of research on the nature of mathematical and logical symbolism, on the one hand, and, on the other, the pragmatic and behavioristic theory that the meaning of a symbol depends how it is used in the context of other signs (especially sentences) and in the context of "stimulating situations" (Quine), which prompt sign users to use or interpret a symbol in a particular manner. While the research on syntactics and semantics has grown out of abstruse problems in the foundations of mathematics and logic, it has found applications in communications engineering, in descriptive linguistics, and even in descriptive ethnography, among other fields. Radcliffe-Brown and Lévi-Strauss were both attracted by the possibility of applying a logical-mathematical concept of structure as sets of similar relations to the analysis of kinship relations and totemic symbols. The pragmatic theory of meaning is better known to anthropologists through Malinowski's "context of situation" theory, first expounded in his 1923 essay "On the Problem of Meaning in Primitive Languages," in which it is identified with Ogden and Richard's "sign-situation" concept. Malinowski also acknowledged his debt to the "moderate" behaviorism of Dewey, G. H. Mead, and Grace De Laguna in a footnote to his 1935 *Coral Gardens* monograph.

The belief that a semiotic theory of logic and mathematics could be unified with a pragmatic theory of empirical science was an underlying motivation for Morris's 1938 monograph on *The Foundations of a Theory of Signs*. In spite of the apparent success of that monograph, or perhaps because of it, Morris's later monograph on *Signs, Language, and Behavior* (1946) was much more heavily weighted with a behavioristic pragmatics than with syntactic or semantic analysis. The effort to restore the balance, at least as defined by Greenberg's schema of research possibilities for Morris's trichotomy, will find support not only in the pragmatic theory of meaning in use from Dewey to the later Wittgenstein and Quine (1981:43–54) but also in the studies of linguistic and cultural patterning by the American configurationalists.

The strongest support of all for such an ecumenical research program in anthropology will be found in Peirce's original theory of signs or semiotics, which contains an early version of Morris's trichotomy and of the language-metalanguage distinction. This distinction between the use and mention of signs was also built into Peirce's threefold classification of signs—iconic signs, which "show" an image or diagram of their object, indexical signs, which "point to" their objects, and symbolic signs, which use conventional symbols to "tell about" their objects. The meaning of intellectual concepts expressed by symbolic signs, no matter how abstract, can be clarified by applying to them Peirce's pragmatic maxim: "In order to ascertain the meaning of an intellectual conception one should consider what practical consequences might conceivably result by necessity from the truth of that conception, and the sum of these consequences will constitute the entire meaning of the conception" (Peirce 5.9, quoted in Morris 1970:21). Because Peirce was intimately associated, as a contributor to them, with modern innovations in symbolic logic and the foundations of mathematics, he came to believe on the basis of his experience that these were "observational" sciences. By observing the iconic and indexical signs in geometrical diagrams and algebraic equations, one can discover new truths (Peirce 1955:135–49).

Without avoiding the formalism and generality of mathematics and logic, Peirce nevertheless anchored his general theory of symbolism in the analysis of idiomatic and colloquial conversations, actual or imaginary.

Morris's trichotomy of syntactics, semantics, and pragmatics has been refined and qualified by Morris, Carnap, and others (Singer 1978:224–25; Carnap 1965; Morris 1955, 1964, 1971). As such, it provides a useful scheme for ordering the diverse anthropological approaches to the study of symbolic phenomena. For example, componential analysis, the construction of folk botanical taxonomies, and kinship "algebras" all tend to abstract from the native speakers and are therefore semantical. Although some of these approaches are sometimes also presented as purely "formal" analyses, they rarely abstract from the objects or meanings designated by the signs. The prominence of references to speakers and hearers in sociolinguistics, psycholinguistics, the ethnography of communication, proxemics, and kinesics places such investigations into pragmatics, which does not preclude syntactic and semantic studies of the relevant sign systems (Hymes 1971; Sebeok et al. 1964; Sebeok 1976).

Beyond such obvious uses of the trichotomy, it also adds greater differentiation and specificity to the use of the language analogy in the interpretation of symbolic phenomena. When we compare Radcliffe-Brown's description and use of the language analogy in *The Andaman Islanders* with the use and development of the analogy by modern linguists, semiologists, and semioticians, we can see how it has been transformed into an instrument for semiotic research. Two assumptions underlie this transformation—first, that languages are semiotic and semiological systems, and second, that linguistic semiotic systems can be taken as models for the analysis of nonlinguistic systems (Greenberg 1957; Burke 1966; Friedrich 1979c; Barthes 1970 [1963]; Silverstein 1975, 1976; Sahlins 1976).

The fruitfulness of the language analogy depends not so much on the obvious pervasiveness of language and other sign systems at the heart of social life as on the less obvious fact that the interpretation of signs presupposes an acquaintance with the objects designated by the signs and with the speakers and hearers of the signs (Peirce 1977:196–97, Nida 1964; Barthes 1970). To interpret social and cultural sign systems as if they were "languages" becomes an operatively fruitful procedure when one has such collateral acquaintance. This condition is not unique to the interpretation of nonlinguistic sign systems; it is equally a condition for the interpretation of linguistic signs. In anthropology such a requirement of experience and observation is called "fieldwork."

Because anthropological fieldwork involves travel, and special experience, training, and study, a semiotic anthropology will contribute to a *descriptive* semiotic. Its methods and results will not be restricted to the formal or quasi-formal domain of *pure semiotic*. Although the definitions, rules, and theoretical constructions of *pure semiotic* will be useful to guide empirical research and analysis, such research and analysis will be something more than a logical deduction from *pure semiotic*. It will include inductive and abductive inference as well, and presuppose acquaintance with nonlinguistic objects and events, and with speakers and hearers.

The assumption that syntactic and semantic analyses of signs can remain at a purely formal level derives from the widespread belief that Peirce's analysis of sign process *(semiosis)* posits an endless chain of signs interpreting and interpreted by other signs. This conception overlooks the presence in his theory of "scientific intelligences," utterers and interpreters, whose symbolic activity includes the production of signs and their interpretations. In other words, the chain of human discourse is punctuated by the acts of sign production and by the human responses to them, immediate emotional responses as well as physical and intellectual reactions. Even the *logical* or *final interpretant* of a sign is not for Peirce just another sign, but a habit of action, or a bundle of such habits, which the pragmatic conception of a theoretical concept envisages. Peirce's semiotic is a *pragmatic* semiotic, quite at home in a world of objects, events, and people, not a "mere" symbolic or linguistic solipsism in search of reality.

If anthropology is a conversation of man with man, as Lévi-Strauss suggested, it should not surprise us that the founding fathers of modern social and cultural anthropology conversed with the "natives" in the field—that Haddon and Rivers listened to the native "yarns" told around campfires in the Torres Straits, that Radcliffe-Brown found a native "ritual idiom" in the ceremonies and customs in the Andamans and in Australia, and that Malinowski discerned for Trobriand agriculture and gardening a *corpus inscriptionum*. Nor is it surprising that the anthropological conversation should include the language and idiom of anthropologists as they talk with one another in the field or at home, in face-to-face exchange or in articles, monographs, letters, and lectures.

What may be a bit surprising is the extent to which the founding fathers of modern anthropology have "conversed" with philosophers, linguists, literary critics, psychologists, and sociologists in their search for a theory of cultural symbolism.[8] Boas reading Kant among the Eskimo of Baffinland and much later talking with Dewey at Columbia; Malinowski in the Trobriands reading notes on Freud sent him by Seligman or, on his return, avidly recognizing his "context of situation" theory of meaning in the proofs of Ogden and Richards's *The Meaning of Meaning* and, after returning to England, finding a kinship with the "moderate behaviorism" of Dewey's, G. H. Mead's, and De Laguna's theory of speech and symbolic communication. Radcliffe-Brown's use of Shand's theory of sentiments and of Durkheim's theory of totemism are well known; his applications of Russell and Whitehead's structural logic of relations and events for the formation of a natural science of society remain to be appreciated. While Lévi-Strauss has acknowledged his contacts with Jakobson (and Saussure's texts) in New York City and with Rousseau and Bergson in the *Tristes Tropiques*, his contacts with the logical and mathematical conceptions of structure seem to have been more indirect (Singer 1984).

These anthropologists' extracurricular conversations have been two-way, as all good conversation should be. Ogden and Richards added Malinowski's essay on "The Problem of Meaning in Primitive Languages" to their book, *The Meaning of Meaning*. Dewey cited Boas and Malinowski in *Experience and Nature*, and De Laguna cited Malinowski in *Speech, Its Function and Development*.

In a classical Freudian slip (or was it a "typo"?), Freud cited Kroeber as "Kroeger" on *Totem and Taboo* (Freud 1949 [1922]:90). Lévi-Strauss's structuralism is clearly discernible in Barthes, Foucault, and Lacan. In a knowledgeable tribute to anthropology and anthropological linguists, W. V. Quine's discussion in *Word and Object* of a theory of "radical" translation refers to Bloomfield, Firth, Jakobson, Leach, Lee, Lévy-Bruhl, Lienhard, Malinowski, Pike, Sebeok, Sapir, and Whorf. Although the description of the "jungle linguist's" procedure in learning the language of a hitherto unknown tribe is obviously hypothetical, the fact that there may not be a primitive tribe who call rabbits "Gavagai" does not lessen the value of Quine's discussion for a theory of cultural symbolism.

Semiotic anthropology, in sum, holds out a good prospect for resolving many of the problems generated by the debates over structuralism in the 1960s. It provides a means of incorporating structural and symbolic anthropology, together with functionalism, empiricism, and naturalism, within a single paradigm for social and cultural anthropology. The conflicts between rationalist and empiricist conceptions of social structure and culture patterns can be reconciled within a theory of signs that includes *indexical signs* of individual existence and interaction, *iconic signs* of structural forms, and *symbolic signs* of intellectual concepts. Persons and selves are essential ingredients in this paradigm as subjects and objects of sign systems. The world of natural objects and events enters the paradigm as a set of independent terms in the triadic sign-relation, as well as the material substratum for sign-tokens, interpretants, and objects.

Perhaps the most significant feature of a semiotic anthropology is that it includes as an intrinsic ingredient a theory of signification and communication. Functionalism, structuralism, structural functionalism, and configurationism, deficient in this respect, borrowed theories of symbolism to make up the deficiency, but their theories of symbolism were never fully integrated with their structuralism or with a theory of communication. After almost one hundred years of looking for structure and pattern in human society, culture, and personality, it may be time for anthropologists to join in that other search which has also interested them—the search for the meaningful and the valuable in structure and pattern, and in individual and collective existence.

2

For a Semiotic Anthropology

During the 1960s and early 1970s, discussions of culture theory showed a preoccupation with the idea that cultures are systems of symbols and meanings. At the least, this preoccupation created a new subfield of cultural anthropology; it has probably also transformed the aims, methods, and subject matter of cultural anthropology and its relations to other disciplines. Leading anthropologists who have articulated this symbolic conception of culture have given different names to the emerging field or subfield. Lévi-Strauss calls it "structural anthropology" and "semiology," Geertz, extending Weber, Dilthey, and Schutz, refers to it as "interpretive anthropology," Schneider simply calls it "a cultural account." In a recently published book, Peacock notes that he and several colleagues introduced the designation "symbolic anthropology" for the new field, while Victor Turner prefers "comparative symbology" as a wider designation to take account of the symbolic genres of advanced civilizations as well as of the ethnographical materials of nonliterate cultures. Turner has also emphasized the need for a processual analysis of symbols in the concrete contexts of social life, in contrast to the formal analysis of symbols as algebraic, logical, or cognitive systems, which Turner regards as characteristic of semiology, semiotics, and linguistics.

Other anthropologists who have contributed to these recent developments of culture theory have not introduced any special designation for the field, but have either aligned themselves with one of the named approaches—Leach, e.g., with Lévi-Strauss's "structural anthropology" and "semiology," Mary Douglas with Victor Turner's "symbology," Margaret Mead with "semiotics"—or, as in Firth's book on *Symbols*, have adopted an eclectic attitude toward the different approaches.

In this chapter I should like to consider two problems that these recent developments in culture theory pose: (1) Why does the tilt of culture theory to semiotics occur just when it does, in the 1960s and early 1970s?

and (2) What kind of general theory of signs and symbols is likely to prove most fruitful and adequate for a general theory of culture?

The answer to the first question will be found, I believe, both in the preceding developments within anthropological theory and in what was going on outside of anthropology. It is perhaps premature to predict the answer to the second question, but an analysis of some of the issues in dispute between the semiotic and semiological theories of signs should enable us to state a case for a *semiotic anthropology* and to prefigure some of its contours.

CULTURE AND SOCIETY AS COMPLEMENTARY CONCEPTS

In trying to sort out and understand the recent proliferation of symbolic theories of culture, it is tempting to see in them different expressions of national character or at least of national traditions in anthropological thought and research. In their joint introduction to the symposium *African Systems of Thought*, the British and French coeditors, Meyer Fortes and Germaine Dieterlen, agreed on two major propositions; first, that there were two broadly contrastive approaches in the symposium papers to the description and analysis of African religious systems. The one approach, characteristic of French ethnography, starts with the total body of knowledge (the *"connaissance"*) "expressed in a people's mythology and in the symbolism of their ritual, reflected in their conceptions of man and of the universe, and embodied in their categories of thought, their forms of social organization and their technology, and constituting a coherent logical system." The other approach, characteristic of British social anthropology, "starts from the social and political relations in the context of which ritual, myth, and belief are found to be operative." It "links the body of knowledge and beliefs of a people with the actualities of their social organization and daily life." A second proposition accepted by the coeditors is that the two approaches are not antithetical but deal with complementary aspects of African religious and ritual institutions. The question then arises as to how these two aspects of African religious systems are interconnected. The editors report that in the symposium discussion, evidence emerged very clearly "for the way in which myth, ritual, concepts of personality, and cosmological ideas penetrate the social organization of a people and are in turn shaped by the latter" (Fortes and Dieterlen 1965:4).

The explicit characterization of the difference between the British and French approaches to the study of ritual and symbolism was introduced and elaborated by Victor Turner (ibid.:9–15). Audrey Richards, in a review of *African Systems of Thought*, sought to pinpoint the social and institutional reasons for the difference between the French and the British approaches. French anthropologists, she pointed out, tend to conduct their field observations in their brief vacation periods extended over many years, while British anthropologists conduct theirs in an intensive year or two of fieldwork. These differences in the ways of doing fieldwork, she suggested, help explain the French and British contrastive approaches to African religious systems (Richards 1967).

In his recent book on *Rethinking Symbolism* Dan Sperber also invokes a national-character kind of explanation for the French semiological approach: "The Frenchman lives in a universe where everything means something, where every correlation is a relation of meaning, where the cause is the sign of its effect and the effect, a sign of its cause. By a singular inversion, only real signs—words, texts—are said, sometimes, to mean nothing at all" (Sperber 1974:83).

Claiming that "semiologism" is an essential aspect of French culture and ideology but not necessarily of all cultures, Sperber argues that "Lévi-Strauss has demonstrated the opposite of what he asserts, and myths do not constitute a language. All these learned terms—signifier and signified, paradigm and syntagm, code, mytheme, will not for long hide the following paradox: that if Lévi-Strauss thought of myths as a semiological system, the myths thought themselves in him, and without his knowledge, as a cognitive system" (ibid.: 84).

Before we become involved in the debate over whether "semiologism" is a French disease, or a British, American, Russian, Polish, or Italian one, it would be advisable to review the historical and analytic aspects of the *culture* concept. Such a review would, I believe, also help clarify Sperber's distinction between semiological and cognitive systems, as well as illuminate the recent tilt of culture theory to semiotics.

In historical perspective, the two contrastive approaches to African religions identified by Fortes and Dieterlen represent a specialized application and transformation of the contrast between *society* and *culture* as global, inclusive concepts. The national affiliations of the two concepts, however, have undergone a sea change. The British anthropologist Edward Tylor was one of the first to formulate a global concept of culture in his famous definition: "Culture or civilization, taken in its wide ethnographic sense, is that complex whole which includes knowledge, belief, art, morals, law, custom, and any other capabilities and habits acquired by man as a member of society" (Tylor 1871).

The inclusive conception of society as a social system and synchronic structure, which became a trademark of British social anthropology, derives from Durkheim, Comte, and Montesquieu, as well as from Spencer and the American anthropologist Morgan (Singer 1968a).

The later vicissitudes of these concepts are equally unrespective of national boundaries: Tylor's culture concept was miniaturized and pluralized by Malinowski in England and by Boas and his students in the

United States. As such, it guided the study first of "primitive" and "tribal" cultures and later of "peasant," "urban," "ethnic," and all sorts of "subcultures." The French sociological tradition, on the other hand, not only led to the concepts of social system and social structure in British social anthropology but also influenced American sociology decisively.

In a joint paper on "The Concepts of Culture and of Social System" published in 1958 *(American Sociological Review)*, Alfred Kroeber and Talcott Parsons proposed "a truce to quarrelling over whether culture is best understood from the perspective of society or society from that of culture." The historical significance of this proposal is that it marks a public and professional recognition of the shift from the global and intellectually imperialistic concepts of culture and social system to an analytical distinction between the two concepts as quasi-independent, complementary, and interrelated:

> We suggest that it is useful to define the concept of *culture* for most usages more narrowly than has been done in most American anthropological tradition and have it refer to transmitted and created content and patterns of values, ideas, and other symbolical-meaningful systems as factors in the shaping of human behavior and the artifacts produced through behavior. On the other hand, we suggest that the term *society*—or more generally, *social system*—be used to designate the specifically relational system of interaction among individuals and collectivities.

By 1958, when the joint Kroeber-Parsons article appeared, the proposed condominious merger of anthropological and sociological concepts of culture and society was beginning to occur in the work of Raymond Firth (1951), Fred Eggan (1955), and Robert Redfield (1955a), among others. In fact, Kroeber himself, who was one of the leading exponents of a global concept of culture that encompassed social relations and social organization, had started to think about a narrower and more differentiated culture concept as early as 1909. As a result of an extended debate with Rivers and then with Radcliffe-Brown over their "sociological" interpretation of classificatory kinship terminologies, Kroeber crystallized a conception of kinship terms as little systems of semantic logic. Almost fifty years after Kroeber made this suggestion, Lounsbury and Goodenough both returned to it in 1956 and developed the method of "kinship semantics," a method from which Goodenough and others extrapolated a general theory of culture as "ethnosemantics" or "ethnoscience" (Singer 1968a).

Rivers and Radcliffe-Brown were similarly stimulated by the debate with Kroeber, and with one another, to crystallize a conception of kinship systems as social systems that included as components kinship terms and categories, kinship behavior and norms, rights and obligations, as well as rules of marriage and descent. For Radcliffe-Brown this conception of kinship system became an exemplary paradigm for his broader concepts of social system and social structure.

The place of the *culture* concept in this paradigm remained somewhat ambiguous for Radcliffe-Brown. He was critical of the survival in American anthropology of Tylor's global-culture concept and referred to it as "a vague abstraction." He preferred to eliminate that concept altogether. On the other hand, Radcliffe-Brown began to construct a fairly precise concept of cultural system complementary to his concept of social structure as early as his 1937 lectures on "A Natural Science of Society." In the published version of the lectures (1957) he analyzed the concept of culture into three aspects: (1) a set of rules of behavior "which exists in the minds of a certain number of people owing to the fact that they recognize it as the proper procedure," and carry it out in behavior, or "social usages"; (2) the existence of certain common symbols and common meanings attached to those symbols—words, gestures, works of art, rituals, and myths are symbols that provide the means of communication between individuals; and (3) common ways of feeling or sentiments and common ways of thinking or beliefs shared by a majority of the people in a society— Durkheim's "collective representations."

These three aspects of culture together make possible a "standardization" or "system" of behavior, sentiment, and belief of individuals in a society. In fact, Radcliffe-Brown uses the term "culture" to refer to just such a standardized *system*, not to the individual acts of behavior or even to a *class* of such acts. But Radcliffe-Brown insists that there can be no independent, autonomous science of cultural systems, for the standardization of behavior, sentiments, and beliefs implies a set of relations between persons, or a social structure. "Neither social structure nor culture can be scientifically dealt with in isolation from one another. . . . You can study culture only as a characteristic of a social system" (Radcliffe-Brown 1957:106–107).

One can read many of Radcliffe-Brown's ethnographic papers—e.g., on joking relations, totemism, the mother's brother and other kinship studies, religion and society, taboo, etc.—as attempts to explore the "functional" connections between culture as collective representations, cultural symbols, rules of behavior and social usages, on the one hand, and social structures as networks of actual social relations on the other. In the 1930s, when he was at the University of Chicago, and in the years immediately following at Oxford, Radcliffe-Brown became sufficiently convinced of the fruitfulness and validity of this approach to attempt an explicit general formulation of it in the lectures on a natural science of society and on social anthropology, and in papers on the concepts of function, social structure, kinship systems, and the comparative method in anthropology (Singer 1984).

For American anthropologists, Radcliffe-Brown's methodological views and their ethnographic exemplifications offered a needed alternative to the Boasian eclectic "descriptive integrations" of observed facts and historical reconstructions. As Redfield pointed out in his 1937 introduction to the volume in honor of Radcliffe-Brown prepared by some of his American students, the alternative presented by Radcliffe-Brown consisted not so much in formulating or discovering general social laws as in providing a guide to research: the formulation of general concepts, classification of problems, and explicit statement of general postulates and propositions. "The propositions are not to be treated as final but are to be challenged, revised, or abandoned as the investigation into special fact guided by them proceeds" (Redfield in Eggan 1955:xiii).

Redfield's description of Radcliffe-Brown's American contributions to social anthropology as a generalizing science is both confirmed and extended by his own study of *The Folk Culture of Yucatan*. And nowhere is Radcliffe-Brown's influence more explicit and striking than in the definitions of culture and society as complementary concepts, which Redfield uses in that study (1941:14–15). His definition of culture as "an organization of conventional understandings expressed in act and artifact" extends some of Sapir's ideas from his 1931 articles on "symbolism" and "communication," as well as Tylor's charter definition. The definitions of "society" and "community," however, were very close to those of Radcliffe-Brown and show the influence of the latter's presence in the Chicago department from 1931 to 1937. Redfield defined "society" as a network of social relations, and "community" as the territorial group that is characterized by a given culture and society.

While these early formulations of Redfield's formed an integral part of the conceptual framework of *The Folk Culture of Yucatan* and of his more special concepts of "folk" culture and "folk" society, they did not become at that time a stimulus for developing a semiotic theory of culture either in Redfield's thinking or in that of other anthropologists. The interest instead turned to processes of acculturation and other forms of culture change generated by the contact of "folk" cultures and societies with modern, Western urban societies and cultures.

After the Second World War, when Redfield became interested in studying and comparing the "great traditions" of living civilizations, he saw a greater need for anthropologists to work with the humanists on their left than with the natural scientists on their right. What is of special interest for the present story, however, is that in developing a "social anthropology of civilizations," Redfield did not abandon the complemen-

tary concepts of culture, social structure, and community or the conception of culture as a system of meanings and values. Rather, he enlarged the
scope of their application and modified their definitions to take account of
history, high cultures, and large organized states. He defined a civilization
as consisting of a *societal structure* of communities of differing size, complexity, and interrelations, and of a *cultural structure* of little and great
traditions in reciprocal interaction. Such complex structures were not
simply conceived as *synchronic* structures but were to be traced through
their persistences and changes as *historic structures*. And just as Firth and
Victor Turner, among others, studied specific social structures through
their *social organizations* in particular places and times, so the societal and
cultural structures of civilizations could be studied in the *social organization
of their cultural traditions* in particular centers and networks. The formation, maintenance, and transmission of these cultural traditions were not
only "organizations of conventional understandings expressed in act and
artifact," but also bodies of knowledge, "more or less pyramidal, more or
less multilineal," embodying distinctive world views and value systems,
cosmologies and religions. The cultivation and understanding of these
bodies of knowledge is socially organized in schools, in churches and
sects, in towns and cities, by cultural specialists, literati, and intelligent-
sia. The French conceptions of culture and civilization as organized
knowledge and the British conceptions of society as social structure and
social organization found their synthesis in Redfield's conception of civilizations as social organizations of great and little traditions and of great and
little communities (Singer 1976).

The Kroeber-Parsons joint article on culture and social system and
Redfield's conceptions of the cultural and societal structures of civilizations indicate that by 1958 culture theory, in the United States, at least,
had reached a phase of explicit formulation that emphasized the structural, symbolic, and cognitive aspects of the culture concept, and its
complementarity with the concept of social structure.

It is noteworthy that Lévi-Strauss, whose work in the 1950s and 1960s
was to make anthropology famous for two new isms—"structuralism" and
"semiologism"—recognized theoretical affinities with some of his predecessors whom in other respects he characterized as practitioners of a natural-science model of empiricism, functionalism, and naturalism. He found
such affinities, for example, in Radcliffe-Brown's 1951 paper on totemism
and wondered if Radcliffe-Brown realized how radical a departure he had
made from his own previous functionalism in developing a theory of
totemism that explained the selection of totemic species because they were
good to think, not because they were good to eat. Lévi-Strauss even
suggested that this out-of-character paper of Radcliffe-Brown's may have
been influenced by the development of structural linguistics and structural

anthropology in the previous decade, 1940–50 (Lévi-Strauss 1963a:89–90).

Meyer Fortes dismissed Lévi-Strauss's suggestion; Radcliffe-Brown's 1951 paper on totemism, Fortes said, covered ground so familiar to his students and colleagues that its publication caused no stir whatever among them (Fortes 1966). While Fortes may have underestimated some of the novel features of Radcliffe-Brown's structuralism and of Lévi-Strauss's, I believe that for both, the roots of a structural and symbolic theory of culture, and of society, can be found in the preceding fifty years' development of culture theory, which has just been sketched. Radcliffe-Brown started to formulate such a theory as early as 1937 and Redfield in 1941. Elsewhere I have tried to show that both of these anthropologists, and Lévi-Strauss as well, did not so much abandon the natural-science model as extend and modify it to take account of history, complex societies, and the "great traditions" of living civilizations. Humanism did not replace science in the development of a structural and symbolic theory of culture and society; it was incorporated into a transformed philosophy and method of science. That transformation began about 1900 with new developments in the foundations of mathematics, symbolic logic, theoretical physics, and the mathematical theory of communication. Structural linguistics and structural anthropology participated in this transformation, as did social and cultural anthropology (Singer 1968a, 1984; Jakobson 1961).

SEMIOTICS AND SEMIOLOGY: A COMPARISON AND CONTRAST

In his Inaugural Address at the Collège de France in 1960 Lévi-Strauss proposed that anthropology devote itself to the study of signs and symbols, to the science that Saussure called "*semiologie.*" In this address Lévi-Strauss conceives of anthropology as a branch of semiology, "the occupant in good faith of that domain of semiology which linguistics has not already claimed for its own, pending the time when for at least certain sections of this domain, special sciences are set up within anthropology" (Lévi-Strauss 1976: 9–10).

Within Saussure's conception of semiology as the study of "the life of signs at the heart of social life," Lévi-Strauss claims for anthropology some of the sign systems mentioned by Saussure—e.g., symbolic forms of politeness, military signals, "mythic language, the oral and gestural signs of ritual, marriage rules, kinship systems, customary laws, certain conditions of economic exchange." The enumeration is not intended to be exhaustive and, indeed, cannot be in view of Lévi-Strauss's broad perspective on man and anthropology, quoted earlier: "Men communicate by means of symbols and signs; for anthropology, which is a conversation of man with man, everything is symbol and sign, when it acts as intermediary between two subjects."

Clearly such a semiotic theory of culture implies, and perhaps presupposes, a philosophical anthropology about the nature of man, and an epistemology about how we can know that nature, which are not made entirely explicit in Lévi-Strauss's writings. The closest he comes to explicit revelation of his position is in the autobiographical travelogue, *Tristes Tropiques*, in which it turns out that the Western anthropologist's vision quest for "true savages" finds only men—conversing with men. When conversation fails because men do not know one another's language, there can only be a dumb silence. When conversation across cultures occurs, it does not matter whether we see the flow of communication as going from us to them or in the reverse direction. In this perspective structuralism and structural anthropology provide a method for the analysis of human communication, which Lévi-Strauss suggests can be analyzed into a unified theory of the exchange of words, of women, and of goods and services.

Two years after Lévi-Strauss's Inaugural Address, Margaret Mead, at the Indiana University conference on paralinguistics, kinesics, and proxemics, having listened to the papers and discussions, tried to describe what the conference was about and to suggest a name for the field,

> which in time will include the study of all patterned communication in all modalities, of which linguistics is the most technically advanced. If we had a word for patterned communication in all modalities, it would be useful. I am not enough of a specialist in this field to know what word to use, but many people here, who have looked as if they were on opposite sides of the fence, have used the word "semiotics." It seems to me the one word, in some form or other, that has been used by people arguing from quite different positions. (Mead in Sebeok et al. 1964)

Despite some expressed preferences for the word "communication" and some argument about whether "semiotics" should be restricted to the nonlinguistic aspects of communication, the organizers of the conference and the editors of its proceedings adopted Margaret Mead's suggestion and incorporated it in the title of the conference proceedings as *Approaches to Semiotics*. In addition, one of the organizers and editors, Thomas A. Sebeok, took this same title for a series of volumes published under his editorship by Mouton from 1969 to 1976. In 1976 he started another series, "Advances in Semiotics," published by Indiana University Press.

"Semiotics" is a plural formed by analogy from "semiotic," Peirce's designation for a general theory of the nature and different kinds of signs. Whether, in adopting "semiotics" as the designation for the study of culturally patterned communication in all modalities, Sebeok and his coeditors were endorsing Peirce's "semiotic" rather than Saussure's "semiology" is not certain. Nevertheless, the apparent convergence between Lévi-Strauss's and Margaret Mead's proposals to bring anthropology within a broader interdisciplinary study of patterned communication is striking both in timing and in content. In view of such consensus it may seem like quibbling to raise the question whether the new field should be called "semiology" or "semiotics." Indeed, some scholars have been using the terms interchangeably, while others have tried to synthesize the pioneering insights of Peirce and Saussure into a comprehensive and integrated point of view (Eco 1976; Jakobson 1967 in 1971; Sebeok 1976). Yet there are many issues in dispute between "semiotic" and "semiological" theories of signs that need to be clarified at the present time. In culture theory, particularly, the differences between Radcliffe-Brown and Lévi-Strauss, between Geertz and Lévi-Strauss, between Victor Turner and Leach, and between Goodenough and Schneider, for example, are not just the expression of personal or national prejudices but spring from differences in underlying conceptions of cultures and societies as systems of symbols and meanings. It would help to sharpen and clarify these differences, I believe, if the two most influential theories of signs, Peirce's *semiotic* and Saussure's *semiology*,were contrasted as well as compared with respect to some features that are especially relevant for culture theory. Such a comparison and contrast between *semiology* and *semiotic* need not be based on a comprehensive and historically detailed study of all writers who have used these terms. For purposes of the present discussion it is sufficient to construct an ideal-typical comparison based on Peirce and Saussure and some of their leading descendants. It may help the reader to follow the comparison and contrast between semiotic and semiology if the major items are summarized in Table 1.

Underlying similarities between Peircean *semiotic* and Saussurean *semiology* are important and have been recognized. Both Peirce and Saussure regarded themselves as pioneers opening up a new field, both aimed at a general theory of signs that would deal with all kinds of symbol-systems, and both analyzed the nature of signs in relational and structural terms rather than as "substances" and "things." Both also regarded linguistic signs as "arbitrary," in the sense that the meanings of such signs generally depend on social conventions and usages rather than on "natural" connections between the signs and the objects they denote.

The differences between semiotic and semiology are equally important and not so frequently recognized. In spite of the shared aim of both semiotic and semiology to become general theories of all kinds of sign systems, in actual practice the two theories differ in subject matter and method, in specific concepts and "laws," as well as in epistemology and ontology.

The subject matter of semiology tends to fall in the domains of natural languages, literature, myths and legends, and folk classifications.

TABLE 1
Comparison of Semiotic and Semiology

Point of Comparison	Semiotic (Peirce)	Semiology (Saussure)
1. Aims at a general theory of signs	philosophical, normative, but observational	a descriptive, generalized linguistics
2. Frequent subject matter domains	logic, mathematics, sciences, colloquial English (logic-centered)	natural languages, literature, legends, myths (language-centered)
3. Signs are relations, not "things"	a sign is a triadic relation of sign, object, and interpretant	a sign is a dyadic relation between signifier and signified
4. Linguistic signs are "arbitrary"	but also include "natural signs"—icons and indexes	but appear "necessary" for speakers of the language (Benveniste)
5. Ontology of "objects" of signs	existence presupposed by signs	not "given," but determined by the linguistic relations
6. Epistemology of empirical ego or subject	included in semiotic analysis	presupposed by but not included in semiological analysis

Semiotic, on the other hand, tends to concentrate on the domains of the formalized languages of mathematics, logic, and the natural sciences, on colloquial speech, and on nonverbal communication, human and animal.

Peirce conceived of semiotic as an "observational science," being dependent on the observations and experience of everyday life. In this respect it was a philosophical and normative science, a branch of logic in fact, in contrast to the special sciences, both physical and psychical, which depend for their observations on travel, special instruments, and training. Linguistics, ethnology, psychology, and sociology he classified as special psychical sciences, to which semiotic as "a quasi-necessary" doctrine of signs can be applied (Peirce CP:3.427–30).

Saussurean semiology also makes use of logical analysis, but since its subject matter consists of natural languages, its methods are descriptive and empirical rather than purely theoretical and analytic. In Peirce's classification, semiology could be a special science, a kind of generalized linguistics, dependent on special observation and comparison, rather than a philosophical science like semiotic.

These differences in subject matter and method between semiology and semiotic can be summarized in terms of a third important difference: semiology is language-centered, while semiotic is interested in the process of communication by signs of all kinds—a process Peirce named *semiosis*.

The language-centeredness of semiology is based on three assumptions: (1) that language is the most important of all sign systems; (2) that all other sign systems presuppose or imply the use of language; and (3) that linguistics, as the scientific study of language, offers the best model for the study of all other sign systems (Barthes 1970 [1963]; Hymes 1971; Jakobson 1971; Lévi-Strauss 1963a).

If these three assumptions are accepted, then a language-centered semiology becomes as broad in scope as Peirce's logic-centered general semiotic, since any kind of sign system, including culture, would then be studied as modeled on language. While this linguistic interpretation of semiology has been seriously proposed by Barthes, among others, the assumptions on which it is based are not self-evident. They need to be taken as hypotheses for discussion and testing, as does the linguistic interpretation of culture.

In one of his letters to Lady Welby, Peirce told her that her concentration on language and on English words was far narrower than his own studies, which "must extend over the whole of general semiotic": "I think that perhaps you are in danger of falling into some error in consequence of limiting your studies so much to language, and among languages to one very peculiar language, as all Aryan languages are; and within that language so much to words" (Welby 1931:312).

Peirce added that there were only three classes of English words with which he had "a decent acquaintance": "the words of the vernacular of the class of society in which I am placed, the words of philosophical and mathematical terminology," and chemical words—"which can hardly be said to be English or any other Aryan speech, being of a synthetic structure much like those of the tribes of our own brown 'red Indians'" (ibid.:313).

In contrast to such a narrow concentration on the meaning of words in one language, Peirce urged a broader science of semiotic, which would also study all kinds of signs—including icons, indices, and symbols—and their relations to their objects as well as to their interpretants. The comparative study of linguistic signs in different languages and of equations, graphs, and diagrams Peirce brought within the scope of his general semiotic, but he regarded the different linguistic forms by which a concept was signified, or an object designated, as "inessential accidents," like the skins of an onion. What was essential was that a thought have some possible expression for some possible interpreter (Peirce CP:4.6).

The semiological and the semiotic analyses of signs are both relational and structural. This point is quite explicit in both Saussure and Peirce. In his search for the basic data for linguistic analysis, Saussure rejected the position that there are given "objects," "things," or "substances" that could serve as the point of departure for linguistics. He insisted instead on the importance of the point of view from which the subject was studied and, in particular, on giving priority to relations: "The more one delves into the material proposed for linguistic study, the more one becomes convinced of this truth, which most particularly—it would be useless to conceal it—makes one pause: that the bond established amongst things is preexistent, in this one area, *to the things themselves*, and serves to determine them" (quoted in Benveniste 1971, "Saussure after Half a Century"; italics in the original). Saussure applied this relational point of view to the analysis of the linguistic sign, which he defined as a relation between an acoustic image and a concept, or, more generally, as a relation between a *signifier* and a *signified* (Saussure 1966:65–78).

In Peirce's semiotic theory a sign is also defined in relational terms but as a triadic relation rather than a dyadic relation, and the definition is intended for any kind of sign, not just for linguistic signs. Peirce's triadic definition of a sign is well known. One version, which seems to be especially lucid and succinct, is the following:

> A sign is in a conjoint relation to the thing denoted and to the mind. If this triple relation is not of a degenerate species, the sign is related to its object only in consequence of a mental association, and depends upon habit. Such signs are always abstract and general, because habits are general rules to which the organism has become subjected. They are, for the most part, conventional or arbitrary. They include all general words, the main body of speech, and any mode of conveying a judgment. (Peirce CP:3.13)

Peirce called such signs "symbols" to distinguish them from signs whose relation to their objects was of a direct nature and did not depend on a mental association. If the sign signifies its object solely by virtue of being really connected with it, as in physical symptoms—for example, meteorological signs and a pointing finger—Peirce called such a sign an *index*. A sign that stands for something merely because it resembles it, Peirce called an *icon*. Geometrical diagrams, maps, and paintings, are in this sense icons, although they may also have conventional and indexical features as well.

The difference between a dyadic and a triadic definition of the sign leads to other important differences. Benveniste has pointed out some confusions in Saussure's conception of the arbitrary nature of the linguistic sign because his concentration on the relation between signifier and signified slighted the object denoted, although in reality, "Saussure was always thinking of the representation of the *real object* (although he spoke of the 'idea') and of the evidently unnecessary and unmotivated character of the bond which united the sign to the *thing* signified" (Benveniste 1971, "The Nature of the Linguistic Sign").

Eco and others have explained Saussure's slighting of the object as springing from his giving primacy to the study of codes, of *langue*, over the study of the messages of *parole* (Eco 1976:60). It is also possible that Saussure's emphasis on "objects," "things," and "substances" as determined by relations rather than as preexisting "givens" influenced his attitude toward naming and denotation.

In any case, Peirce, who was a major contributor to the development of a logic of relations, felt no compulsion to omit objects from his definition of a sign. On the contrary, "objects" enter essentially into his definition of a sign and into many of his classifications of signs. "A *Sign* or *Representamen*, is a First which stands in such a genuine triadic relation to a Second, called its *Object*, as to be capable of determining a Third, called its *Interpretant* to assume the same triadic relation to its Object in which it stands itself to the same Object" (Peirce 1955:100).

I would suggest that Peirce was able to include objects in his relational analysis of signs and sign processes or semiosis because in his logic of relations, or relatives, he regarded objects as whatever was denoted by the subject of a relational statement. If such a statement contained two subjects, the relation was dyadic; if three subjects, then the relation was triadic; if *n* subjects, then the relation was *n*-adic.

From Peirce's logical point of view, the ontological status of the "objects" denoted by the subjects of the statement is the same whatever their number. Peirce's ontology of "objects" is not, however, simply one of logical or conceivable "objects"—although these are included. His ontology contains as well the "real" objects of the external world in two senses: (1) that such objects are indicated or denoted by the subjects of the statements as indexical signs. Without the indices we would not know what we were talking about, no matter how detailed our verbal descriptions or graphic our maps and diagrams. A proposition would then become a predicate with blanks for subjects. The object of a sign is "that with which the sign presupposes an acquaintance in order to convey some further information concerning it" (Peirce 1955:100; CP:3.414–24). (2) Peirce also distinguishes between the "immediate object" of a sign and its "dynamical object." The latter is the object as it will eventually be determined by a community of scientific investigators, while the "immediate object" is the object that an index calls to the immediate attention of an interpreter. "Look, it's raining!" would usually send the listener to the window to see the immediate object of the statement, while the meteorologists' reports would be concerned with the dynamical object (ibid.).

The epistemological differences between semiology and semiotic are as striking as their differences with respect to the ontology of "objects." I shall confine my comments on these to the roles of the empirical ego or subject in both theories.

Lévi-Strauss has accepted Ricoeur's characterization of structuralism as "Kantism without a transcendental subject," but neither he nor Ricoeur has indicated the role of the empirical subject. Although Lévi-Strauss declared that anthropology is "a conversation of man with man," he has been accused of neglecting just those face-to-face interactions considered essential for fieldwork by many social anthropologists (e.g., Geertz 1967 in 1973).

Some of Lévi-Strauss's formulations frequently seem to justify such charges. If "the myths think themselves in me," and I do not think them, then there is "decentering" of the empirical ego in structural and semiological anthropology in favor of a centering on signs and symbols.

Fortes has suggested an interesting interpretation of the difference between Lévi-Strauss and Radcliffe-Brown, which bears on this epistemological point. Lévi-Strauss's structural analysis, Fortes says, is "message-oriented," while Radcliffe-Brown's, and that of British social anthropology, is "actor-oriented" (Fortes 1966).

Fortes attributes the source of the general distinction between "message-oriented" and "actor-oriented" analysis to an article of Jakobson's. Drawing on Bohr's complementarity principle, and on Ruesch, MacKay, Cherry, and others, Jakobson distinguishes between two kinds of observers. The first of these is outside the system, "the most detached and external onlooker," who, having no knowledge of the code, acts as a cryptoanalyst and attempts to break the code through a scrutiny of the messages in Sherlock Holmes fashion.

In linguistics Jakobson regards cryptoanalysis as "merely a preliminary stage toward an internal approach to the language studied, when the observer becomes adjusted to the native speakers and decodes messages in their mother tongue through the medium of its code" (Jakobson 1971: 575). Such an observer becomes a "participant observer," who is placed within the system.

Fortes undoubtedly saw in the two kinds of observers, the cryptoanalyst and the participant observer, the difference between Lévi-Strauss and Radcliffe-Brown, respectively, and possibly that between French and British anthropology in general. Jakobson does not himself make such an application of the distinction, although some well-known criticism of Lévi-Strauss as a poor fieldworker (e.g., by Maybury-Lewis) and Lévi-Strauss's description in *Tristes Tropiques* of his dramatic silent encounter with the Mundé would seem to lend plausibility to such criticism.

The dismissal of Lévi-Strauss as a poor fieldworker is much too easy a polemical tactic, as was the same criticism of Radcliffe-Brown by Firth, Needham, and others. Functionalist social anthropology and participant observation in face-to-face interactions are accepted by Lévi-Strauss, especially as practiced by Mauss and the British school of social anthropology

(Lévi-Strauss 1976:5–9). That, however, is for him only the foundation on which to erect a structural and semiological anthropology. Fieldwork provides the empirical data—including native terminologies and texts—from which structural and semiological analysis constructs the unconscious categories and structures behind the level of observed facts. In these constructions the existence of subjects and their face-to-face interactions with one another and the anthropologist are presupposed, but abstracted from in structural analysis.

In a metaphor reminiscent of Kroeber, Lévi-Strauss calls structural anthropology the astronomy of the social sciences, since it studies societies and cultures at a distance, through the telescope, rather than with the microscopic observation of face-to-face community studies. In Lévi-Strauss's semiological telescope, everything looks like sign and symbol. But the hidden meanings are not observable through either a telescope or a microscope. They must be deciphered by the French Sherlock Holmes from the fragmentary empirical clues he finds in primitive myths, masks, and marriage practices.

In Peircean semiotic there is no transcendental ego, but there is an empirical ego. Peirce's critique of the prevailing Cartesianism of modern philosophy denies that we have the powers of introspection and intuition, of thinking without signs, of universal doubt. One's self is not a thinking substance whose existence is guaranteed by thinking—*Je pense, donc je suis.* All knowledge of the internal world is derived from hypothetic inferences from knowledge of external facts. "What passes within we only know as it is mirrored in external objects" (Peirce 1955:308).

Becoming aware of an inner world is a developmental process deriving from observation and experience of the external world and of other people. "We first see blue and red things. It is quite a discovery when we find the eye has anything to do with them, and a discovery still more recondite when we learn that there is an *ego* behind the eye, to which these qualities belong" (ibid.).

The *ego* exists in and is formed from these interactions with the external world and with other people. It is a phase in the dialogue with others and with oneself. ". . . A person is not absolutely an individual. His thoughts are what he is 'saying to himself,' that is, saying to that other self that is just coming to life in the flow of time. When one reasons, it is that critical self that one is trying to persuade; and all thought whatever is a sign, and is mostly of the nature of language" (ibid.: 258).

Eco quotes from one of Peirce's early lectures a passage in a somewhat similar vein to support the thesis that semiotics either defines subjects of semiotic acts in terms of semiotic structures or cannot deal with the empirical subjects at all (Eco 1976:316). This is an unwarranted conclusion to draw from the Peirce passage, as well as from Eco's own preceding acceptance of a Peircean semiotic. Empirical subjects are included in Eco's definition of the field of semiotics and of the subject matter of his book: "In this book semiotics has been provided with a paramount subject matter, *semiosis*. Semiosis is the process by which empirical subjects communicate, communication processes being made possible by the organization of signification systems" (Ibid.).

Why, given such a definition of semiosis, Eco should place the empirical subject beyond the semiotic threshold is puzzling. By accepting this limit, Eco seems to think that semiotics "fully avoids any risk of idealism" (ibid.:317).

Peirce did not exclude the empirical subject from his doctrine of semiotic, and yet he avoided an idealistic conception of the self. By locating the existence and development of the empirical ego within the process of communication, external and internal, he laid the foundations for a social theory of language, mind, and self, which was developed by William James, John Dewey, G. H. Mead, C. H. Cooley, Jean Piaget, and Charles Morris and came to be known as "symbolic interactionism" (Parsons 1968).

Peirce would probably have accepted a good deal of this theory, for he regarded the dictum of the old psychology, "which identified the soul with the ego, declared its absolute simplicity, and held that its faculties were names for logical divisions of human activity," as "all unadulterated fancy." He looked instead to a new psychology, whose observation of facts "has now taught us that the ego is a mere wave of the soul, a superficial and small feature, that the soul may contain several personalities and is as complex as the brain itself, and that the faculties, while not exactly definable and not absolutely fixed, are as real as are the different convolutions of the cortex" (Peirce 1955:52).

FOR A SEMIOTIC ANTHROPOLOGY

In retrospect, the tilt of culture theory to semiotics and semiology in the 1960s was no accident. It was a logical next step that followed important developments in anthropological theory as well as in other disciplines. By the 1950s some anthropologists and sociologists had recognized and explicitly formulated the concepts of culture and society as complementary, quasi-independent, and interconnected systems. This formulation represented a contraction of the long-standing definitions of culture and society as all-inclusive and rival concepts. The more restricted formulations tended to define "culture" as some kind of symbol system and "society" as sets of social relations among individual actors or among groups of actors. The specification of what kinds of symbol systems cultures were made of and how these were related to social action, to individual personalities, and to ecological conditions began to be explored in the 1960s and 1970s in the work of Lévi-Strauss, Geertz, Schneider, Leach, and Victor Turner, among others. These explorations in culture theory coincided with and drew on a veritable explosion in the general theories of signs and symbols, and particularly in the *semiology* of Saussure and in Peirce's *semiotic*, both of which had become international and interdisciplinary movements.

Lévi-Strauss has acknowledged Saussure as a source for his semiology and structural anthroplogy, and he also acknowledges Jakobson and Trubetskoy, structural linguistics generally, nonmetrical mathematics, cybernetics, the theory of games, and much else. The Bloomington conference on paralinguistics, kinesics, and proxemics encompassed a similar sweep of disciplines and specialized developments in psychology, medicine, philosophy of language, ethnology, literary and art criticism, and other fields. This interdisciplinary scope of discussion was also characteristic of the 1960s conferences and publications on semiotics and semiology in the Soviet Union, Poland, France, Italy, Israel, the United States, and elsewhere (Sebeok 1975).

As a result of these developments culture theory now confronts two major options—whether to become a branch of *semiology*, as Lévi-Strauss, Barthes, and Leach have proposed, or to follow a Peircean *semiotics*, as Margaret Mead, Sebeok, and Geertz have done to some extent. The choice between these options, and the consequences of each choice, can be clarified by an ideal-typical comparison of semiology and semiotics as general theories of signs, as well as through a historical study of their associations with culture theory.

The publication of some of Peirce's letters to Lady Welby and other selections from his writings in the appendixes to Ogden and Richards's *Meaning of Meaning* brought his semiotic theory to the notice of anthropologists as early as 1923. Malinowski, for example, whose essay on "The Problem of Meaning in Primitive Languages" was also included as an appendix to the Ogden and Richards volume, adapted the use of Ogden and Richards's semantic triangle, which was a simplified version of Peirce's semiotic triad. Lloyd Warner in turn extended the triangle to his analysis of Murngin totemism (1937) and then to his study of "Yankee City" Memorial Day and Tercentenary ceremonies (1959).

Lévi-Strauss's structural analyses of South and North American Indian myths and legends have shown the possibilities of a semiological anthropology. He has also proposed application of the approach to other culture domains—kinship and marriage, ritual, economic exchange, cuisine—within a unified theory of communication. Jakobson, who approves of that proposal, also points out that it requires different levels of analysis for different cultural domains (Jakobson 1971). Boon and Schneider (1974) have shown how these different levels operate in Lévi-Strauss's treatments of myth and kinship. Barthes (1970 [1963]), Leach (1976), and others have interpreted semiology as a generalized linguistics and have suggested how it can be applied to food, clothes, furniture, architecture, and traffic signals as "languages" and "codes."

Without wishing to deny the fruitful ingenuity of a semiological analysis of culture, or accepting Sperber's criticisms of Lévi-Strauss as a semiologist, I would urge the application of Peircean semiotic to the problems of culture theory and suggest that we call such explorations "semiotic anthropology." In one important respect, at least, a semiotic theory of signs has a distinct advantage over a semiological theory: it can deal with some of the difficult problems generated by acceptance of the complementarity of cultural and social systems. Because semiology limits itself to a theory of signification and linguistic codes, it cannot deal with the problems of how the different cultural "languages" are related to empirical objects and egos, to individual actors and groups. The existence of such extralinguistic relations is, of course, recognized by semiologists, but the study of them is relegated to other disciplines—psychology, sociology, economics, geography, and history. They do not enter directly and essentially into a semiological analysis.

In a semiotic anthropology, on the contrary, it is possible to deal with such extralinguistic relations within the framework of semiotic theory, because *a semiotic anthropology is a pragmatic anthropology*. It contains a theory of how systems of signs are related to their meanings, as well as to the objects designated and to the experience and behavior of the sign users.

Peircean semiotic is a "pragmatic semiotic," as Morris aptly calls it (Morris 1970:16,23). Morris refers particularly to the important point that " . . . pragmatism, more than any other philosophy, has embedded semiotic in a theory of action or behavior. The relation of a sign to what it signifies always involves the mediation of an interpretant, and an interpretant is an action or tendency to action of an organism" (ibid.:40).

This formulation of the pragmatic aspect of semiotic reflects the extensions added by James, Dewey, Mead, C. I. Lewis, and Morris himself. It has, however, a foundation in Peirce's formulation of the fundamental maxim of pragmatism: "The most perfect account of a concept that words can convey will consist in a description of the habit which that concept is calculated to produce. But how otherwise can a habit be described than by a description of the kind of action to which it gives rise, with the specification of the conditions and of the motive?" (in ibid.:24).

This particular formulation of the pragmatic maxim, as Morris notes, coincides with Peirce's definition of the *final interpretant* of intellectual concepts and is therefore an essential component of his semiotic. Peirce also distinguishes two other kinds of interpretants, the *emotional interpretant*, which is a kind of first impression created by the sign in the mind of the interpreter, and the *energetic interpretant*, which is an interpreter's direct reaction to a sign, expressed in verbal or nonverbal behavior.

There are two other pragmatic features implied by Peirce's semiotic theory of signs: the very definition of a sign in terms of a triadic relation of sign to object and interpretant includes an essential reference to the sign user. Similarly, Peirce's conception of sign processes *(semiosis)* as a process of growth and development of symbols from other symbols depends on the persuasive force of signs in the mind of the interpreter.

"Pragmatics" has gotten a bad name in contrast to the more rigorous "syntactics" and "semantics" because it has not until recently been greatly formalized and also because it has been regarded as a vague residual category. As a result, there have emerged two counter tendencies aiming to redefine "pragmatics"—to restrict it to (1) a study of specific indexical signs (Jakobson 1971; Silverstein 1976), or (2) a formalization of a theory of indexical signs (Montague 1974). It is to be hoped that these useful recent developments will not lead us to abandon Peirce's broader conception of a pragmatic semiotic or discourage its application to the problems of a semiotic anthropology. For, as the reclusive Yankee Yogi explained to Lady Welby, a new scientific field, such as the study of signs, can be best delimited in terms of a community of scholars prepared to devote themselves to that field.

> I smiled at your speaking of my having been "kindly interested" in your work, as if it were a divergence—I should say a deviation—from my ordinary line of attention. . . . It has never been in my power to study anything—mathematics, ethics, metaphysics, gravitation, thermodynamics, optics, chemistry, comparative anatomy, astronomy, psychology, phonetics, economics, the history of science, whist, men and women, wine, meteorology, except as a study of semiotic. . . . How . . . rarely I have met any who cares to understand my studies, I need not tell you. . . . (Welby 1931:304–305)

> I am satisfied that in the present state of the subject, there is but one general science of the nature of Signs. If we were to separate it into two,—then according to my idea that a "science"—as scientific men use the word, implies a social group of devotees, we should be in imminent danger of erecting two groups of one member each! Whereas if you and I stick together, we are, at least, two of us. . . . We shall have to try to seduce one of the linguists to our more fundamental study. (Peirce CP:8.378)

In the sixty-five or more years since Peirce wrote these words, the dialog-ical community of scholars devoting themselves to semiotic studies has multiplied manyfold. There are many signs that some members of this community are prepared to explore the application of Peirce's quasi-necessary doctrine of signs to the problems of anthropology.

3

Signs of the Self

The growth of interest in the 1940s and 1950s in the study of the human being as a cultural, social, and psychological universal led a few anthropologists, especially Hallowell and Redfield, to start thinking about a phenomenological conception of the self and the person (Hallowell 1955; Redfield 1955, 1962). This trend, while significant and important, did not convert many anthropologists to a phenomenological approach or produce a generally accepted anthropological theory of the self. The idea of describing another society-culture and its members from an "inside" point of view (on the self-axis, that is)—from the point of view of selves who appear in their own experience as well as in that of anthropological observers—seemed at that time too "subjective" and "unscientific."[1] A few anthropologists, notably Ruth Benedict, Margaret Mead, Paul Radin, and some other contributors to the personality and culture movement, were sympathetic to a phenomenological approach but were inclined to use it, if at all, for purposes of anecdotal illustration rather than as a staple method of anthropological observation, analysis, and report. Personality in "personality and culture" studies was an *object* of anthropological discourse— rarely a *subject* and participant in it (Singer 1961:66).[2] The situation began to change in the 1960s, when a renewed interest in post-Kantian phenomenology, combined with interest in Eastern philosophies and religions, stimulated new exploration of the role of the self in many different fields (Geertz 1966a; Kaplan 1968; Schutz 1962).

With the virtual explosion in the 1960s of the idea that cultures are systems of symbols and meanings, the stage was set for the development of a theory of the self as a system of symbols and meanings (Burke 1966; Douglas 1966, 1970; Munn 1973; Schneider 1968; Singer 1968; Turner 1967; Umiker-Sebeok 1977; White 1962; White and Dillingham 1973). It is true that none of the many varieties of "symbolic anthropology" in the 1960s addressed themselves directly to a theory of the self or person. It was inevitable, however, that once two members of the trinity (cultural and social systems) became signs and symbols, the third (the personality system) would soon follow (Lacan 1968; Piaget 1971; Shands 1978; Sebeok 1979; Singer 1978). The extent to which that is taking place is suggested by Spiro's protest in his paper "Whatever Happened to the Id?" that the trend has gone too far, that not everything is sign and symbol (Spiro 1979). One answer to Spiro's question is that the Id, especially sexuality and aggression, has been culturally constituted but need not be interpreted out of existence by a semiotic anthropology!

I have suggested in chapter 2 that, since it has a number of advantages over Saussure's semiology for the solution of anthropological problems of meaning and communication, Peirce's general theory of signs should be applied explicitly, under the rubric of *semiotic anthropology*. The present chapter explores the thesis that an application of Peirce's general theory of signs will produce a semiotic conception of the self that is also a phenomenological and a pragmatic conception. Since this feature of Peirce's theory of signs is not familiar to many anthropologists—or to many nonanthropologists, for that matter—its presentation here should be of value for the further development of culture theory. In addition, a semiotic conception of the self is consistent with the social and cultural nature of the self, as a matter of logical consistency in Peirce's formulations and in the later formulations of James (1961), Baldwin (1957), Cooley (1929 [1909], 1922), and Mead (1922, 1925). It will be shown not only that these later formulations add a specific social and cultural content to Peirce's semiotic conception of the self, but also that these specifications are themselves grounded in a semiotic analysis (see chap. 4).

In 1866, Peirce delivered a series of lectures at the Lowell Institute, in which can be found adumbrations of his semiotic theory of the self. In the manuscript that the editors of the *Collected Papers* have identified as Lecture XI of the Lowell Institute series, Peirce announces that in order to illustrate the advantages of the study of logic for philosophy, he has selected for discussion a loftier and more practical question of metaphysics—"What is man?" After putting the question within the field of inductive logic, he asks, "To what real kind does the thinking, feeling and willing being belong? We know that externally considered he belongs to the animal kingdom, to the branch of vertebrates and the class of mammals; but what we seek is his place when considered internally, disregarding his muscles, glands and nerves and considering only his feelings, efforts and conceptions" (Peirce CP:7.582).

Peirce obviously accepted one part of Darwinian evolution but preferred to treat separately the application of the question to the feeling, thinking, willing human being. This is not to say that he believed in a Cartesian dualism of mind and matter. Far from it; as we have noted, he considered his approach anti-Cartesian and phenomenological. His short preliminary answer to the question indicates the path along which his more specific answer will be found: "We have already seen that every state of consciousness [is] an inference; so that life is but a sequence of inferences or a train of thought. At any instant then man is a thought, and as thought is a species of symbol, the general answer to the question what is man? is that he is a symbol" (CP:7.583).

At first reading, that answer will strike many as a poetic metaphor right out of the romantic visions of American and German transcendentalism. Peirce admits that it is a metaphor, occasionally quotes Emerson's line "Of Thine Eye I am Eyebeam," and acknowledges his early affiliations with the Concord School (Peirce CP:6.102; 1955:339). He also acknowledges the influences on his thinking of German philosophical anthropology—Kant, Hegel, Schiller, and Schelling. He studied Kant's *Critique of Pure Reason* for two hours a day for three years (1955:1–2). While critical of those sources, especially of Hegel's logic, he nevertheless took some of their ideas as a point of departure for his own.

For Peirce a metaphor is a special kind of sign, the interpretation of which requires a knowledge of the theory of signs, or semiotic, his theory of logic and inference, and his phenomenological classification of the three categories of being and of consciousness (ibid.:105).[3] A poetic quotation from Emerson may have been a pithy indication of some of his New England intellectual affiliations, but the lines of poetry he quotes most frequently are those from which the title of this book is taken: "Most ignorant of what he's most assur'd,/His glassy essence. . . ."

When we read Peirce's Lowell Lecture XI carefully, we find that his metaphor that man is a symbol is not merely based on a poetic line or two from Emerson and Shakespeare, nor is it only another answer to the German philosophical anthropologists' question *Was ist der Mensch?* In this, as well as in other papers, Peirce carefully developed what he considered the true and exact analogy between man and symbol. He was able to show that most of the distinctive traits of human beings have their parallels in words: consciousness, feeling, perception, conformity to law, the power of attention. Even the unity of thought, the *I think*, has its parallel in the unity of symbolization that is consistency, and the power of creation has its counterpart in the power of symbols to create other symbols within themselves:

> Perception is the possibility of acquiring information, of meaning more; now a word may learn. How much more the word *electricity* means now than it did in the days of Franklin; how much more the term planet means now than it did in the time [of] Hipparchus. These words have acquired information; just as man's thought does by further perception. But is there not a difference, since a man makes the word and the word means nothing which some man has not made it mean and that only to that man? This is true; but since man can think only by means of words

or other external symbols, words might turn round and say, You mean nothing which we have not taught you and then only so far as you address some word as the interpretant of your thought. In fact, therefore, men and words reciprocally educate each other; each increase of a man's information is at the same time the increase of a word's information and *vice versa*. So that there is no difference even here. (CP:7.587)

Peirce's summary of "the true analogy" between man and word is remarkable for its concision and its content:

A man denotes whatever is the object of his attention at the moment; he connotes whatever he knows or feels of this object, and is the incarnation of this form or intelligible species; his interpretant is the future memory of this cognition, his future self, or another person he addresses, or a sentence he writes or a child he gets. (CP:7.591)

To my mind this is the seed from which grew Peirce's semiotic and empirical conception of the self, out of a philosophical anthropology deeply influenced by German objective idealism. I do not say that the transformation can be seen in its entirety in this one short passage or even in the whole of the Lowell Lecture XI. In the lecture, read pragmatically, however, in the light of the consequences Peirce later developed from the man-sign thesis, we can discern the semiotic conception of the self. I do not expect to persuade readers of the correctness of my interpretation of Peirce on this occasion. They may find useful, however, a brief summary of the interpretation and of the applications of such a theory in contemporary anthropological research.

Peirce's starting point is the sensing, thinking, feeling, willing self of nineteenth-century philosophy and psychology. That self, however, is no longer for him a permanent Cartesian mental substance with the powers of introspection, intuition, and universal doubt, which is dispelled by the clear and distinct ideas of its own existence, the unity of the "I think." Instead, Peirce finds a "phenomenological" self without the powers of introspection, intuition, of thinking without signs, of conceiving the absolutely incognizable. All our "knowledge of the internal world is derived by hypothetical reasoning from our knowledge of external facts," by means of multiple chains of signs that make up the inferences (CP:5.264–68, 280–317).

Given such an anti-Cartesian point of departure, Peirce confronted—as have other modern philosophers—the problem of finding the locus, identity, unity, and continuity of the self among the rapidly changing "phenomena" of a stream of consciousness.[4] His solution to the problem was to look in the sign-processes themselves for the answer. For Peirce, the locus, identity, and continuity of the self was not to be found in the individual organism, whether in the pineal gland or in the organism as a whole. It was, rather, an "outreaching identity," which connected the feelings, thoughts, and actions of one individual with those of others through the processes of semiotic communication (CP:7.591). The self was thus both a product and an agent of semiotic communication, and therefore social and public.

THE SELF AS OBJECT AND SUBJECT OF SEMIOTIC SYSTEMS[5]

It is probable that Peirce's anti-Cartesian approach to the self-concept may have been suggested to him by his reading in Kant. As early as 1787 Kant denied the intuitive character of the "I think," in the *Critique of Pure Reason:* "In the representation I, the consciousness of myself is not an intuition, but merely an intellectual representation produced by the spontaneous activity of a thinking subject" (1855:168–69). Peirce's development of the approach, however, advanced considerably beyond Kant and included several novel contributions. Notable among these in the present context are the ways in which Peirce escaped from the subjectivism that has dominated modern philosophy since Descartes, according to Whitehead. One of these ways was to include in his three phenomenological categories of being and consciousness the category of secondness, or brute, matter-of-fact interaction with the world. This enabled Peirce to retain the distinction between an *inner* and *outer* world *within* a phenomenological description of the self and the world in terms of degree of muscular effort exerted (Peirce 1955:276). In his classification of signs, the counterpart of secondness is the indexical kind of sign, which directs attention to single objects or collections of objects by blind compulsion or physical proximity. Without the use of indices to denote the objects, the speaker would not be able to identify what he was talking about. Even with the use of indices, it is still necessary for the listener to have "collateral observation" and "collateral information" about the object in order to become better acquainted with its location and characteristics.

Peirce's analysis of the sign-function or sign-action, which he called *semiosis*, as consisting of an irreducibly triadic relation of object, sign, and interpretant, also escapes from subjectivism and solipsism since it assumes that the objects may exist in the outer world independently of the signs they determine and independently of the persons whose interpretations are determined by the signs (Peirce 1977:190–91, 196).

In the case of linguistic symbols, such as words that depend on conventional definitions and customary usages of the symbolizers, Peirce subjects their interpretations to the control of his pragmatic maxim: "Consider what effects, that might conceivably have practical bearings, we conceive the object of our conception to have. Then, our conception of these effects is the whole of our conception of the object" (Peirce 1955:31).

The repetition of "conception" in this formulation, as well as in other formulations, was a deliberate attempt by Peirce to emphasize that his maxim did not appeal to the concrete sensory effects of an object, as James interpreted pragmatic meaning, but depended on the general and conditional consequences of an intellectual concept (Peirce 1955:287–88). At the same time, Peirce described his variety of pragmatism as an application of the experimental method of science to ascertain the meanings of hard words and of abstract concepts (Peirce 1955:271). From the illustrations Peirce gives of the application of the method, such as the scratch test for hardness, one must conclude that the pragmatic meaning of a concept did include concrete sensory effects and that the experimental method made use of indexical signs to identify and measure degrees, magnitudes, and numbers of specific observations. The barometer, plumb line, spirit level, weather vane, pendulum, and photometer are cited by Peirce as respective indices of observed specific pressure, vertical and horizontal directions, wind direction, gravity, and star brightness. And even the final interpretant of an intellectual concept comes to rest in concrete habits of action or in changes thereof. In this sense, Peirce's pragmatism includes the later operationalism. Peirce, I believe, would agree but would add that no single test or single collection of tests can exhaust the meaning of an intellectual concept (Peirce 1955:109, 286).

The coordination of his semiotic with his pragmatism and phenomenology not only enabled Peirce to avoid falling into subjectivism but also allowed him to start constructing a social and semiotic theory of the self consistent with science and common sense. Such a conception of the self is not transparently implied by Peirce's analogy between man and symbol or even by his anti-Cartesianism. It is a conception, however, that is implicit in Peirce's semiotic theory and can be derived from it with the help of several principles that are occasionally stated explicitly in Peirce's writings. Although these principles are partially independent, taken together they converge on the conception of the self as an essential component of semiotic systems.

One of the most important of these principles is that of the reflexiveness or self-reference of all signs. Peirce formulates this principle explicitly in an 1868 paper, "On Some Consequences of Four Incapacities":

> . . . whenever we think, we have present to the consciousness some feeling, image, conception, or other representation, which serves as a sign. But it follows from our own existence (which is proved by the occurrence of ignorance and error) that everything which is present to us is a phenomenal manifestation of ourselves. This does not prevent its being a phenomenon of something without us, just as a rainbow is at once a manifestation both of the sun and of the rain. When we think, then, we ourselves as we are at that moment, appear as a sign. (Peirce 1955:233; CP:5.283)

This formulation is a difficult one to interpret. The notion that we think by means of signs is familiar enough in Peirce as well as in Leibniz, Berkeley, and others. But that everything that is present to our minds should appear as a sign of ourselves as well as a sign of something without us is a less familiar notion. Peirce's effort to explain it in the same 1868 paper in terms of the belief that a thought-sign of an outward thing can refer to this thing only through denoting the previous thought is psychologically problematic introspection and does not prove that the thought-sign is also a sign of the self, except in the sense that one thought-sign has been preceded by an earlier thought-sign and will be followed by a later thought-sign.

Peirce's own statement that "at no one instant in my state of mind is there cognition or representation, but in the relation of my states of mind at different instants there is," shows the difficulty of inferring self-reference from thoughts that refer to outward objects. Peirce's further comment, however, that we ought to say that "we are in thought, and not that thoughts are in us," "just as we say that a body is in motion, and not that motion is in body," is a valid conclusion from his analysis (Peirce 1955:236; CP:5.289n).

Fortunately, it is not necessary to wait until psychology can confirm Peirce's theory that "every thought, however artificial and complex, is, so far as it is immediately present, a mere sensation without parts, and therefore, in itself, without similarity to any other, but incomparable with any other and absolutely *sui generis*." And a confirmation would not in any case explain the thinking subject, for "every thought, in so far as it is a feeling of a peculiar sort, is simply an ultimate inexplicable fact" (Peirce 1955:236; CP5.289).

It is sufficient for a semiotic conception of the self to assume, as Peirce does, that trains of thought are mediated by signs and are species of inference. And even if not all signs are signs of the self, as Peirce's principle of reflexive reference implies, *some* signs can and do refer to the self either as object or subject of the signs, or both. This principle follows from Peirce's triadic analysis of the sign-function, or semiosis, and from the dialogical nature of that function.

I have argued in chapter 2 that Peirce's analysis of the sign-function as a triadic relation of sign, object, and interpretant includes an ontology of objects as well as an epistemology of subjects who conceive or know the objects through the mediation of the signs. The objects in Peirce's ontology comprise not only imaginary and conceivable objects but single existing things or collections of such things. In this respect, as we have noted, Peirce's semiotic differs from Saussure's semiology, which defines the sign-function as a dyadic relation of signifier and signified that dispenses with both independent objects and subjects.

Let us now apply Peirce's semiotic analysis to the self as an object of signs. We shall not try to deal with all the kinds of signs defined and classified by Peirce, for that classification is complex and numerous, and included sixty-six kinds of signs in one of his latest versions. I shall restrict the present discussion to his trichotomy of indices, icons, and symbols, for that remained one of his most important and useful classifications and contained the ancient one of "deictic, mimetic, and symbolic" signs, which goes back at least to Plato and Aristotle (Peirce 1977:85n.30; Burks 1948–49; Whittier 1970).[6]

The trichotomy of iconic, indexical, and symbolic signs is based on Peirce's analysis of three kinds of relations that a sign may have to its object—resemblance, contiguity, and association by convention. An iconic sign resembles its object in some respect (e.g., a picture or a diagram); an indexical sign is contiguous with its object or physically related to it (e.g., a weather vane); and a symbol stands for its object because it is so interpreted by convention and usage (e.g., the word *dog*). In Peirce's triadic analysis of the sign-relation, the diagram and the weather vane are also interpreted, but the interpretations rest on "natural" relations of the signs to their objects.

While iconic, indexical, and symbolic signs may refer to all sort of things—natural landscapes, plants and animals, houses and vehicles, and the starry heavens above—an important subset of these signs refers to human persons, e.g., personal and family portraits are iconic signs of persons; personal pronouns and names are indexical signs of persons; verbal descriptions of people are symbolic signs. All these signs are, in one sense, signs of the self, and selves are objects of these signs. Peirce's analysis of such signs and how they indicate and symbolize their objects, separately and in combination, applies the tools of modern logic to show how nonverbal and nonpropositional signs can be combined to make statements. A portrait, for example, as an iconic sign makes no assertion; nor does a proper name as an indexcial sign. But put the name on the portrait and the result is a statement that this is a portrait of the person named.

More generally, the self as an object of a sign-relation is denoted by the indexical signs (cf. the grammatical subjects and objects of a sentence). The character of the self is signified by the iconic signs (as the predicate of the sentence). The indexical and iconic signs are conjoined by a symbol to make a statement about one or more persons. The sentence "Ezekiel loveth Huldah," constructed by Peirce, illustrates the general analysis and its application to the self as object. Ezekiel and Huldah are indexical signs that denote two persons, and "the effect of the word 'loveth' is that the pair of objects denoted by the pair of indices Ezekiel and Huldah is represented by the icon, or the image we have in our minds of a lover and his beloved" (Peirce 1955:113).

So far I have argued that Peirce's analysis of the sign-function in terms of the triadic relation of sign, object, and interpretant, together with his

classification of signs into iconic, indexical, and symbolical, provides a
semiotic means for denoting persons as objects, signifying their characteristics, and making propositional statements about them. I have also suggested that the concept of the self as an object of a semiotic system remains
significant and effective, even if Peirce's principle of the reflexive reference
of all signs present to the mind cannot be psychologically validated. Now,
what about the self as the subject of a semiotic system? I do not mean the
grammatical subject of a sentence, for that, as already explained, is an
indexical sign, which denotes something (including persons) as objects. I
mean the thinking subject whose spontaneous activity produces the representation *I*, as Kant said. This is a more difficult problem than the
semiotic representation of the self as an object. Eco, for example, has
denied that the sign-creating subject can be included within semiotic:
"What is behind, before or after, outside or *too much* inside the
methodological 'subject' outlined by this book might be tremendously
important. Unfortunately it seems to me—at this stage—beyond the
semiotic threshold" (Eco 1976:317).

Although he recognizes that some semiotic approaches (Kristeva 1973,
for example) transcend the threshold by attempting to study "the creative
activity of a semiosis-making subject," Eco nevertheless insists that empirical subjects who communicate by means of the process of semiosis can be
defined only in terms of semiotic structures. Either they are among the
possible referents of objects of the message or text, or, if presupposed by
the statements, they have to be "read" as an element of the conveyed
content. Otherwise, the subjects do not exist at all as far as semiotics is
concerned, although they may be studied by other disciplines (Eco
1976:314–17).

Curiously, Eco quotes in support Peirce's analogy of man and sign and
his statement that "my language is the sum total of myself; for the man is
the thought" (ibid.:316).

Another approach to the problem of how the thinking, feeling, acting
subject is related to language and symbolism has been suggested by
Ricoeur (1974). After reviewing in historical perspective the challenges
that both structuralism and psychoanalysis present to the philosophical
ego, Ricoeur suggests that the linguist Benveniste's analysis of the first-,
second-, and third-person pronouns offers a new basis for a "Hermeneutics of the I am" as well as for a reconciliation between structuralism,
psychoanalysis, and philosophy.

For Ricoeur, the essential feature of Benveniste's article on pronouns is
the interpretation of *I*: "The signification of *I* is singular in each instance;
it refers to the occurrence of discourse which contains it and refers solely
to it. *I* signifies 'the person who is uttering the present instance of the
discourse containing *I*'" (Benveniste 1971:218, 226; Ricoeur 1974:225).

This interpretation of the first-person pronoun establishes a connection between the linguistic representation "I" and the speaking subject, and, in Ricoeur's version, with the thinking, feeling subject as well. The interpretation explains how a grammatical code, the classification of pronouns, is actually used to construct a message: "Outside the reference to a particular individual who designates himself in saying *I*, the personal pronoun is an empty sign that anyone can seize: the pronoun is waiting there, in my language, like an instrument available for converting the language into discourse through my appropriation of this empty sign" (Ricoeur 1974:255).

The personal pronouns, as Benveniste and Ricoeur recognize, form only one group of signs that, together with demonstratives and adverbs of time and place, do not signify a class of objects but are "indicators," which "do not name but indicate the *I*, the *here*, the *now*, the *this*; in short, the relation of a speaking subject to an audience and a situation." "What is admirable," Benveniste adds, is that "the language is organized in such a way that it allows each speaker to appropriate the entire language by designating himself as the *I*" (Benveniste 1971:266).

Benveniste's "indicators" sound very much like some of Peirce's indexical signs, and there is some evidence in Benveniste's article that he may have been influenced by Peirce through Morris. The notion is also closely related to that of "shifters" (Burks 1948–49; Jakobson 1971; Silverstein 1976). Peirce did not, however, regard the self-designation of the *I* as a primordial creative act that allows each speaker to appropriate the entire language and to "posit" the ego and the world. The consciousness of the self and that of the world do not for him emerge as simultaneous and instantaneous creations from the utterance of "I." Ontogenetically, at least, the appearance of self-consciousness and consciousness of the external world are gradual developments, very much dependent on the child's nurturance, interactions, and communication with others. Peirce's contributions to developmental psychology were not very extensive, but he did introduce two principles that were to become crucial for the further growth of a semiotic theory of the self. One of these principles was the dialogical structure of sign-action, or semiosis, and the other was the social-symbolic nature of personal identity.

THE DIALOGICAL STRUCTURE OF THE SIGN-RELATION

We may now generalize these observations and point out an important feature of Peirce's classification of iconic, indexical, and symbolic signs— that it combines a theory of signification with a theory of communication. This feature is not only built into the classification of signs, their objects, and interpretants; it is also explicitly discussed by Peirce in his references to the "utterer," or the producer of a sign, and the "interpreter" of the sign. The triadic action of signs does not take place in a vacuum; it is a segment in a process of communication and exchange between the "utterer" and the "interpreter." In the case of two persons communicating, the triadic relation of sign-object-interpretant may be considered reducibly pentadic, with the addition of "utterer" and "interpreter," as a comparison with exchange relations shows (Peirce 1977:190–91).

In one of his latest writings, in a letter to Lady Welby, Peirce explains his use of the word "sign" in the widest sense, "for any medium for the communication or extension of a Form (or feature)" (ibid.:196). He also specifies that such communication requires that "the Form be embodied in a Subject independently of the communication; and it is necessary that there should be another subject in which the same form is embodied only in consequence of the communication" (ibid.).

The implication of this explanation of "sign" for the relationship between "utterer" and "interpreter" is embodied in an explicit classification of the kinds of interpretants, or meanings, of a sign, thus integrating the analysis of signification with the analysis of communication:

> There is the *Intentional* Interpretant, which is a determination of the mind of the utterer; the *Effectual* Interpretant, which is a determination of the mind of the interpreter; and the *Communicational* Interpretant, or say the *Cominterpretant*, which is a determination of that mind into which the minds of utterer and interpreter have to be fused in order that any communication should take place. This mind may be called the commens. It consists of all that is, and must be, well understood between utterer and interpreter at the outset, in order that the sign in question should fulfill its function. . . . it is out of the nature of things for an object to be signified (and remember that the most solitary meditation is dialogue,) otherwise than in relation to some actuality or existent in the commens. (Ibid.:197)

Peirce's semiotic conception of the self is not only logical; it is "dialogical." The self is an interlocutor in a dialogue with other selves as well as a signified object and interpretant of a specific code of signs. In the letter to Lady Welby just cited, Peirce extends this dialogical conception to inner thought: "A thought is a very special variety of sign. All thinking is necessarily a sort of dialogue, an appeal from the momentary self to the better considered self of the immediate and of the general future" (ibid.:195).

The full reach of Peirce's dialogical conception of self, as both agent and product of dialogue, is indicated in one of his later papers on pragmatism:

> Two things here are all-important to assure oneself of and to remember. The first is that a person is not absolutely an individual. His thoughts are what he is "saying to himself," that is, is saying to that other

self that is just coming into life in the flow of time. When one reasons, it is that critical self that one is trying to persuade; and all thought whatsoever is a sign, and is mostly of the nature of language. The second thing to remember is that the man's circle of society (however widely or narrowly this phrase may be understood), is a sort of loosely compacted person, in some respects of higher rank than the person of an individual organism. (Peirce 1955:258; CP:5.421)

PERSONAL IDENTITY AS SOCIAL AND SEMIOTIC

What happens to personal identity in the dialogical process of talking to oneself and talking to others? Having renounced an immediate intuition of the Cartesian *cogito*, Peirce tries to build a conception of personal identity from the complex of feelings, ideas, and actions that come together within a single organism and in the relations between organisms. Personality is "some kind of coordination or connection" of ideas and feelings. It has to be "lived in time," and "so far as it is apprehended in a moment, it is immediate self-consciousness." For Peirce, however, personality was not simply a "stream of consciousness" but a "bundle of habits" guided by the "developmental teleology" of "a general idea, living and conscious now, and already determinative of acts in the future to an extent to which it is not now conscious."

Peirce added that the reference to the future is "an essential element of personality. Were the ends of a person already explicit, there would be no room for development, for growth, for life: and consequently there would be no personality." (The quotations are from Peirce's essay on "the law of mind," published in 1892 and reprinted in Peirce 1955 as well as in the *Collected Papers*:6.102–63.)

This conception of personality is not restricted by Peirce to the person of the individual organism but includes "the loosely compacted person" of a man's circle of society. The wider application of the personality concept implies that there is some form of communication between individual organisms that underlies the compacting of "higher rank persons." Although he did not rule out the possibility of telepathy and "other modes of continuous connection between minds than those of time and space," Peirce adhered to a naturalistic explanation of interpersonal communication of ideas and feelings: "when an idea is conveyed from one mind to another, it is by forms of combination of the diverse elements of nature, say by some curious symmetry, or by some union of a tender colour with a refined odour. To such forms the law of mechanical energy has no application" (Peirce 1955:351). He also maintained that "feelings are communicated to the nerves by continuity, so that there must be something like them in the excitants themselves."

Consistently with the above theory of interpersonal communication, Peirce held that the recognition by one person of another's personality "takes place by means to some extent identical with the means by which he is conscious of his own personality. The idea of the second personality, which is as much as to say the second personality itself, enters within the field of direct consciousness of the first person, and is as immediately perceived as his ego, though less strongly. At the same time, the opposition between the two is perceived, so that the externality of the second is recognized" (ibid.).

Peirce admits that the phenomena of intercommunication between two minds have been "unfortunately little studied." He was impressed, however, by "the very extraordinary insight which some persons are able to gain of others from indications so slight that it is difficult to ascertain what they are," and believed that his theory explained such insight (ibid.:351–52; CP:6.548–52). A fascinating account of an incident in which Peirce himself believed he showed such extraordinary insight has been described and discussed by Thomas Sebeok and Jean Umiker-Sebeok (1979).

Peirce's theory of personality and of personal identity has the important consequence that the self, whether considered as the object of a semiotic system or as the subject and interlocutor in such a system, is not identical with the individual organism. The self may be less or more than the individual organism, less when in the flow of time the inner dialogue brings a new phase of the self into life, and more when in dialogue with other organisms there emerges one loosely compacted person.

Under these circumstances, personal identity is not confined to the consciousness of one's body, the "box of flesh and blood," but extends as well to "social consciousness," the consciousness of living others with whom one is in sympathetic communication, and to "spiritual consciousness," the consciousness of others who are no longer living but whose ideas and feelings are still present among the living. Personal identity is an "outreaching identity" (CP:7.591). The boundaries of personal identity, in Peirce's theory, are somewhat indefinite and variable and depend on the social and cultural "outreach" of a particular individual's consciousness.

Peirce wrote before anthropology developed its concepts of social, cultural, and personality systems, and he seems not to have been familiar with Tylor's charter definition of culture. Nevertheless, he anticipated later anthropological ideas about the role of social and cultural factors in the development of many cultural achievements, e.g., Gothic pointed architecture, and the independent and simultaneous development of many modern inventions and discoveries, such as the principle of the conservation of energy, the mechanical theory of heat, the kinetic theory of gases, the doctrine of natural selection, the periodic law of chemical elements, the telegraph, the telephone, and ether as an anesthetic. Individual genius did not seem to him an adequate explanation of such developments (ibid.:6.306–17).

These views of cultural historical developments—including the idea that there are "natural" periods in cultural evolution of about five hundred years each—are similar to Kroeber's, except that for Peirce the developments are supra-individual but not super-organic. For Peirce the innovation and diffusion of cultural developments depend on the power of sympathy as it affects a whole people or community or particular individuals (Peirce 1955:366–67). For Kroeber the role of individual and collective psychology in the innovation and diffusion of cultural forms belongs not to the study of cultural history but to the subcultural disciplines of psychology and social psychology (Kroeber 1963).

That Peirce's conception of personal identity is based on a psychology of personality that is at once social and cultural is apparent in the passages I have quoted from the cosmological papers in the early 1890s. These passages do not by themselves suffice to show that such a conception of personal identity implies a semiotic, phenomenological, and pragmatic theory of the self. Taken together, however, with the quotations I cited earlier from the 1905 essay on "What Pragmatism Is," and from the Peirce-Welby correspondence, these passages do indicate that in his later years Peirce was moving toward an integrated and consistent theory of personal identity. How Peirce's theory was extended by the later development of symbolic interactionism is the subject of chapter 4 (cf. Lincourt and Hare 1973).

INTERPRETANTS AND INTERPRETERS

One possible objection that may be urged against my analysis of the self as the subject and object of semiotic systems is that I assume personal users of signs, as utterers and interpreters, in addition to the interpretant of a sign in Peirce's triadic semiosis. Dewey severely criticized Morris for making a similar assumption (Dewey 1946). He called it "a gratuitous introduction of an interpreter," a misinterpretation that "not only does not describe pragmatism in any way whatever, but falls . . . wholly outside of Peirce's theory of signs and meaning and of anything involved in that theory."

> To Peirce, "interpreter", if he used the word, would mean *that which interprets*, thereby giving meaning to a linguistic sign. . . . I do not believe that it is possible to exaggerate the scorn with which Peirce would treat the notion that *what* interprets a given linguistic sign, can be left to the whim or caprice of those who happen to use it . . . the interpretant, in Peirce's usage, is always and necessarily *another* linguistic sign—or, better, a set of such signs. (Dewey 1946:87)

Since Morris convincingly showed in his reply to Dewey that Peirce did indeed use the words "interpreter" and "interpretant" in more or less the manner Morris had attributed to him and that these usages were an integral part of his pragmatism, there is no need to repeat Morris's reply (Morris 1948–49). I would like, however, to comment on another aspect of Dewey's argument that bears directly on the semiotic conception of the self and seems to me internally inconsistent.

On the one hand, Dewey emphasizes, quite properly, that in Peirce's theory of signs there is no such thing as a sign in isolation, that every sign is a constituent of a sequential set of signs, and that a "thing" has no meaning—is not a sign—apart from membership in this set. The meaning of earlier signs in the sequential movement of signs is provided by later ones until a *(logical)* conclusion is reached (Dewey 1946:88).

All this is familiar Peirce doctrine and was not denied by Morris. But Dewey draws from it a conclusion unfavorable to Morris's "translation" of "interpretant" into a personal user as its interpreter, and his formulation of *semantics* as a relation of signs to "things." Since signs as such are connected with other signs, argues Dewey, signs cannot refer to "things": "a designatum of a sign which is not itself a sign is an absurdity" (ibid.:84).

Dewey does admit, however, that Morris's statement that "Things may be regarded as the designata of indexical signs" approximates, except for the word "designata," "the actual theory of Peirce concerning how one kind of sign, but *not* word, sentence, or linguistic sign, refers to things" (ibid.:89).

What this aspect of Dewey's argument amounts to, then, is that "linguistic signs, constituting *thought* and conferring generality, continuity, and law," cannot refer to "things" without "getting into connection with indexical signs" (and some form of secondness). This, again, is good Peirce doctrine, and Dewey cites Peirce's examples of physical pointing and all demonstratives and personal pronouns—"this," "that," "I," "you," etc.—as indexical signs and reflections of secondness (ibid.:90).

Nor would Morris disagree with this, as Dewey's own statement makes clear: "This perceptual-manipulative behavioral event determines the indexical sign which brings us into connection with things, something it is impossible, according to Peirce, for symbols, linguistic signs, or, in Morris' words, for a sentence, to do" (ibid.:91).

Dewey also recognizes, at least by implication, that the *emotional* and *energetic* interpretants of iconic and indexical signs, respectively, are not simply further signs but the interpreter's experience of qualities and interactions (ibid.:92). Even the *logical* interpretants of intellectual concepts and linguistic signs find a resting place in the final interpretant, the interpreter's habits. Such habits constitute the regularities in the interpreter's character and personality, capable of change and growth through the elimination of old habits and the learning of new ones.[7]

Although we may have no powers of introspection and have to infer the self from observation of external facts, including signs, we also observe that symbolic as well as iconic and indexical signs are forms of communication that are intrinsically social. To paraphrase Peirce somewhat, a self denotes by an indexical sign whatever is the object of its attention at the moment, it connotes with an iconic sign whatever it knows or feels of this object, and it incarnates in a symbol this form or intelligible species. Its interpretant is the future memory of this cognition, its future self, another person whom it addresses, a sentence it writes, or a child it gets.

The problem of distinguishing the "interpretant" of a sign from the "interpreter," raised by Dewey, has been reopened in recent years by several Peirce specialists (Thompson 1953, Zeman 1977). The editor of the new edition of the Peirce papers has suggested a new view of the problem based on several little-known Peirce passages (Fisch 1978). The most important of those passages is from a 1908 letter to Lady Welby: "I define Sign as anything which is so determined by something else, called its Object, and so determines an effect upon a person which effect I call its Interpretant, that the latter is thereby mediately determined by the former. My insertion of 'upon a person' is a sop to Cerberus, because I despair of making my own broader conception understood" (Fisch 1978:55; Peirce 1977:80–81).

On the basis of this and several other passages he cites, Fisch suggests that Peirce's "sop to Cerberus" may be "lapsing from sign-talk into psych-talk" because he feared that his readers would not understand *formal semiotic* language (Fisch 1978:56). The suggestion is ingenious and important; it is very apt to be misunderstood. To forestall a misinterpretation of Peirce, I should like to add a word or two about the meaning of "formal semiotic."

Peirce usually refers to semiotic as "formal" in a sense "very much like mathematical reasoning." It is a process of "abstractive observation" and generalization, by which he arrives at "conclusions as to what *would* be true of signs in all cases, so long as the intelligence using them was scientific" (CP:2.227–29; Peirce 1955:98–99). The fact that the reasoning is *formal* does not exclude its also being empirical, for it is based on the observation of "diagrams" and "outline sketches," from which one can reach new conclusions, just as in the case of reasoning with the help of mathematical diagrams (ibid.). For Peirce, "formal" analysis means relational analysis (Singer 1978:213–18; Peirce 1977:190–93).

The mathematical analogy is restated in two passages that Fisch quotes. In these, Peirce compares the process of arriving at an abstract notion of a sign by stripping away "all reference to the mind" and then giving "a mathematical definition of a mind, in the same sense in which we can give a mathematical definition of a straight line. . . . But there is nothing to compel the object of such a formal definition to have the peculiar feeling of consciousness" (Fisch 1978:56).

That "peculiar feeling of consciousness" is, of course, for Peirce an essential characteristic of the human mind and of mental signs, as he makes clear in the Lowell Lecture XI, as well as in his later writings on psychology. As long, however, as he is concerned with a mathematically *formal* definition of mind, he need not refer to the psychology of feeling and personality, although *informally* he has a good deal to say, in the *metalanguage* of English, about that psychology (Peirce 1977:195–96).[8] Such informal discourse, based on "collateral observation" of the object of the sign, human psychology in this case, is presupposed for a correct use and interpretation of the formal definition.

In spite of its *formal* character, semiotic is a phenomenological science not only in the sense that it is observational; it is phenomenological also in Peirce's special sense of being based on "phaneroscopy," the description of what "is present to the mind, quite regardless of whether it corresponds to any real thing or not." Peirce "never entertained a doubt that those features of the phaneron" that he "found in [his] mind are present at all times and to all minds" (CP:1.284–87; Peirce 1955:74–75). His phenomenology, and especially his three phenomenological categories of consciousness and of being, are thus based on an "honest, single-minded observation of the appearances."

A possible implication that there is a science of reality behind the appearances, a realm of Kantian things-in-themselves, *noumena*, in addition to the realm of *phenomena*, is rejected by Peirce. His is a Kantianism without a transcendental subject, to paraphrase Ricoeur's characterization of Lévi-Strauss. Unlike Lévi-Strauss, however, Peirce's Kantianism includes an *empirical* subject. The signs of the self, its manifestations, *are* the real self, which emerges along with the external world by a process of fallible inference from "the parish of percepts" (in Peirce 1955:248–49, 308–309).

IMPLICATIONS FOR RESEARCH

A theory of the self based on Peirce's semiotic, or general theory of signs, is obviously neither a set of self-evident truths arrived at by introspection and intuition, nor a set of empirical generalizations that have been confirmed with a high decree of confidence. It is a tentative theory, fallible and incomplete, supported by several lines of argument and research and with important implications for further research. I should like to indicate briefly what some of these implications are—cultural, social, and psychological—and how they can be further developed and empirically tested in a semiotic anthropology.

For his article reviewing 1950s linguistic research on the concept of person, Hymes took as his text Hallowell's statement that "the concept of person, like the concept of self, may be expected to appear as a cultural universal," and then added, "it would seem to be a linguistic universal" (Hymes 1961:335). This topic has stimulated much discussion and research in the last thirty years, especially in the newer subdisciplines of language and culture, ethnolinguistics, sociolinguistics, and psycholinguistics. It has provided one of the major motivations for a review and reappraisal of the Sapir-Whorf hypothesis (Hoijer 1954) and for interesting new research on the speech and linguistic styles of individual personalities (Redfield 1975; Friedrich and Redfield 1978; Friedrich 1977, 1979; Silverstein 1979). Much of this recent research is relevant for the interpretation and testing of a semiotic theory of the self, especially Peirce's dictum that "my language is the sum total of my self" (CP:5.314). In considering the bearing of recent research on a Peircean theory of the self, and vice versa, one should remember that the theory is not simply a formal theory—whether syntactic or semantic—but a pragmatic, phenomenological, and semiotic theory. Even when considering such well-known grammatical categories as personal pronouns, Boas's 1911 observation is still relevant—that "the three personal pronouns—I, thou, and he—occur in all human language. . . . The underlying idea of these pronouns is the clear distinction between the self as speaker, the person or object spoken to, and that spoken of" (quoted in D. R. Miller 1961:280).

Benveniste's rediscovery of this truth testifies not only to the value of Boas's observation but also to the continuing relevance of Peirce's general theory of signs. By looking at personal pronouns pragmatically as indexical signs, Peirce was led to develop a "dialogical" analysis of language and meaning as a process of communication between the utterers and interpreters of signs. This analysis, enriched by European functionalism, opened the way for the growth of an "ethnography of communication," a growth to which Hymes, Gumperz, and others have contributed (Hymes and Gumperz 1970; Cherry 1966).[9]

In this context, consider Lévi-Strauss's declaration in his Inaugural Address at the Collège de France that anthropology as a conversation of man with man provides in its studies of the exchange of messages, commodities and services, and women an integrated science of communication (Lévi-Strauss 1976). As Jakobson has pointed out, however, while commending Lévi-Strauss's aspiration, a unified science of communication will have to incorporate "semiotic proper," "that is the study of sheer messages and their underlying codes, plus those disciplines wherein messages play a relevant yet solely accessory role" (Jakobson 1971:575).

A unified science of communication that incorporates semiotic proper provides the basis, as Margaret Mead observed, for "semiotics" as a study of patterned communication in all modalities (Sebeok 1974).

The conversation of man with man is only one of the dialogues in Peirce's semiotic theory of the self. There is also the inner dialogue of the self with its self. This is, as discussed previously, a dialogue "between two phases of the ego, . . . what one is saying to that other self that is just coming into life in the flow of time" (Peirce CP:4.6, 5.421). Jakobson thinks that Peirce's notion of "inner speech" is "astutely conceived"; it is "a cardinal factor in a network of language and serves as one's connection with the self's past and future" (Jakobson 1974:33).

The inner dialogue between two phases of the ego also provides a bridge from the outer dialogue of interpersonal relations to the intra-personal relations studied by the psychologist, psychiatrist, and novelist. Sullivan (1953), Bateson and Ruesch (1968), and others have attempted to rethink for psychiatry an interpersonal relations approach. In the work of Volosinov, Baxtin, and Vygotskij this had led to a direct application of semiotic analysis to the inner dialogue (Matejka 1973:171–74; see also Lincourt and Olczak 1974).

How both inner and outer dialogues are acquired by human beings in society is a problem about which Peirce does not have a great deal to say, except for his adherence to his general principle that knowledge about the ontogentic development of the self must come through observation and inference from "external" facts, not from intuition. This is supported by developmental theories of the self formulated by James, Cooley, Mead, and Baldwin in their studies of the dialogue of the "I" and the "me," and in the more recent theories of Piaget, Kohut, Lee, and Kohlberg.

In the revised edition of the Harvard *Guide to Modern Psychiatry*, a comprehensive article on theories of personality observes that Erikson's theory of identity has been a useful contribution but fails in the end to integrate personality with society and culture (Meissner 1978:134). This defect, I would suggest, is not unique to Erikson; it is a direct consequence of retaining a Cartesian dualism of body and mind, of individual and society, and of the self and the world. An integrated theory of identity is bound to elude us as long as we remain Cartesians. Peirce, who took seriously a logic of vagueness, avoided the dilemma by regarding matter and mind as two aspects of the same stuff. Matter, he wrote, is mind hidebound with habits. Since a self is not confined to a box of flesh and blood, he was able to develop a semiotic conception of it as a "loosely compacted person." The compacting is made of the sympathetic feelings through which social and cultural consciousness are communicated. In this sense an individual organism may be several persons, and the loosely compacted person may include several organisms. The problem, then, is not a conflict between personal identity and a sociocultural identity, for they are both personal and sociocultural. The problem is, rather, the empirical one of discovering the bonds of feeling that hold people together or tear them apart, and what their interrelations and conditions are. I am now engaged in comparative cultural research into this identity problem in India and in the United States within the framework of a Peircean semiotic (Singer 1977; chapters 5, 6).

There is much in contemporary social and cultural anthropology, sociology and social psychology, psychology, psychiatry, and linguistics that is relevant for research on a semiotic theory of the self. In fact, several developments have been moving in that direction: for example, "symbolic anthropology," "symbolic interactionism," "ethnolinguistics and psycholinguistics," and "egopsychology" (Firth 1973; Peacock 1975; Dolgin, Kemnitzer, and Schneider 1977; Devereux 1976; Kohut 1977; Boon 1972).

An increasing recognition of the value of combining phenomenological with objective perspectives has also been transforming fieldwork methods and monographs (Redfield 1955a; Geertz 1966a; Schneider 1968; Sahlins 1976; Rabinow 1977; Riesman 1977; Srinivas 1976; Beteille and Madan 1975).

In spite of these developments, the theory of the self is still beset by many of the dilemmas that have haunted it for several hundred years: materialism vs. mentalism, objective vs. subjective, determinism vs. chance and free will, quantitative vs. qualitative, collective vs. individual, cognition vs. feeling and action. One reason for the persistence of the dilemmas is the persistence of Cartesian dualism. When we recognize that it was over one hundred years ago that Charles Peirce started to lay the foundation for a semiotic theory of the self that transcends the Cartesian dilemmas, we shall be in a position to achieve a unification of the human sciences. It may also be possible to achieve such a unification within the framework of a revised Cartesianism, as Popper and Eccles (1977) have proposed. But that would still leave the self divided among three interacting worlds, not unlike the three quasi-independent systems of personality, society, and culture.

Cassirer has noted the cultural significance of the anti-Cartesian revolution:

> The great thinkers who have defined man as an *animal rationale* were not empiricists, not did they ever intend to give an empirical account of human nature. By this definition they were expressing rather a fundamental moral imperative. Reason is a very inadequate term with which to comprehend the forms of man's cultural life in all their richness and variety. But all these forms are symbolic forms. Hence instead of

defining man as an *animal rationale* we should define him as an *animal symbolicum*. By so doing we can designate his specific difference, and we can understand the new way open to man—the way to civilization. (Cassirer 1976 [1944]:25–26)

4

Personal and Social Identity in Dialogue

We must not begin by talking of pure ideas—
vagabond thoughts that tramp on the public roads
without any human habitation,—but must begin
with men and their conversation. (Peirce CP:8.12)

About two years ago at a birthday party for an eight-year-old boy named Simon, I was surprised to hear him sing with the rest of the company as the birthday cake was brought in, "Happy birthday to you, happy birthday, dear Simon, happy birthday to you," and then by himself, "Happy birthday to me, happy birthday, dear Simon, happy birthday to me."

A day or two later, when I described to some colleagues Simon's shift from "you" to "me" in the song and commented that this was a way of accenting the self-reference, a senior anthropological linguist challenged my interpretation and suggested that one couldn't be sure that there was *any* self-reference in the boy's words, that he might only have been joining in a kind of ceremonial chant.

My first inclination was to insist that I had directly "observed" the self-reference, that everyone else also "observed" it, and that the words themselves obviously indicated the self-reference. However, as other colleagues, several of them also anthropological linguists, took a skeptical approach and cited the problematic character of the limited technical literature on the use of pronouns and deictic expressions, I began to have second thoughts and started to do a little research on psychological observation and the relation of the use of personal pronouns to personal and social identity. The present chapter represents the outcome of that research.

Since the chapter was stimulated by several events as serendipitous as

Simon's birthday party, I shall mention briefly the circumstances of their occurrence:

(1) In chapter 3 I had already included the section on personal identity when the discussion with colleagues reopened the question for me and led me to reread what Peirce and some of his commentators, especially Murphey and Goudge, had to say. I was surprised to find that in some of the Peirce papers I had used for the section on personal identity in "Signs of the Self" (the "cosmological" papers of the early 1890s), Peirce had tried to construct a theory of collective as well as individual personality on the basis of a physiologically based psychology with practically no explicit reference to his semiotic or to pragmatism. This discovery posed the question of how Peirce integrated his personality theory with his semiotic and pragmatic theory of the self to produce a social psychology that does not presuppose physics and physiology. The discussion of the dialogue of the interpeters and utterers of signs in "Signs of the Self" was a major clue to the answer, but the details and the role of pronouns as indexical signs had to be worked out.

(2) Max Fisch, the general editor of the new critical edition of Peirce's papers, sent me in August of 1979 some comments on the "Signs of the Self" chapter, in which he called my attention to Peirce's undergraduate writings on I, It, and Thou and his 1863 essay on "The Place of Our Age in the History of Civilization" published in Wiener 1958, with the correct reading of the following memorable paragraph on p. 13: "First there was the egotistical age when man arbitrarily imagined perfection, now is the idistical stage when he observes it. Hereafter must be the more glorious tuistical stage when he shall be in communion with her" (Fisch to Singer, August 29, 1979). Later Fisch sent me a few pages from Peirce's early formulations on the three pronouns as names for his three categories and the introduction to volume I (1857–66) of the new edition of the Peirce papers.

When Fisch came to speak in Chicago at the Center for Psychosocial Studies on November 6, 1979, he used as a basis for his talk his presidential address to the Semiotic Society of America, Bloomington, Indiana, October 6, 1979. Upon reading in Fisch's address that "Peirce began where most of us begin, with a model which, taken by itself, would suggest too narrow a definition; the model, namely, of conversation between two competent speakers of the same natural language," I was encouraged to think that the dialogical interpretation of sign process was the pathway to the social psychology of personal identity.

(3) A preliminary portion of the present chapter was presented and discussed at the Conference on New Approaches to the Development of the Self (Center for Psychosocial Studies, Chicago, Mar. 29–Apr. 1, 1979). Following the conference, I discussed with the research staff at the

center the relationship of Peirce's theory of personal identity to the later theories of James, Baldwin, Cooley, and Mead.[1]

While the chapter may not faithfully reflect all the dialogues that stimulated it, this prologue may help explain its development.

TOWARD A SOCIAL AND SEMIOTIC PSYCHOLOGY
OF PERSONAL IDENTITY

In "Signs of the Self" I suggested that Peirce's conception of personality and personal identity was both social and semiotic. This interpretation, however, was based on combining several different sources: some of Peirce's "cosmological papers" published in *The Monist* in 1891 to 1893, his paper "What Pragmatism Is" (CP:5.421), and his correspondence with Lady Welby (1977). If we consider only his views in the "cosmological papers," we find a much narrower conception of personality and personal identity as some kind of coordination of feelings and ideas within the individual organism, and some kind of connection between these feelings and ideas in different organisms. Murphey (1961:347) has suggested that Peirce uses two languages in his "cosmological papers"—the language of psychology and the language of physics—as representing the inside and the outside views of the mind. In spite of recognizing a parallelism between the terms of the two languages (feeling, will, habit; chance, haecceity, love), Murphey thinks that Peirce regarded the psychological language as more fundamental than the physical.

If Murphey's interpretations are correct, they would imply that Peirce's conception of personal identity in the cosmological papers rests on a psychophysical parallelism or on a physiological psychology, but not on a semiotic and a social psychology. Murphey avoids this conclusion by arguing that Peirce reaffirms in the cosmological papers his earlier theory that man is a sign (ibid.:344). The evidence for this interpretation is inconclusive. There is only one reference to the earlier semiotic theory in the cosmological papers, and this is ambiguous: "Long ago, in the *Journal of Speculative Philosophy*, I pointed out that a person is nothing but a symbol involving a general idea; but my views were, then, too nominalistic to enable me to see that every general idea has the unified living feeling of a person" (CP:6.270).

This passage is hardly sufficient ground for concluding that Peirce abandoned his semiotic theory in the early 1890s. It is not inconsistent, however, with the impression that Peirce's conception of personality and personal identity in the cosmological papers had not yet freed itself from psychophysics and physiological psychology to become the genuinely semiotic and social psychological conception of the late papers.

In a letter to William James (c. 1909), Peirce contrasts the physiological approach of "Psychology Proper" to the phenomenological approach of "Phaneroscopy," as he calls it:

> On the one hand "a sort of physiology of the mind"—
> An account of how the mind functions, develops, and decays, together with the explanation of all this by motions and changes of the brain, or in default of this kind of explanation, by generalizations of psychical phenomena, so as to account for all the workings of the soul in the sense of reducing them to combinations of a few typical workings—
> On the other hand "phaneroscopy"—or a description of what is before the mind or in consciousness, as it *appears* in the different kinds of consciousness, which I rank under three headings. . . . (CP:8.303–305; emphasis in original)

The three headings are Peirce's three categories considered as kinds of consciousness: First, *Qualisense*, "consciousness of the quality of feeling," "the sort of consciousness of any whole regardless of anything else, and therefore regardless of the parts of that whole"; Second, *Molition*, "a double consciousness of exertion and resistance"; and Third, *Recognition of Habit*, "a consciousness at once of the substance of the habit, the special case of application, and the union of the two."

In view of Peirce's preference for a phenomenological over a physiological description, it seems justified to interpret his statements about personal identity and personality, especially in the cosmological papers, in phenomenological terms without seeking direct parallels in physiology, physics, or chemistry. If personal identity is primarily defined in terms of consistency and continuity of feelings, actions, and ideas, as Peirce defines it in the cosmological papers, we can accept this definition without necessarily accepting Peirce's definitions of physiological and physico-chemical analogues. In this manner the question of how much, if any, of the physical organism enters into personal identity can be left open as we explore the semiotic and social aspects of consistency and continuity in personal identity.

ON THE SEMIOTICS OF DIALOGUE

As we have noted, Lévi-Strauss has defined anthropology as a conversation of man with man and has also proposed that a study of the exchange of words be joined to the study of the exchange of women and goods and services to bring linguistics, social anthropology, and economics into a unified science of communication. This conception would not be identical with the inclusive view of symbolic interaction that Firth attributed to Parsons, G. H. Mead, and Schneider, according to which "all relations of people to one another are mediated and defined by systems of culturally structured symbols" (Firth 1973:196–97). Levi-Strauss's unified science of communication would restrict itself to a structural analysis of the relations abstracted from the specific conversations of specific people in specific social contexts. As Jakobson has said of Lévi-Strauss's aspiration, a unified science of communication would have to incorporate "semiotic proper," "that is the study of sheer messages and their underlying codes, plus those disciplines wherein messages play a relevant yet solely accessory role" (Jakobson 1973:36). Margaret Mead's suggestion that "semiotics" can be used to designate the study of patterned communication in all modalities comes closer in spirit and scope to the more inclusive view and to symbolic interactionism than to Lévi-Strauss's unified science of communication.

Most of the symbolic interactionists have a good deal to say about conversation—as a distinctive form of human symbolic interaction and as both the nursery of human personality and the forum for its expression. Before discussing the relation of personality and personal identity to conversation, I should like to describe briefly the semiotics of conversation as it has been developed within the symbolic interactionist tradition. While several different contributions need to be distinguished and different theoretical positions recognized, the most comprehensive and general semiotic theory of conversation as a form of symbolic interaction was formulated in the writings of Charles S. Peirce. Not only are his writings sprinkled with fragments of colloquial conversation to illustrate his abstract and sometimes abstruse analyses, but, as Fisch has recently observed, Peirce took the model of conversation as a starting point for his general theory of signs. In this model, at least two competent speakers of the same natural language, such as English, interpret one another's sounds, with some assistance from lip movements and gestures (Fisch 1979).

As Royce, who was significantly influenced by Peirce's theory of signs, implied, "the objects of knowledge are public and therefore interpretation is social. The metaphor of conversation appropriately suggests the manner in which interpretative processes are generated and developed" (Royce in Fuss 1965:106; 1913:159).[2] For Peirce the appropriate suggestion was that of a dialogue between the utterers and interpreters of signs. Fisch believes that Peirce's emphasis on the dialogical nature of conversation and of thought was probably suggested to him by some of Plato's Dialogues (Fisch Preface). Fisch is probably right about Peirce's source of suggestion, but it is relevant to point out that modern linguistics and information theory also use the dialogical model of communication. Lyons, a linguist, for example, specifies "the canonical situation of utterance" in terms that, while not identical with Peirce's semiotic, in effect describe a colloquial conversation between two interlocutors that "involves one-one, or one-many, signalling in the phonic medium along the vocal auditory channel, with all the participants present in the same actual situation able to see one another and to perceive the associated non-vocal paralinguistic features of their utterances, and each assuming the role of sender and receiver in turn" (Lyons 1977:2.637).

Writing as a communications engineer, Cherry not only constructs a similar dialogical paradigm for human communication but also points out the parallels with Peirce's semiotic analysis (Cherry 1966:89, 110).

Peirce's semiotic analysis of conversation is based on a concept of sign-action or sign-process that is irreducibly triadic: a sign is determined by an object and in turn determines an interpretation, or interpretant, in the mind of a person. An essential feature of Peirce's theory is that the interpretation of the sign assumes the same relation to the object as the sign itself has.

That Peirce's conception of the sign-process ("semiosis") is essentially dialogical has not been sufficiently recognized because his most general definitions of "sign" and sign-process tend to omit mention of persons and their interaction. In these formulations he defines a sign as something (a First) that is determined by an object (a Second) to determine an interpretant (a Third) to assume the same relation to the object that the sign has. There are at least three reasons why Peirce omitted reference to persons in such abstract definitions: (1) he wanted to demonstrate that it is possible to give a mathematically formal definition of "sign" (and of "mind"), just as mathematicians were beginning to define "number" and "line" formally without explicit reference to the usual interpretations of these terms; (2) he wanted to distinguish a semiotic analysis in terms of signs from a psychological analysis in terms of persons and personality; and (3) he wanted to leave open the possibility that there might be nonhuman intelligences capable of triadic sign-action.

Peirce never denied, however, that sign-processes in the case of human minds are mediated by the interpersonal interactions between the utterers and interpreters of the signs. The fact that some "natural signs," as in meteorology or in medicine, might not have been produced by utterers did not alter his conception of human semiosis as a social and dialogical process. And even his most formal and abstract definitions and classifications of signs were usually accompanied by informal comments in the English metalanguage about the personal utterers and interpreters of the signs (cf. Singer 1980a:497–98; Fisch 1978:55–56).

For Peirce, not only are human sign-processes essentially dialogical and social, but many of the ingredients of the processes, also, are dialogical. As he often writes, "a sign addresses somebody" (Peirce 1955:99). Indexical signs, particularly, direct someone's attention to some thing or to some person. The use of *selectives*, as Peirce calls them, "some," "any," etc., usually occasions a question-and-answer dialogue: "Man is mortal."

"What man?" "Any man you like" (CP:5.505).

Symbolic signs are implicated in the dialogues of verbal discourse. Peirce's emphasis on the systemic and endless nature of such discourse should not obscure the fact that language is for him part of a vast semiotic system and is intrinsically social and dialogical. Individual signs should be interpreted as items in such sign systems and not in isolation, and every interpretation will generate further interpretations indefinitely. Peirce, however, is neither a formalist nor a linguistic solipsist; the human sign-processes are limited at any given time by the utterers' and interpeters' sensory experience and by their habits of action. While he envisions an enlargement of experience and the growth of new habits, Peirce also envisages the possibility of a complete destruction of the species and an end to human semiosis (CP:8.45–46).[3] In the meantime, the criteria for the meaning and truth of signs, and for the reality of the objects designated by them, will depend on the eventual consensus arrived at by the community of all investigators. Such a consensus will be the result of the continuing dialogues between the utterers and interpreters as they bring their respective interpretations and previous experience into a shared understanding (see p. 63).

INNER DIALOGUE AND OUTER DIALOGUE

The dialogues between the utterers and interpreters of signs, their objects and interpretants, characterize human conversation and human communication generally in Peirce's conception of sign-process. He also extends this kind of semiotic analysis to thinking, which he sees as "talking to oneself." Fisch cites Peirce's use of the colloquial "I says to myself, says I" as a confirmation of this interpretation; but even when he addresses others, his conversation is often imaginary: "I say to people,—imaginary interlocutors, for I have nobody to talk to,—you think that the proposition that truth and justice are the greatest powers in this world is metaphorical. Well, I, for my part, hold it to be true" (CP:8.272, in a 1902 letter to James).

All thinking, according to Peirce, takes the form of an inner dialogue: "your self of one instant appeals to your deeper self for his assent" (CP:6.338 [1909]). The inner dialogue is "conducted in signs that are mainly of the same general structure as words" (ibid.), but not only words, or linguistic symbols, for "the substance of thoughts" also includes icons, which "chiefly illustrate the significations of predicate thoughts" and indices, "the denotations of subject-thoughts" (CP:6.338). The subject is singular and is known by the compulsion and insistency that characterize experience, while the matter of the predicate is known by the senses and feeling, and its structure by reason (CP:6.340).

Peirce's analysis of thought as an inner dialogue between an old self and a new self just coming into being, in which indexical signs denote subjects, iconic signs signify predicates, or "forms of fact," and the two are brought together by verbal symbols, seems to be a consistent extension of his semiotic analysis into the subjective inner world of the self. But is this extension consistent with his anti-Cartesianism, declared in the 1860s, to the effect that all knowledge of mind and the self is based on the observation of external facts and not on intuition and introspection?

Peirce's lectures on pragmatism in the 1900s and his correspondence with Lady Welby indicate that he remained consistently anti-Cartesian to the end. His distinction between an inner world of "thought" and an outer world of external facts was not ontological but phenomenological and depends ultimately on the degree of muscular effort that is required to overcome the resistance of external facts (Peirce 1955:86, 276, 283). The similarity of the inner dialogue of thought to the semiotic structure of conversation is not the result of a preestablished harmony between the inner and outer worlds but simply the result of the fact that the interlocutors (or "selves") are products of, as well agents in, both inner and outer dialogues. They are the objects designated by, as well as the subjects creating, the semiotic systems constituting the dialogues.

PERSONAL IDENTITY: PRIVATE AND PUBLIC

Just how the intrapersonal dialogue (self-consciousness and thought) comes to have a semiotic structure similar to that of interpersonal dialogue (consciousness of and communication with others) is for Peirce, as it is for most other symbolic interactionists, a question that cannot be answered by introspection but only by empirical observation and inference. "Introspection is wholly a matter of inference. One is immediately conscious of his feelings, no doubt; but not that they are feelings of an *ego*. The *self* is only inferred" (CP:5.462 [1905]).

If immediate consciousness (of feelings, powers and capacities, actions) precedes consciousness of self, then selves must appear relatively late in individual experience. Peirce accepted this implication and cited an observation by Kant in support: "There is no known self-consciousness to be accounted for in extremely young children. It has already been pointed out by Kant that the late use of the very common word 'I' with children indicates an imperfect self-consciousness in them" (CP:2.227 [1868]). But, Peirce added, children manifest powers of thought (CP:2.228) before they are self-conscious.

Peirce then went on to describe, in the same 1868 paper, a plausible course of experience in a child's encounter with others and the world that leads it to develop the consciousness of a private self to which all sorts of qualities are attributed. Essential to Peirce's explanation of the rise of selves in individual experience is the notion that the child discovers in his interactions with others that his perceptions, actions, and judgments are often the result of ignorance and error (for example, the notion that fire does not burn) and, therefore, must suppose a private self that is fallible (CP:5.234). The discovery assumes that the child already understands verbal commands and testimony such as "don't touch the hot stove; it will burn you" (CP:5.227–37).

In the child's experience of surprise when he fails to heed commands and testimony, there is a discovery of the external non-ego as well as of the inner ego. Peirce speaks of a "double conciousness," of an ego and a non-ego "directly acting upon each other at the instant of surprise" (CP:5.421). The ego represents "the expected idea suddenly broken off"; the non-ego, "the strange intruder in his abrupt entrance" (CP5.52–53). In the *first instance*, we attribute a quality of feeling to a non-ego and "only come to attribute it to ourselves when irrefragable reasons compel us to do so" (CP:5.57).

The interplay between ego and non-ego in the experience of interaction and surprise becomes for the mature, reflective adult analogous to the inner dialogue of the old self and new self coming into being in the flow of time: "The perceptual judgment, then, can only be that . . . the *non-ego*, something over against the *ego* and bearing it down, is what surprised him. But if that be so, this direct perception presents an *ego* to which the smashed expectation belonged, and the *non-ego*, the sadder and wiser man, to which the new phenomenon belongs" (CP:5.58).

The ever-widening circles of interaction and surprise that correct and revise the ego's familiar expectations with the non-ego's novelties are circles of society and of social relations and imply a personal identity that is social in form if not in content.

> Two things here are all-important to assure oneself of and to remember. The first is that a person is not absolutely an individual. His thoughts are what he is "saying to himself," that is, is saying to that other self that is just coming into life in the flow of time. When one reasons, it is that critical self that one is trying to persuade; and all thought whatsoever is a sign, and is mostly of the nature of language. The second thing to remember is that the man's circle of society (however widely or narrowly this phrase may be understood), is a sort of loosely compacted person, in some respects of higher rank than the person of an individual organism. (Peirce 1955:258; CP:5.421)

If self-consciousness and the consciousness of others emerge from the child's interactions with others, then the individual's sense of personal identity is social in origin. That an individual's personal identity may consist of *private* feelings, thoughts, and actions is admitted by Peirce in his early as well as later papers. From an 1868 paper: " . . . by self-consciousness is meant a knowledge of ourselves . . . the self-consciousness here meant is the recognition of my *private* self. I know that *I* (not merely *the* I) exist" (CP:5.225). From an 1893 paper: "It is plain that intelligence does not consist in feeling in a certain way, but in acting in a certain way. Only we must acknowledge that there are inward actions—what might be called potential actions, that is, actions which do not take place, but which somehow influence the formation of habits" (CP:5.286).

Peirce anticipates here the concept of "incipient response," which was to play so important a part in G. H. Mead's and Morris's behavioristic analyses of symbolic interactions mediated by gestures. Peirce emphasized, however, the role of imagination and fantasy:

> The whole business of ratiocination, and all that makes us intellectual beings, is performed in imagination. . . . Mere imagination would indeed be mere trifling; only no imagination is *mere*.
> "More than all that is in thy custody, watch over thy phantasy," said Solomon, "for out of it are the issues of life."

The apparent paradox of a personal identity private in content and public and social in origin did not compel Peirce to retreat to a Cartesian intuition and introspection. By maintaining that all thinking is by means of signs, that it takes the form of an inner dialogue structurally similar to and continuous with the outer dialogue of conversation with others, Peirce was able to develop a concept of personal identity that is not confined to the individual organism but that extends as far as his social and cultural consciousness and his circle of society. The individual's consciousness of self and of others is a "double consciousness," in which the consciousness of others may precede the consciousness of self, and, in any case, develops with the individual's interactions with others and with the world as selves emerge from these interactions.

THE DRAMA OF FIRST, SECOND, AND THIRD PERSONS

A crucial link in Peirce's social theory of personal identity is the assumption that there are signs symptomatic or indicative of self-consciousness that are observable to others. In his early papers Peirce takes this assumption for granted, when, for example, he accepts Kant's observation of the child's late use of the pronoun "I" as evidence for the relatively late appearance of a self. His whole theory of indexical signs and of pronouns as a kind of indexical sign was developed in his later papers on semiotic to deal with this problem now known to linguists as "person deixis."

Lyons's explanation of "deixis" is probably widely accepted by linguists as "the location and identification of persons, objects, events, processes and activities talked about, or referred to, in relation to the spatiotemporal context created and sustained by the act of utterance and the participation in it, typically, of a single speaker and at least one addressee" (Lyons 1977:2.637).

The application of this concept of deixis to expressions referring to persons, for example to pronouns, proper names, and definite noun phrases, has become known through the work of Benveniste and other linguists (Silverstein 1976). Such applications depend on interpreting first- and second-person pronouns as indexical signs that refer to the speaker and hearer respectively, in the situation of utterance. It is probable that these interpretations of "person deixis" were influenced, at least indirectly, by Peirce's theory of indexical signs (cf. Singer 1980a:493; and Burks 1948–49:686: "Thus a token of 'I' means *the person uttering that token*: in other words, it is part of the symbolic meaning of 'I' that one finds the object indicated by a token of this type by proceeding from the token to the speaker" [italics in original]).

Burks's formulation is fairly close to Benveniste's, although it does not refer explicitly to the situation of utterance. Peirce himself, however, does this in several passages on pronouns and proper names:

> The pronoun, which may be defined as a part of speech intended to fulfill the function of an index, is never intelligible taken by itself apart from the circumstances of its utterance. (CP:5.153 [1903])

> When we express a proposition in words we leave most of its singular subjects unexpressed, for the circumstances of the enunciation sufficiently show what subject is intended. . . . (CP:5.153)

> A proper name has a certain denotative function peculiar, in each case, to that name and its equivalents; every assertion contains such a denotative or pointing-out function. (CP:5.429 [1905])

The interpretation of self-referring pronouns, proper names, and definite descriptions of persons as indexical signs identifies the utterer of the expression as its object but does not necessarily identify the expressive and social functions of the signs. Peirce specified three criteria for any indexical sign: that it not resemble its object, that it direct attention to its object, and that it refer to individual objects or individual collections of objects (Peirce 1955:108). The use of personal pronouns and other signs of person meets these three criteria, but that is not sufficient to determine which personal pronouns will be used by a particular speaker on a particular occasion. Nor will the use of a particular pronoun tell us whether the speaker is following a customary role of usage or is also intending an application to himself. Pronouns, in other words, cannot be interpreted as "indicators" and "symptoms" of personal or subjective conscious meanings without making additional theoretical assumptions.

One common assumption is that of *egocentricity*. Lyons, who adopts this assumption quite explicitly, explains it as follows: "The speaker, by virtue of being the speaker, casts himself in the role of ego and relates everything to his viewpoint. . . . Egocentricity is temporal as well as spatial, since the role of the speaker is being transferred from one participant to the other as the conversation proceeds, and the participants may move around as they are conversing" (1977:2.638).

The debatable status of this assumption becomes apparent if we ask whether it is based on an empirical survey of conversations, a hypothesis, or a normative rule. Suppose some speakers cast themselves in the role of the second person, or the third person; what happens to the doctrine of egocentricity—in honorific terms of address, for example?[4]

The context of Lyons's discussion clearly indicates that his assumption of egocentricity derives from a broader theory, which correlates the grammatical categories of personal pronouns with the social roles of a drama:

> The grammatical category of person depends upon the notion of participant roles and upon their grammaticalization in particular languages. . . . The Latin word "persona" (meaning "mask") was used to translate the Greek word for "dramatic character" or "role", and the use of this term by grammarians derives from their metaphorical conception of a language event as a drama in which the principal role is played by the first person, the role subsidiary to his by the second person, and all other roles by the third person. It is important to note, however, that only the speaker and addressee are actually participating in the drama. The term "third person" . . . does not correlate with any positive participant role. (Ibid.)

Given this dramatic theory of language and the personal pronouns, it is easier to understand the assumption of egocentricity, although the question can still be raised: do all languages and all speakers grammaticalize the speaker's reference to himself in the first person?[5]

There is some evidence that Peirce answered this question in the negative, at least in his earliest papers. Accepting the social drama of the three personal pronouns, he regarded the second person, and not the first person, as the most important social role, and defined "Tuism" as the doctrine that "all thought is addressed to a second person, or to one's future self as a second person," a definition he wrote for the *Century Dictionary* of 1891 (Fisch Introduction).

In a paper he wrote as a sophomore at Harvard, Peirce connected the I, the It, and the Thou with Schiller's three drives or impulses respectively, the formal I-impulse toward the infinite, the sensuous It-impluse toward the particular, and the harmonizing Thou-impulse (Fisch, personal communication). Peirce also used these three pronouns to designate three historical eras, the egotistical age, his own "idistical" age, and a coming "tuistical" age (Wiener 1966; Fisch 1979; Introduction).

Peirce's use of the three pronouns to name the ethos of an age, and individual personality types, seems to have anticipated the psychoanalytic typology of Id, Ego, and Superego later developed by Freud (1927, 1953 [1930]), Groddeck (1961 [1923]), and other analysts. This is especially striking in Peirce's interpretation of the Trinity in terms of the three persons.[6]

Peirce's chief interest in the three pronouns I, It, and Thou, however, was in their use as names for his three phenomenological categories, names that he eventually replaced by the designations Firstness, Secondness, and Thirdness. After he introduced the latter names, he seems to have lost interest in the drama of the pronouns and their family romance. Perhaps he felt that the pronouns were sufficiently provided for by being analyzed as indexical signs.

PRONOUNS OF PERSONAL AND INTERPERSONAL IDENTITY

Despite his assumption of egocentricity in person deixis, Lyons asserts that "every utterance is, in general and regardless of its more specific function, an expressive symptom of what is in the speaker's mind, a symbol descriptive of what is signified and a vocative signal that is addressed to the receiver" (1977:1.52).

He sees an "obvious connection" between Bühler's and Jakobson's analysis of an utterance's descriptive, expressive, and vocative functions, and the analysis of the typical situation of utterance as a drama in which three roles are given grammatical recognition by means of the category of person (ibid.). If this connection is valid, can the particular social role be inferred from the particular personal pronoun used? Although Lyons summarizes the Bühler-Jakobson theory of functions in neutral terms: "an utterance is primarily descriptive, expressive, or vocative in function according to whether the reference is made primarily to one of the three components rather than the other two of a typical speech act—the speaker, the addressee or the external situation to which reference is made," in fact he collapses the social and expressive functions into a joint function, that of establishing and maintaining a social relationship and expressing a symptom that "covaries with the characteristics of the speaker." In effect, this means that personal pronouns that express a personal identity also serve to establish interpersonal relations, and conversely. "For it is only by virtue of our membership of social groups that we are able to interact with others, and in doing so, to establish our individual identity and personality" (ibid.:1.51).

This conclusion is remarkably similar to Peirce's position on pronouns and proper names as indexical signs. Peirce may have lost interest in I, It, and Thou, but he did not lose interest in his doctrine of "Tuism." On the contrary, he expanded "Tuism" from a doctrine about the dialogical nature of thought and "inner" speech, to embrace the dialogical nature of all signs, conversation, and triadic social relations such as giving and exchange.[7] Such an expansion and generalization of his tuistic doctrine was a relatively easy step for Peirce, in view of his analysis of all sign-action as a triadic relation of sign, object, and interpretant, and his conception of an indexical sign in dynamical connection with the utterer and interpreter of the sign as well as with the sign's object. Following such an analysis of sign-action, it is plausible to assume that thinking, which for Peirce is carried on by means of signs, and significant social communication are similar in semiotic structure.

Peirce did not live to test and develop his indexical theory of personal pronouns. Beyond the incidental illustrations and his suggestions of how indexical signs combine with iconic and symbolic signs to form statements (for indices are expressive and do not assert anything), the development and application of the theory is now on the agenda of literary scholars, linguists, anthropologists, and social psychologists.[8] As this development proceeds, it will undoubtedly continue to draw inspiration from Pierce's pioneer contributions and also from the symbolic interactionists who followed him. That personal identity should still be so strongly associated with the relationship between the pronouns "I" and "me," and interpersonal identity with the relationship of "I" and "you," is a legacy not only from Peirce but also from James, Royce, Baldwin, Cooley, and Mead, all of whom accepted Peirce's anti-Cartesian approach to the self. For all of them, the inner dialogue of the self was a dialogue between an immediately experienced "I" and a remembered social "me," just as the outer dialogue was a public conversation between an "I" and a "you," a conversation in which both "I" and "you" express alternating social roles in symbolic, face-to-face interaction.

Both dialogues are social in origin and to some extent in content, because the boundary between "I" and "me" is relative, as is that between "I" and "you." Having rejected, with Peirce, both a Cartesian self and a Kantian transcendental ego, the symbolic interactionists turned to empirical distinctions and observable processes. James, who was probably the first to distinguish the I and the me as the subject self and the object self, was quick to add that "the identity of the *I* with *Me*, even in the very act of their discrimination, is perhaps the most ineradicable dictum of commonsense" (James 1961:43).[9]

His famous description of the social self as a man's me extends the boundaries of that self "to all that he *can* call his"—"not only his body and his psychic powers, but his clothes, and his house, his wife and children, his ancestors and his friends, his reputation and works, his lands and horses, and yacht and bank-account" (James 1961:44).

Despite James's well-known individualism and pluralism, he was apparently not quite the nominalist about the self that Peirce accused him of being, particularly if we take seriously his practical identification of the I and the me, and of me and mine: "Between what a man calls *Me* and what he simply calls *Mine* the line is difficult to draw. We feel and act about certain things that are ours very much as we feel about ourselves" (ibid.:43).

A somewhat similar emphasis on the social nature of "I" was expressed by Cooley, who based his opinion on close and systematic observation of his own children's use of "self-words":

> "I" is social in that the very essence of it is the assertion of self-will in a social medium of which the speaker is conscious. . . . "I" is addressed to an audience—usually with some emphasis—and its purpose is to impress upon the audience the power ("I make go"), the wish ("I go play sand-pile"), the claim ("my Mama"), the service ("I get it for you") of the speaker. Its use in solitude would be inconceivable (though the audience may, of course, be imaginary).
>
> To put it otherwise, "I" is a differentiation in a vague body of personal ideas which is either self-consciousness or social consciousness, as you please to look at it. In the use of "I" and of names for other people, the *ego* and *alter* phases of this consciousness become explicit. (Cooley 1908:342)

Mead said his account of the "I" and "you" dialogue was more objective than Cooley's subjective and ethnocentric account. Mead claimed to analyze the development of mind and self from early conditions shared with animal behavior: a "conversation of gestures," the matrix for significant communication. But Mead also used introspective and phenomenological descriptions in his concept of role-playing.[10] Cooley, on the other hand, makes room for historical studies of preconditions, "primary groups" (neighborhood, play groups, family) in face-to-face interaction (Mead 1930a).

In retrospect, Peirce's semiotic analysis of the inner and outer dialogues and of their interconnection through an indexical theory of pronouns bypasses the controversy between mentalism and behaviorism. Personal pronouns act by "blind compulsion" on the human nervous system, as indexical signs, but they also signify properties when joined to icons by verbal symbols such as "Happy Birthday." Cooley observed that "you" was often used for "I" in early childhood. If a two-year-old can redirect the self-reference from "you" to "I," it should not surprise us that an eight-year-old redirects it from "you" to "me"!

CORPORATE PERSONALITY AND COLLECTIVE IDENTITY

In one of his cosmological papers, "Man's Glassy Essence," Peirce introduced a concept of corporate personality that he drew as a consequence from his theory that the necessary condition for the existence of a person is that his feelings "should be in close enough connection to influence one another" (CP:6.271). That something like a personal consciousness, and a corporate personality, should emerge "in bodies of men who are in intimate and intensely sympathetic communion" seemed to Peirce a logical consequence of his theory that could be tested by observation and experiment. He cited "ordinary observations" of *esprit de corps*, national sentiment, sympathy, and the mind of corporations as giving evidence, at first appearance, of "the influence of such greater persons upon individuals" (CP:6.271). The gathering of thirty thousand young people of the Society for Christian Endeavor seemed to him to generate "some mysterious diffusion of sweetness and light" (ibid.). Further evidence of such corporate personality, he suggested, should be looked for in the Christian church, where Christians "have always been ready to risk their lives for the sake of having prayers in common, of getting together and praying simultaneously with great energy, and especially for their common body" (ibid.).

In making these suggestions Peirce was aware of the common-sense belief that personality and personal consciousness do not extend beyond the individual's body, and he seems to have anticipated and replied to that view when he writes in the same paper: "It is true that when the generalization of feeling has been carried so far as to include all within a person, a stopping-place, in a certain sense, has been attained; and further generalization will have a less lively character" (ibid.).

Peirce gave a more explicit reply to the common-sense point of view in his notes on William James's *Principles of Psychology*: quoting selected passages from the work, he asked James critical questions about them. The confrontation between Peirce and James is particularly dramatic on the issue of "personality" and personal identity and the communication of thought between individuals. James was emphatic that "no thought ever comes into direct sight of a thought in another personal consciousness than its own. Absolute insulation, irreducible pluralism, is the law" (CP:8.81). To this Peirce asks: "Is not the direct contrary nearer the observed facts? Is not this pure metaphysical speculation? You think there *must* be such isolation, because you confound thoughts with feeling-qualities; but all observation is against you. There are some small particulars that a man can keep to himself. He exaggerates them and his personality sadly" (ibid.).

James strongly insisted that the "breaches" between the thoughts belonging to different personal minds are "the most absolute breaches in nature," that "neither contemporaneity nor proximity in space nor similarity of quality and content are able to fuse thoughts together which are sundered by this barrier of belonging to different personal minds . . . the personal self rather than the thought might be treated as the immediate datum in psychology" (quoted in CP:8.82).

To this direct challenge to his own concept of a corporate personality formed from the connection of feelings and thoughts between different individuals, Peirce replied in a half-ironic tone, calling the tongue the "very organ of personality":

> Everybody will admit a personal self exists in the same sense in which a snark exists; that is, there is a phenomenon to which that name is given. It is an illusory phenomenon; but still it is a phenomenon. It is not quite purely illusory, but only mainly so. It is true, for instance, that men are selfish, that is, that they are really deluded into supposing themselves to have some isolated existence; and in so far, they have it. To deny the reality of personality is not anti-spiritualistic; it is only anti-nominalistic. It is true that there are certain phenomena, really quite slight and insignificant, but exaggerated, because they are connected with the tongue, which may be described as personality. The agility of the tongue is shown in its insisting that the world depends upon it. The phenomena of personality consist mainly in ability to hold the tongue. This is what the tongue brags so about.
>
> Meantime, physicians are highly privileged that they can ask to see people's tongues; for this is inspecting the very organ of personality. It is largely because this organ is so sensitive that personality is so vivid. But it is more because it is so agile and complex a muscle. (CP:8.82–85)

James was not the only psychologist to express skepticism about the existence of a corporate personality. Baldwin's *Dictionary of Philosophy and Psychology*, originally published in 1902, defined a "Tribal Self" in terms of "the psychological factors involved in the organization of a social group (tribe), when conceived after the analogy with the individual's mental organization in the form of a personal self," but then added that "the conception is often vague and stands upon much the same plane as that of general (or social) will" (Baldwin 1957:714–15).

In a more general definition of social unit, Baldwin adopts a relational point of view, anticipating Durkheim, Radcliffe-Brown, and the later sociological and anthropological theories:

It is true that the individual is the unit of the social group . . . but he is not the social unit, since the social is a relation of individuals. . . . There is no general social unit and it is doubtful whether in the social sciences any final unit of analogy will ever be discovered in terms of which all the phenomena of the class can be quantitatively increased. . . . The phrase "fundamental social fact" . . . better expresses the scope of this field. (Baldwin 1957:541)

Contrary to Peirce, who himself contributed some articles to it on logic and signs, Baldwin's *Dictionary* seemed to restrict the definitions of personality and personal identity to the individual, even when considering the essentially legal Roman conception of the person as the subject of rights and the Christian conception of the absolute moral worth of personality (Baldwin 1957:282–83). Baldwin's own theory emphasized the role of social factors in personality formation.

In the context of the cosmological papers, Peirce formulated his concept of corporate personality in psychological terms and not semiotically, analogously to the practice he followed in his formulation of an individual personality concept. The latter semiotic formulations were later developed for an inner dialogue of "I" and "me" and an outer dialogue of "I" and "you." Peirce himself suggested these formulations, although they were discussed more explicitly by James, Baldwin, Cooley, and Mead. Is there an analogous discussion of dialogues between corporate personalities?

Peirce occasionally refers to the use of "we" and "our" as indicating evidence for the existence of corporate personality. ". . . the constant use of the word 'we'—as when we speak of our possessions in the Pacific—our destiny as a republic—in cases in which no personal interests at all are involved, show conclusively that men do not make their personal interests their only ones, and therefore may, at least, subordinate them to the interests of the community" (CP:5.355). This statement is reminiscent of his assumption in the early papers that the use of "I" is a symptom of self-consciousness, and implies that the use of "we" or "our" is to be interpreted as a symptom of a collective consciousness or a collective identity. There is not much along these lines in the cosmological papers and not a great deal more in Peirce's later papers. The symbolic interactionists who came after Peirce were more explicit about the formation of a corporate personality. Cooley, for example, wrote about the "we" ideal in terms that would have pleased Peirce: "I am aware of the social group in which I live as immediately and authentically as I am aware of myself; and Descartes might have said 'we think', *cogitamus*, on as good grounds as he said *cogito*" (Cooley 1929 [1909]: 9). "Children and savages . . . see themselves and their fellows as an indivisible, though various, 'we', and desire this 'we' to be harmonious, happy, and successful" (ibid.:33–34).

Cooley's theory of how the individual is molded by the primary group of face-to-face association in family, play group, and neighborhood to develop a social self and to bring under the discipline of sympathy the "passions of lust, greed, revenge, the pride of power" is too well known to require elaboration here. So is Mead's equally familiar behavioristic variant of the theory, which sees a socialized self emerge from play and organized games via role-playing and taking the role of a "generalized other."

The controversy between the followers of Cooley and of Mead over the issue of introspective mentalism and scientific behaviorism can be resolved by recalling Peirce's non-Cartesian approach to the relation of mind and matter: "Viewing a thing from the outside, considering its relations of action and reaction with other things, it appears as matter. Viewing it from the inside, looking at its immediate character of feeling, it appears as consciousness" (CP:6.268).

Applying Peirce's approach to a semiotic analysis of corporate personality, I would suggest that the appropriate dialogue is a "we-they" dialogue, and that it is both inner and outer. It is an inner dialogue insofar as it is viewed from the inside, as feeling and immediate consciousness, and an outer dialogue insofar as it is viewed from the outside as a social interaction. Following the analogy with Peirce's analysis of the ego–non-ego (or "I and you") dialogue, we can construct the hypothesis that in the "we-they" dialogue, "we" and "they" are experienced practically simultaneously as a contrast, that "we" appears as familiar, and "they" as strange and surprising. The element of surprise introduced by "they" gives the dialogue the quality of a physical encounter, but as "they" become familiar the dialogue is raised to a level of feeling and consciousness.

The alternating reversal of "I" and "you" in conversation with others does not seem to have an exact analogue in the "we-they" dialogue, for two reasons. It is much more difficult to shift from a "we" to a "they" than from an "I" to a "you" in a conversation. A particular "we-they" contrast is usually associated with a heavy load of associated contrasts, for example: "natives-foreigners," "old-timers–newcomers," "Northerners-Southerners," and all sorts of religious, racial, national, and class contrasts. Where these contrasts are intensely and emotionally felt, they are not quickly picked up or dropped; it is therefore difficult for "us" to take "their" point of view or to see "ourselves" as "others" see "us." Analogous resistance may occur in an "I-you" dialogue, but it is not usually as heavily loaded or highly charged.

The difficulty (or ease) with which a "we" can shift to a "they" and back to a "we" depends not only on the felt emotional intensity of a particular "we-they" contrast but on the legal and customary constraints surrounding distinctions of race, religion, ethnicity, social class, and sex. Where the constraints are rigorous, and conversion, even at an individual level, is followed by severe penalties, intergroup dialogues of "we-they" will be slow to start and intermittent in their course. Role reversals on ritual and ceremonial occasions are associated with intermittent "conversations of gestures" and of words across the boundaries of age and sex, class and caste, race and religion (Marriott and Singer in Singer 1968b; Turner 1969, especially chap. 5).

Another obstacle to a smooth-flowing "we-they" dialogue is an "I-we" dialogue. This is especially so in a highly individualistic society, where individual self-interest and independence are major social values. The conflict between individual and society then becomes a major preoccupation. In the second half of the nineteenth century, Peirce saw the United States dominated by a "gospel of greed," which exaggerated the beneficial effects of selfishness and needed to be replaced by a "gospel of love."

This sentiment was to blossom in Peirce's cosmological papers of the 1890s into a doctrine of "evolutionary love" (*agapastic* evolution as distinct from *tychastic* evolution by chance, and from *anancastic* evolution by necessity). It was also expressed in his doctrine of *Tuism*, that all thought and conversation is addressed to a second person, and was embodied in his social theory of logic, which held that an identification with the interests of the unlimited community is an indispensable condition for the validity of all reasoning.

> Each of us is an insurance company. . . . But, now, suppose that an insurance company, among its risks, should take one exceeding in amount the sum of all the others. Plainly, it would then have no security whatever. . . . If a man has a transcendent personal interest infinitely outweighing all others, then, upon the theory of validity of inference just developed, he is devoid of all security, and can make no valid inference whatever. What follows? That logic rigidly requires, before all else, that no determinate fact, nothing which can happen to a man's self, should be of more consequence to him than everything else. He who would not sacrifice his own soul to save the whole world is illogical in all his inferences, collectively. So the social principle is intrinsically rooted in logic. (CP:5.354)

In his social sentiments and interpretation of "evolutionary love," Peirce was out of step with the individualism and social Darwinism of his times. His position, however, did find some support in Cooley, as already indicated, and in Josiah Royce. A contemporary of Peirce's who heard his lectures and corresponded with him, Royce restated many of Peirce's arguments in more popular language and based them, as Peirce did, on modern logic and a semiotic doctrine of interpretation (see especially Royce 1913). As for corporate personality, Royce was even more confident of its existence and its influence on the individual person than Peirce:

> For me, at present, a genuinely and loyally united community, which lives a coherent life, is in a perfectly [literal] sense a person. . . . On the other hand, any human individual person, in a perfectly literal sense, is a community. The coherent life which includes past, present and future and holds them reasonably together, is the life of what I have also called . . . a Community of Interpretation, in which the present, with an endless fecundity of invention, interprets the past to the future. (Royce in letter to Mary W. Calkins, March 20, 1916, in Royce 1970:644–46)

Royce gave this position a theological application and identified it with Pauline Christianity and the Christian view of a community as a person, not merely as an aggregate. The process in question was not, for Royce,

> . . . merely theological, and is not merely mystical, less merely mythical. Nor is it a process invented merely by abstract metaphysicians. It is the process which Victor Hugo expressed in *Les Misérables*, when he put into the mouth of Enjolras the words: *"Ma Mère, c'est la république."* As I write you these words, Frenchmen are writing the meaning of these words in their blood, about Verdun. The mother which is a republic, is a community, which is also a person,—and not merely an aggregate, and not merely by metaphor a person. (Royce 1970:647)

The individual's sacrifice to a nation in time of war represented for Royce during the First World War, as it did for Peirce during the Civil War and the Spanish-American War, compelling testimony to the existence of corporate personality and a collective identity. That national loyalty and patriotism could and should be generalized to the interests of an unlimited World Community was a matter of faith for both Royce and Peirce. In an article published after the First World War on "National-Mindedness and International-Mindedness," Mead took a more realistic view of the problem of reconciling the diversity of interests in a modern community with national unity and international peace. He saw nothing in an industrial civilization "to sweep the individual into emotional realization of his identity with the community . . . loyalties to the family, business, or schools, the more intense they are, the more exclusive they are" (Mead 1929:388). Applying his social-psychological theory of how selves are formed, Mead found that a self is an interaction between two parts of our nature—the *fundamental impulses*, i.e., "The primitive, sexual, parental, hostile, and cooperative impulses out of which our social selves are built up," and the power we get from language to control our thinking and our conduct through talking to ourselves and taking the role of the *generalized other* (ibid.:396). "We import the conventions of the group into our inner sessions and debate with ourselves. But the concatenated concepts which we use are ours because we are speaking in the language of the outer universe of discourse, the organized human world to which we belong" (ibid.:395).

The unity of society, and of the self, Mead believed, derived from two sources, the identity of fundamental emotional and hostile impulses, "a unity from below"; and the "sophisticated self-consciousness" of a unity-in-diversity among the members of a highly organized industrial society (ibid.:396). "[Because] every war will now become a world war and will take as its objective not the destruction of hostile forces but of enemy nations in their entirety . . . it has become unthinkable as a policy for adjudicating national differences. It has become logically impossible" (ibid.:400).

Recognizing that wars may still arise, Mead concluded that we cannot any longer think of our international life in terms of warfare and appeals to the unity from below, to "our diaphragms and the visceral responses which a fight sets in operation" (ibid.:402). Instead, he wrote:

> We are compelled to reach a sense of being a nation by means of rational self-consciousness. We must *think* ourselves in terms of the great community to which we belong. We cannot depend upon feeling ourselves at one with our compatriots, because the only effective feeling of unity springs from our common response against the common enemy. No other social emotion will melt us into one. Instead of depending upon a national soul we must achieve national mindedness. (ibid.:401; emphasis in original)

The kind of corporate personality and collective identity discussed by Peirce, Royce, and Mead is essentially a phenomenon of wartime and shows two characteristic features: it grows and declines as a war fever waxes and wanes, and it involves not only a conflict between a nation and its enemies, "we-they," but also a conflict between the national interest and the interest of its citizens and diverse constituent groups, "I and we," particularly when sacrifices are called for. Semiotically, the conflict gets expressed in an "I-we" dialogue as well as in a "we-they" dialogue. Pericles' Funeral Oration and Lincoln's Gettysburg Address are classic and eloquent rhetorical expressions of such dialogues. They are not, of course, restricted to wartime conditions but may also be expressed during periods of religious enthusiasm, political reform, national memorials, and celebrations, as Peirce, Royce, and Mead suggest. (For Durkheim's and Warner's analogy with totemic rituals, see chap. 5 on "Emblems.")

Durkheim's distinction between mechanical and organic solidarity, and the related social theories of Maine, Morgan, Tönnies, Weber, and Redfield, among others, indicate that a corporate personality and collective identity change with the forms and foundations of political, social, and economic organization and are not independent and unchanging biological and psychological "givens" of social and cultural structure and organization (Singer 1961).

It may well be that the grammatical distinction between the exclusive "we" ("I and they") and the inclusive "we" ("I and you"), which occurs in many languages, represents a linguistic expression of fluctuating "I-we" and "we-they" dialogues that are associated with social and cultural changes. Benveniste, who does not necessarily share this interpretation, points out:

> "We" is not a quantified or multiplied "I"; it is an "I" expanded beyond the strict limits of the person, enlarged and at the same time amorphous. As a result there are two opposed but not contradictory uses—outside of the ordinary plural. On the one hand the "I" is amplified by "we" into a person that is more massive, more solemn, and less defined; it is the royal "we". On the other hand, the use of "we" blurs the too sharp assertion of "I" into a broader and more diffuse expression: it is the "we" of the author or orator. (Benveniste 1971:203)

A recent study of the rhetoric of autocracy and democracy in Nepal illustrates how these conflicting tendencies in the "I-we" dialogue under changing social conditions are reflected in the king's speeches:

> The ambiguity characterizing the King's position is also mirrored in the philosophy that is the vehicle through which he puts forth his political strategy. Panchayat Democracy is a vague concept blending traditional authority and power politics. . . . The greater specificity in King Birendra's speeches (when compared to those of his father) does not reflect a fundamental change in the King's position, but rather the King's stronger control of the country. But this has been achieved without abolishing the ambiguous nature of his rule, and can be seen in his use of the word "we", for instance. Just as Mahendra did, Birendra uses "we" in reference to himself as the exalted ruler—the traditional ruler—and as the ruler merging with his people—the politician who promises to do his share of the work in cooperation with his electorate. (Borgström 1980:49. For another more personal interpretation of the use of the royal "we," see note 5 to this chapter.)

TOWARD A CONVERSATION OF CULTURES AND A CIVILIZATION OF THE DIALOGUE

Writing in the frigid Cold War atmosphere of 1953, Robert Redfield asked whether it would be untactful to suggest that America needs a hearing aid. Quoting Mrs. Trollope and de Tocqueville, he acknowledged that "we Americans have long been known as a talkative people" (Redfield 1963:232–240). Redfield suggested that our national habit needed to be balanced by listening: "I do not think that we listen enough to what other people are trying to say to us about themselves, and I do not think we listen enough to the sound of what we say in the ears of him to whom we say it. We are guided chiefly in deciding what to say by the conceptions we have of what those others ought to like about us if they were just like us. And they aren't."

The art of listening to other peoples and the art of talking need to be cultivated for our own safety: "Mutual security depends on mutual understanding, and for understanding you have to have a conversation. . . . In the Big Room where all peoples meet much of the talk is just the loudest voices shouting what they mistakenly imagine the others might find impressive to hear." The Big Room is a Hall of Nations, in which each people is conceived as if it were a single person. "Of course each of these is really a multitude of voices (except perhaps the Russian); each is a myriad voice coming to us from real individuals of many sorts speaking through books, travel, newspapers, and personal contact."

As we listen to the nations in the Big Room, what should we listen for? Redfield suggested three things: National Character ("the collective personality or the group heritage or perhaps just the persisting peculiarities that make the people distinguishable from their neighbors"), Mood ("the response they make to a marked turn in their fortunes"), and Human Nature ("the qualities that all men share with one another . . . pride, shame, enjoyment of the company of those are who are near and dear, delight in children, and laughter, a certain satisfaction in one's work well done, anger in the face of an injustice—however justice may be conceived . . .").

> While today some of us reassert the traditional American emphasis on self-reliance, striving to keep the control of our affairs in our own hands and out of the control of either powerful business or bureaucratic government, we can use this human impulse of ours to understand the mood of those Asiatics and Middle Easterners who want to keep the control of their affairs in their own hands—and out of ours. Their situation has at least this additional cause for calling up the human disposition to run one's own life: we to them are foreigners, and, as part of Western industrial civilization, conquerors.

Redfield believed that improving the art of carrying on the "little conversations" with the peoples of the world would meet and combine with the more organized discipline of the "great conversation" carried on by great books and plain and sensible conversation. As between two individuals, so a conversation between two nations must be based on the perception of both difference and likeness:

> To talk as free men each must in effect say: "You have a different view from mine, but we are both reasonable and human creatures, and I should like to know what your view is." . . . At home and abroad to talk and then to listen, to listen with the help of reason and then reasonably to talk, is to strengthen us just where we can be so much stronger than the Soviets. It is to build the community of free minds, "the civilization of the dialogue."

When Redfield published this article in 1953 in the *Saturday Review*, he had already launched a cooperative scholarly effort to study the differences and likenesses among some of the world's civilizations and cultures (Chinese, Islamic, Indian, Middle American) with a view both to improving the "little conversations" among them and to building the "civilization of the dialogue" from the carrying on of the "great conversation" among their "great traditions." It is notable that this effort, to which he devoted the last seven years of his life, extended his earlier studies in Tepoztlán and Yucatan of what happens to the folk society and culture in a modern, urban setting. The integration of the earlier and later approaches was achieved in his conception of a "social anthropology of civilizations" and in a conversation of cultures implied by that concept.

Redfield's development of a social anthropology of civilizations contributed to a revision of the classical anthropological and sociological theories of cultural and social change. Redfield's studies and concepts "demonstrated the importance and feasibility of looking at the process of modernization from the point of view of the traditional societies, their own values and world views, their changing moods and biographies. . . . In his later thought Redfield came to see that the struggle for independence and the desire to recover some continuity with their ancient indigenous civilization was for the traditional non-Western societies an inseparable part of the process of modernization" (Singer 1976:247–48).

Although Redfield's research and thinking antedated the structural and symbolic theories of the 1960s and 1970s, his definitions of culture and society were implicitly structural and semiotic: "In so far as any defined human aggregate is characterized by social relations, it is a society; in so far as it is characterized by conventional understandings, it exhibits a culture; and in so far as it may also be said to occupy a territory, it is a community" (Redfield 1941:15–16; for further discussion of Redfield's structuralism, see Singer 1976:222–29).

In one of his last writings, "Art and Icon," Redfield explicitly applied Peirce's icon-concept to the interpretation of a Dogon carving of twins in order to illustrate the difference between ethnographic and aesthetic analysis of exotic cultural objects (Redfield 1962).

Another and more semiotic cultural analysis of the conversation of cultures is Geertz's *Person, Time and Conduct in Bali*. Utilizing Schutz's framework of phenomenological distinctions between the directly experienced social reality of "consociates" in a face-to-face situation of a "we-relationship," and the indirectly experienced social reality of "contemporaries," "predecessors," and "successors," Geertz showed that Balinese society "dampens the intimacy implicit in face-to-face relationships" by ceremonializing social intercourse, pulverizing the flow of time into an absolute present, and depersonalizing concrete individuals into stereotyped, faceless persons. The result is "a glancing hesitant confrontation of anonymous persons brought physically very close and kept socially very distant" (Geertz 1966:60).

That this represents a cultural transformation of Schutz's conceptual scheme is noted by Geertz: " . . . the most striking thing about the culture patterns in which Balinese notions of personal identity are embodied is the degree to which they depict virtually everyone—friends, relatives, neighbors and strangers; elders and youths; superiors and inferiors; men, women, chiefs, kings, priests, and gods; even the dead and unborn—as stereotyped contemporaries, abstract and anonymous fellowmen" (ibid.:42). These patterns represent "the symbolic de-emphasis, in the everyday life of the Balinese, of the perception of fellowmen as consociates, successors, or predecessors in favor of the perception of them as contemporaries" (ibid.:53).

While this is a dominant cultural pattern supported by Balinese perceptions of people, time, and conduct, Geertz admits that there are subdominant counter-patterns in close fit with Schutz's scheme: "Of course people in Bali *are* directly, and sometimes deeply involved in one another's lives; *do* feel their world to have been shaped by the actions of those who came before them and orient their actions toward shaping the world of those who will come after them" (ibid.:43; emphasis in original).

"But it is not these aspects of their existence as persons—their immediacy and individuality, or their special, never to be repeated, impact upon the stream of historical events—which are culturally played up, symbolically emphasized: it is their social placement, their particular location within a persisting, indeed an eternal, metaphysical order" (ibid.).

The illuminating paradox to which Geertz calls attention is that Balinese formulations of personhood are in our terms depersonalizing. We might also ask whether the formulations of a Balinese phenomenologist would omit Schutz's category of "consociates" altogether.

The interest of Geertz's study is not exhausted by these general comments but resides just as much in the ethnographic details and their ex-planatory value. He points out, for example, that in Balinese naming patterns, it is the conventionalized public titles, human and divine, that "comprise the present expression of the Balinese concept of personhood in the image of what they consider themselves at bottom to be. . . ." Com-pared to these, other symbols of personhood are secondary: personal names are secret, birth-order names are used mainly for children and adolescents, kinship terms are not used in face-to-face situations, parents address one another by their children's names, and status titles form a pure prestige system (ibid.:20).

The Balinese sense of shame and the absence of climax in interpersonal relations in this culture are also given ingenious explanations by Geertz in terms of this dominant cultural pattern. Rather than summarize these explanations here, I would prefer to draw one or two implications of the semiotics of dialogue for a semiotics of culture.

In order to understand and participate in the kind of "conversations of cultures" described by Redfield, one would need to know national charac-ter, changing national moods, world-view and value systems, group per-sonality types, and the great and little traditions of a civilization. Geertz's conversation with Balinese culture, although more particularized, requires almost as wide-ranging a knowledge of naming systems, conceptions of time and its calendrical expression, the etiquette of ceremonial conduct, kinship terminology, political organization, and the psychology of social relations. If we are going to communicate with people from other cultures, we shall need to know how their social and cultural structures and organi-zations extend and transform the canonical situation of utterance in a face-to-face situation. This kind of knowledge is more specialized than that provided by Peirce's general theory of signs and a semiotics of dialogue based on that theory. It calls for the results of such special disciplines as linguistics, ethnology, social and cultural anthropology, and geography. Peirce readily acknowledged the difference between semiotic as a general theory of signs on the one hand and its application to specialized fields on the other. Although he had an imposing knowledge of many languages and had read widely in history and geography, he undertook few original cultural studies comparable to his studies in astronomy, physics, mathe-matics, logic, or psychophysics. His studies of Shakespearean pronuncia-tion and of the psychology of great men may be an exception to this general observation. Nevertheless, his general theory of signs offers many fruitful suggestions for social and cultural anthropology and for linguistic anthropology. This is especially true of his semiotic analysis of dialogue and its application to a conversation of cultures. Without trying to discuss the applications already made of Peirce's semiotic to a study of dialogue and conversation, I should like to summarize those features of a semiotics of dialogue which still provide a novel and fruitful framework of concepts and hypotheses for empirical research on personal and sociocultural identity.

By relating personal identity and corporate personality to their linguistic expression, especially in particular pronouns such as "I" and "we," Peirce raised the problem to a semiotic level of analysis and directed attention to a phenomenological and pragmatic approach to the self, and away from transcendental, psychophysical, and psychophysiological approaches.

His interpretation of the use of personal pronouns (as well as proper names and definite descriptions) as indexical signs of, or pointers to, individual and group utterers and interpreters of the signs makes it possible to analyze a dialogue as a five-termed relation of utterer, sign, object, interpretant, and interpreter. Such a formulation also makes possible the location of individual and social identities as objects of as well as participants in a dialogue.

Peirce's observation that ego and non-ego are experienced practically simultaneously, along with the opposition between them, and that the non-ego is experienced as something external and strange, provides a basis for distinguishing an inner dialogue of "I" and "me," an outer dialogue of "I" and "you," and a dialogue of corporate identities, of "we" and "they." Since this observation, in Peirce's analysis, is also the foundation for self-consciousness and the consciousness of others, it provides the point of departure for the structure of inferences that underlies the development of a self.

The pronouns (and other signs) form systems that may grow indefinitely. These systems not only consist of discrete lexical sets, but are also sociocultural patterns and systems whose meanings are limited by the experience and habits of the actors. Pairs of pronouns such as "I-me," "I-you," and "we-they" represent a notation for kinds of dialogues; in Peirce's terms, they are "iconic diagrams," whose relational structure is similar to the structure of social relations among the individuals or groups denoted by the pronouns.[11]

As systems, the pairs of pronouns, or the triads and tetrads, that occur in dialogues include iconic signs and symbols as well as indices. The inclusion of icons and symbols provides the link for Peirce to feelings and concepts:

> A concept is not a mere jumble of particulars;—that is only its crudest species. A concept is the living influence upon us of a *diagram*, or *icon*, with whose several parts are connected in thought an equal number of feelings or ideas. The law of mind is that feelings or ideas attach themselves in thought so as to form systems. (Peirce CP:7.467)

The pragmaticist grants that a proper name (although it is not customary to say that it has a meaning) has a certain denotative function peculiar, in each case, to that name and its equivalents; and . . . he grants that every assertion contains such a denotative or pointing-out function. In its peculiar individuality, the pragmaticist excludes this from the rational purport of the assertion, although *the like* of it, being common to all assertions, and so, being general and not individual, may enter into the pragmaticistic purport. (Peirce 1955:263)

While Peirce's youthful interest in "I," "It," and "Thou" was associated with his desire to write a natural history of words, and then with his search for names for his three categories of Firstness, Secondness, and Thirdness, he also saw the possibility of using the pronouns as names for individual and social types. This possibility is envisaged in his prophecy of the coming of a tuistical age that will succeed the "sensate" generation of the idistical age, and the "me" generation of the egotistical age. Whether Peirce's prophecy comes to be fulfilled or not, his doctrine of Tuism has already shown us the path to a semiotic analysis of thinking, conversation, and social relations generally. The road to a semiotics of culture winds through the semiotics of dialogue.

EPILOGUE

One bridge between a Peircean semiotics of dialogue and a semiotics of personal and social identity in culture and society has already been started in the work of several anthropologists. I have in mind not only such contributions as those of Redfield and Geertz to a conversation of cultures, but also the neglected and pioneering contributions of Lloyd Warner to a semiotic anthropology, especially in his monograph dealing with an Australian group, *A Black Civilization* (1937) and in the last monograph of his "Yankee City" series, *The Living and the Dead: A Study of the Symbolic Life of Americans* (1959). Although lacking the linguistic sophistication of a Silverstein or a Lyons, Warner's early formulation of the dialogical nature of symbolic and social interaction approximates fairly closely Lyons's definition of a "canonical situation of utterance." Warner analyzes the social situation into a mutual and reciprocal exchange of signs between two actors, a sender and a receiver, within a context of culturally defined sign interaction. The context is one in which the actors interpret and attribute meaning to the signs and to the objects indicated by them and thus "invest themselves into the signs" (Warner 1959:470). The signs exchanged include gestures, actions, houses and gardens, photographs, and emblematic systems, as well as words and other kinds of signs (ibid.: 469–70, 474, 476, 477, 484).

While Warner's model allows the interaction between two individuals to represent the "whole web of society's relations," he also discusses how possible extensions of the model permit "delayed sign exchange" between the "here and now" of the immediate action-context in face-to-face interactions and remoter contexts in the past and future (ibid.:468, 471–73). His classification of the different types of action-contexts into *moral, supernatural,* and *technical,* and of the associated symbol systems (e.g., duties and rights, myths and rituals, skills and tools) suggests how each action-context can be viewed as part of larger action systems, the totality of which makes up the social system of the community (ibid.:479–80).

For two reasons, the questions of a "private" language of thoughts and of a "private" self do not pose epistemological problems for Warner's model: (1) private and individual interpretations of a sign are "largely dependent on the previous use of the sign in public exchange" (ibid.:465); and (2) each actor interprets the meaning of the sign to himself as he communicates it to the other actor (ibid.:464). "Hidden signs," including, for example, the manifest content of dreams, reveries and visions, and supernatural experiences, can take objective form in concrete visible symbols, such as a cross or an animal totem, or remain as invisible signs within the "internal conversation" of one individual (ibid.: 468–70).

Warner sometimes calls the concrete, visible symbols "emblems" or "emblematic systems" (ibid.:266, 474). In this usage he is following Durkheim, who developed the analogy between such emblems as flags and heraldic designs, and totems. Extrapolating from Durkheim's conception of totems and emblems as sacred collective representations, Warner interprets myths and rituals as largely evocative symbol systems that express and refer to a collective identity. "Such a collective representation symbolizes for men what they feel and think about themselves as animals and persons" (ibid.:485). The sacred emblems link the individual to a collective identity that takes on a supernatural reality. Warner puts this as follows: "The sacred world is not just a reified symbolic expression of the realities of the society, but also an expression of the ongoing life of the human animal. Men can fully realize all they are as members of a species and a society at the supernatural level. Here they can love and hate themselves as gods and be loved and hated by the deities they have created" (ibid.:488).

Although he regarded his own work as a work of science, using science's technical tools and logical referential symbol systems, Warner did not seem to share the impression of many scientists that "science will ultimately conquer the whole world of religious life" (ibid.:489). "The individual who has lost his faith can no longer express his hope and fears, his sense of belonging and togetherness and thereby his feeling of 'wholeness', for the sacred symbols which combine the emotional world of the species and the moral world of the society are the only ones now available that can function in this manner" (ibid.:490).

I shall discuss Warner's application of Durkheim's emblem theory of totemism to the sacred and secular symbolic life of a New England urban community in chapter 5. I should like to conclude the present chapter with a few comments on the relation of Warner's model for a semiotics of culture to Peirce's general theory of signs and his dialogical analysis of sign action. The number of elements in Warner's model that incorporate something of Peirce's general theory is quite striking: his analysis of sign action into signs, objects, and interpretations in a social situation that consists of at least two actors, as sender and receiver of the signs, has already been noted. In both there is also a wide range of signs included beyond the verbal signs and an inclusion, as well, of feelings and values, in addition to denotative and referential meanings. That no sign can be interpreted in isolation but must be seen as part of a system of signs and their meanings ("symbol systems" for Warner) is another shared feature between the two thinkers.

Warner's statement that "the attribution of meaning to an object by an individual depends on previous experience of the individual with the object itself or with signs of the object" (Warner 1959:467), and the corollary that "signs of the future cannnot reach much beyond the present and past meanings on which they are founded" (ibid.:473), are virtual restatements of Peirce's principle of "collateral information". Peirce's idea that individual organisms acquire selves in the course of interacting with one another in sign situations, and that selves so formed are not restricted to the "box of flesh and blood" but encompass the "loosely compacted persons" from one's "circle of society," finds fuller elaboration in Warner, who draws for his model of "social personalities" in symbolic interaction on the ideas of Durkheim and Mauss, Malinowski and Radcliffe-Brown, as well as Freud, Jung, Piaget, and G. H. Mead, among others (ibid.:449–51).

The echoes of Peirce in Warner are all the more remarkable considering that Warner nowhere mentions Peirce. Since Warner was quite conscientious about acknowledging and citing his sources, we must assume that Peirce was transmitted to him indirectly through Ogden and Richards's *The Meaning of Meaning* and some of the American pragmatists, including Mead and Morris, whom Warner does cite. Through his reading in these and the other authors he mentions, Warner might well have picked up the Peircean doctrine that man is a symbol, and the suggestion that human symbol systems, such as "Yankee City" Memorial Day ceremonies and Australian totemism, evoke and express the emotions of hate, fear, pity, and love much as a Greek drama does for its audience (ibid.:476–77, 506).

5

Emblems of Identity from Durkheim to Warner

The relevance of Peirce's semiotic for an analysis of emblems will be found in his definition of a sign as a triadic relation of sign, object, and interpretant; his distinction between iconic or mimetic, indexical or deictic, and symbolic signs; his conception of the self as a semiotic system that is formed in a matrix of social relations; and his generally phenomenological and pragmatic approach to questions of epistemology and ontology. The implications of Peirce's semiotic for a semiotic anthropology in general, and for a semiotics of emblems in particular, remain to be fully developed (Singer 1978, 1980a; Sebeok 1976).

Although several specific studies have been made of special emblematic signs, for example, flags, horse brands, and Russian icons (Firth 1973; Waddington 1974; Uspensky 1976), the application of Peirce's general theory of signs to the formulation of a semiotics of emblems has hardly begun. Some useful suggestions toward such an application are put forward by Jakobson, in his discussion of the distinction between visual and auditory signs (1971:334-37), by Lyons on "secondary iconization" (1977:2.102-104), by Wallis on "semantic enclaves" (1975), and by Eco on "stylization" (1976:191-217, 238-41).

Peirce himself did not, as far as I know, analyze emblems of identity semiotically. However, he did mention a *standard* or *ensign*, a *badge*, and a *church creed* as examples of "symbols" in ancient Greek usage in order to justify his proposed definition of "symbol" as a conventional sign (Peirce 1955:113-14). While a "symbol" is for Peirce a *kind* of thing and denotes a *kind* of thing, and therefore a law or regularity of the indefinite future, "a law necessarily governs or 'is embodied' in individuals, and prescribes some of their qualities" (ibid.:112). Consequently, both an icon, which signifies a quality, and an index, which denotes an individual, may be constituents of a symbol. A symbol without an associated icon and index would not exhibit the qualities signified or identify the objects denoted (ibid.:114). It is in this particular respect that Peirce's semiotic is especially suited for an analysis of emblems such as banners and badges, concrete sign complexes that combine symbols, icons, and indices. A national flag, for example, is a "symbol" as a product of national agreement, but it also includes iconic features in its insignia (stars, a cross, a crescent, hammer and sickle, for example) and indexical features in its unique combination of color bars and insignia. Any particular national flag can then be analyzed as a member of a *system* of symbols in which the permutations and affiliations of elements can be specified and traced synchronically and historically. The American Congress's resolution of 1777, for example, that the flat of the thirteen United States contain in its union "thirteen stars, white in a blue field, representing a new constellation," removed the two crosses in the Grand Union Flag showing the tie to the Union Jack and Great Britain (cf. Firth 1973:chap. 10).

The suggestion, extrapolated from Peirce, that emblems are conventional signs, or "symbols" by his definition, does not exclude iconic and indexical signs from emblems. On the contrary, the conventional feature of an emblem may consist in an agreement to include certain "natural signs" such as iconic insignia and indexical indentifiers (cf. Silverstein 1976:27ff).

It is useful to distinguish between the *manifest* and the *latent* identities of an emblem. The manifest identity is signified or shown by the iconic signs of the emblem, say a crescent moon or a star in a national flag. The latent identity of an emblem, however, is not restricted to any of the familiar celestial objects signified by the insignia but includes as well the association of people whose badge of membership is a particular kind of flag and insignia, to continue with the example of national flags. The manifest identity of an emblem is usually quite transparent from the iconic features of the emblem, the qualities they exhibit, and the objects denoted. The latent identity is not usually transparently visible, except to those already familiar with the emblem and its conventional meaning. Strangers need to infer the latent identity from attached proper names, verbal legends, and similar explanations. The latent identities of the elephant and the donkey as symbols of the Republican and the Democratic parties respectively, for example, are quite familiar to most Americans; to foreigners, only the manifest identities of these symbols would be obvious, while their latent identities as political badges would need to be learned.

One of the major theses of Durkheim's emblem theory of totemism can be reformulated and clarified in terms of the relationship of the manifest and latent identities of totemic emblems. The plants, animals, and other natural phenomena represented by the totemic emblems are the manifest identities of these emblems, while the clan, the moiety, the groups of men or of women, the individual whose badge the totemic emblem becomes, are the latent identities of the emblem (cf. Nadel 1964:263).[1] Lévi-Strauss's interpretation of totemism in terms of homologies between two systems of differences, natural and cultural, is in fact an assertion that the differences between the manifest identities of the emblems form a system that is homologous to the system of differences between the emblems' latent identities, the social groups and individuals. Lévi-Strauss asserts such homologies as a "postulate"; whether they can also be empirically demonstrated will be critically discussed.

How it is possible for the nonverbal features of an emblem—especially its iconic signs—to make a statement of identity is explained by Peirce in his discussion of the object of an icon:

> Now the object of an Icon is entirely indefinite, equivalent to "something." . . . A pure picture without a legend only says "something is like this." . . . To attach a legend to the picture makes a sentence . . . analogous to a portrait we will say of Leopardi with Leopardi written below it. It conveys its information to a person who knows who Leopardi was, and to anybody else it only says something called Leopardi looked like this. (Peirce:CP 8.183)

The use of an emblem to make a statement of identity need not involve a verbal legend or other verbal expression, since the iconic and indexical signs in the emblem, as well as previous acquaintance with the objects of the emblem and with the conventional usages, may be sufficient to make an identity statement. The wearing of religious, political, or fraternal insignia, for example, often serves to make statements of identity, although when there is doubt or dispute concerning the interpretation of the emblems, verbal explanations are quickly introduced. "In America, hats are the sign of individuality. The hat says who you are. . . . Hard hats and the flag go together like motherhood and apple pie; they're one and the same" (*Chicago Tribune*, March 17, 1980).

The electrician in Ohio who explained his and some of his colleagues' refusal during the Iranian hostage crisis to remove American flag decals from their hard hats even under threat of being fired expressed a popular and widespread belief that the display of certain kinds of emblems "says something" and makes a statement of identity. In this instance the electricians, by placing the flag on their hard hats, were saying that they were patriotic Americans who supported the hostages in Iran. Because their verbal explanations are available, the interpretation of the "message" can be verified. This interpretation of identity statements made by emblems is not always so transparent. Why, for example, did the same electricians refuse to accept the company's offer of cloth flags to sew on their clothes?

Peirce's emphasis, in the Leopardi example and in many others, on the necessity for a previous or "collateral" acquaintance with the object of the sign—"no sign can be understood"—or at least ". . . no *proposition* can be understood—unless the interpreter has 'collateral acquaintance' with every object of it" (Peirce: CP 8.183)—explains as well the necessity for anthropological fieldwork and reports of it in monographs, in order for us to understand emblems of identity. A purely formal or structural analysis of emblems must be supplemented by a contextual study if we are to become acquainted with the objects the emblems denote and the identities they refer to.

Iconic signs in emblems represent their objects by some mode of similarity or analogy. In Peirce's semiotic there may be three kinds: *images*, or pictures that represent their objects through a resemblance in qualities; *diagrams*, which represent the relations between the parts of their objects by analogous relations in their own parts (i.e., as homologies); and *metaphors*, which represent a parallelism in their objects with themselves. Although iconic signs may occur naturally, they are often the products of human construction, for example, the designs "an artist draws of a statue, pictorial composition, architectural elevation, or piece of decoration" are iconic signs by the contemplation of which an artist "can ascertain whether what he proposes will be beautiful and satisfactory" (Peirce 1955:106). In a similar manner, Peirce suggests, mathematicians construct geometrical diagrams and algebraic arrays as iconic signs by the observation of which they can discover new truths (ibid.:106–107, 135–49).

Iconic signs do not of themselves assert anything; they signify a character, but taken together with indexical and symbolic signs, they become predicates of propositional statements, just as Peirce explains with the example of Leopardi's portrait and the legend. Since (pre-abstract) paintings and diagrams depend on conventional rules for their interpretation, according to Peirce, they include indexical and symbolic as well as iconic signs. For this reason Jakobson speaks of "symbolic icons" (1971:129).

A semiotic analysis of emblems as constructed signs will thus require an understanding of the characters they signify, of the objects they denote, and of the system of conventional signs ("symbols") they use to make statements about the relations of emblems, objects, and characters. Such understandings will be realized in the dialogues between the designers of the emblems (the "utterers") and the viewers (the "interpreters") in the context of ongoing social interactions.

These preliminary remarks will explain why a semiotic exploration of emblems of identity looks for such emblems in the anthropological studies of Australian totemism and of "Yankee City" Memorial Day ceremonies and Tercentenary celebrations.

The study of emblems as multimedia symbolic representations in the context of cultural performances also provides a semiotic approach to the study of art and ritual forms as cultural systems (Geertz 1973, 1976; Turner 1967; Redfield 1962:468–489; Wolf 1958). The conception of cultural performances emerged in my Madras studies when I found that "the social organization of tradition," in Robert Redfield's words, included a wide variety of religious and secular performances in which people exhibited their culture. When I applied the cultural performance concept to the study of American identity, Lloyd Warner's "Yankee City" monograph, *The Living and the Dead,* suggested both a valuable base line and the important concept of "emblem" as a Durkheimian collective representation, and as "condensed" (in Freud's 1938 and Sapir's 1931 sense) and primarily visual symbols of the culture (Warner 1959:449–50, 474–76). By emphasizing constructed emblems of identity, I hope to make explicit what is largely implicit in Durkheim and Warner: that the natural objects denoted by emblems are the manifest objects of the emblems, and that there are also the utterers and interpreters of an emblem who denote through the use of that emblem a particular social group with which they identify or from which they separate themselves. In this respect, the use of an emblem implies an assertion or denial of membership in a particular social group.

It is encouraging to see that the increase in space flights is leading to an increasing use of images of the planet earth as an emblem of humanity. These images are becoming for some people magic cosmic diagrams, *mandalas,* and *yantras,* through which to assert one's membership in the human species.

DURKHEIM'S EMBLEM THEORY OF TOTEMISM

When we first began the revisits to "Yankee City" in 1974, we were attracted to a well-organized annual nine-day celebration of "Yankee Homecoming." The festivities usually included a great variety of community events—flea markets and fashion shows, arts and crafts fairs, concerts, lunches and suppers, road races and dances, house tours and historical presentations, family and high-school reunions, and much else. The "Homecomings" began in 1957 as a commercial promotion, but their success has turned them into a set of genuine community-wide affairs, enlisting the cooperation of many local organizations and volunteers. The nine-day celebrations, from the end of July through the first week of August, have come to replace July Fourth celebrations; the last day's "Jimmy Fund" Parade, with its marching bands and colorful floats, draws crowds of spectators lining High Street from an early hour, many returning "home" from newer residences. Along with the special Bicentennial historical reenactments and other special events added in 1975 and 1976, the "Yankee Homecomings" constitute cultural performances in which the citizens of Yankee City not only engage in summer fun and games but also "collectively state what they believe themselves to be." The phrase quoted is used by Lloyd Warner in his monograph *The Living and the Dead* to characterize the major theme of the five days devoted in July 1930 to "historical processions and parades . . . games, religious ceremonies, and sermons and speeches" in the city's celebration of the Tercentenary of the Massachusetts Bay Colony. "At that moment in their long history, the people of Yankee City as a collectivity asked and answered these questions: Who are we? How do we feel about ourselves? Why are we what we are? Through the symbols publicly displayed at this time when near and distant kin collected, the city told its story" (1959:107).

In Singer 1977, I have compared the 1930 Tercentenary and the 1970s Yankee Homecoming and Bicentennial as cultural performances and have also discussed the meaning of the persistent local interest in the historical authenticity of the place, some of the people and their houses, antiques, costumes, and reenactments. In the present chapter I should like to approach some of these questions from the point of view of the special symbols and symbolic representations, which Warner called "emblems," that symbolize collective and individual identities in the city. In addition to the "Yankee Homecomings" and Bicentennial activities that we observed and studied in the summers of 1974, 1975, and 1976, I shall also draw on observations during these and later years of an urban renewal and restoration project, interviews of selected families in 1977, and archival research in 1978. Separate papers about the 1977 and 1978 observations, interviews, and research will be published elsewhere.

The Concise Oxford Dictionary of Current English (Sixth Edition 1976) lists two major meanings for "emblem": (1) symbol, typical representation of a person or a quality, and (2) heraldic device or symbolic object as a distinctive badge. The Random House College Dictionary (Revised Edition 1980) gives a more expanded version of the first meaning as a symbol—an object, or a representation of it, symbolizing a quality, state, class of persons, etc. The second meaning emphasizes the figurative aspect of an emblem: "a sign, design or figure that identifies or represents something: *the emblem of a school.*" The Random House Dictionary lists as a third meaning "an allegorical picture, often inscribed with a motto supplemental to the visual image with which it forms a single unit of meaning."

Both dictionaries also give "emblematize" as a verb—to serve as an emblem, to represent by an emblem. Emblems as allegorical pictures or diagrams with some didactic motto in words were well known in the Renaissance through "emblem books" (Praz 1964). These are only indirectly connected with the emblems of identity that are the subject of this chapter. The carving of allegorical drawings and mottos on gravestones that are otherwise identified by name and town and city seals connects the two kinds of emblems.

The first dictionary definitions of "emblems" as symbols representative of a person, a group, or a quality are familiar enough in popular usage. The stars and stripes, the wheel flag, the red flag with its hammer and sickle are emblems in this sense, as are other national flags. That the same countries may also be symbolized by national animals, such as the American bald eagle and the Russian bear, or by cartoons and effigies of their leaders is only a slight extension of this definition of "emblem." The frequent groupings of emblems such as the cross and the crescent or the swastika and the Star of David suggest a symbolic expression of opposition and antagonism between the groups symbolized by the emblems. Sometimes the antagonism may be confined to flag and effigy burning, but it may also turn into national and religious wars, holocaust, and genocide.

The conversation of emblems, fortunately, can be carried on peacefully without aiming at or resulting in mutual destruction. In designs of postage stamps and playing cards, of chess pieces, institutional seals, and the symbols of political parties, in the corporate logo, and the baseball or football letter on the cap, uniform or sweater, the clashing of "emblems" may sometimes lead to physical injuries for a few individuals without disrupting the mass drama of identification and counteridentification.

Coats of arms and other heraldic devices are no longer current emblems, although in their day they performed some of the same functions—to announce and embellish an identity of an individual, a family, an office—to record and authenticate it, to recall and distinguish it; in short, to symbolize in a concrete, visible form a complex and not immediately visible identity. That such emblems also strengthen and sometimes create the identifications, if not the identities, symbolized is a truth increasingly recognized in symbolic studies. That heraldic emblems form *systems* of designs whose variations and permutations must be great enough to avoid duplication and confusion was already known to heralds as early as the thirteenth century and has been restated by a modern herald with a structuralist accent (Wagner 1978:26; Musée Guimet 1964; Tarn 1976).

Warner and other anthropologists who have used the term "emblem" have undoubtedly been acquainted with the dictionary definition and popular usages of the term. These definitions have not, however, been the chief source of anthropological interest or usage. That interest derives from the association of emblems with totemism in Australia and North America. The first serious and systematic development of an emblem theory of totemism was probably Durkheim's, in his *Elementary Forms of the Religious Life* (1947 [1915]). "The totem is a name first of all, and then, . . . an emblem" (110).

Durkheim himself notes that the analogy of totems with flags and heraldic devices has often been made; he frequently quotes his ethnographic sources, Spencer and Gillen and Schoolcraft among others, on the analogy.[2] He states the heraldic analogy quite explicitly: "The nobles of the feudal period carved, engraved and designed in every way their coats-of-arms upon the walls of their castles, their arms, and every sort of object that belonged to them; the blacks of Australia and the Indians of North America do the same thing with their totems" (Durkheim 1947: 113–14). He then cites ethnographic examples from both North America and Australia of painted totemic emblems on shields, ensigns, and helmets and clan totemic designs on ornaments, paintings, and tents, or on the door posts, walls, and woodwork of houses when society became sedentary. Canoes, utensils, funeral piles, the grounds and trees near tombs, and coffinlike hollowed wood are engraved with totemic designs (ibid.:114–15). Painting bodies with totemic designs is also a very general custom in religious ceremonies, rites of initiation, and funerals (ibid.:115–19).

Closely related to the painting or tatooing of totemic emblems on the body are the practices that imitate the totem in some respect—hair style, cosmetics, garments, bodily movements. "It is a very general rule," Durkheim writes, "that the members of each clan seek to give themselves the external aspect of their totem" (ibid.:116). Among the Omaha, for example, members of the turtle clan wear their hair shaved off except for six bunches, two on each side of the head, one in front and one behind, to imitate the legs, head, and tail of a turtle.

Durkheim also stated the analogy between totem and flag quite explicitly and used it to illustrate and, perhaps, guide his own analysis of the symbolic nature of the totem and its psychological effects. The flag was for him the paradigmatic example of a simple, definite, and easily representable symbol whose emotional effects depend on a "transference of sentiments" aroused by what the flag symbolizes. "The soldier who dies for his flag, dies for his country; but as a matter of fact, in his own consciousness, it is the flag that has the first place. . . . He loses sight of the fact that the flag is only a sign, and that it has no value in itself, but only brings to mind the reality that it represents; it is treated as if it were this reality itself. . . . Now the totem is the flag of the clan . . . " (ibid.:220).

Durkheim's emblematic theory of totemism has undergone much criticism and development since the publication of the *Elementary Forms*. One of the leading specialists on Australian totemism, W. E. H. Stanner, has called Durkheim's theory "a brilliant muddle" (Stanner 1965:236). Even Stanner, however, thinks highly enough of Durkheim's contribution to want to preserve it from that oblivion to which he would consign all other early works on totemism (ibid.). Stanner's own analysis of the "totemic sign-function" into the four elements of *living men*, serving as *interpreters* of signs (totems and totemic places), by the use of sign *vehicles* that form and express affective conceptions of *sign-objects*, which are the significations of the Dream Time Marvels, is itself an indirect testimonial to both Durkheim's early insight into Australian totemism as a part of "a vast social symbolism" and his conception of it as a "language" (Durkheim 1947:126–27n4; Stanner 1965:228, 232). Nancy Munn's brilliant study of Walbiri graphic signs as a semiotic system is also a kind of fulfillment, if not a complete verification, of Durkheim's theory of totemic emblems (Munn 1973:77, 177, 216, 217; Durkheim 1947:126–27, 230–34; Yengoyan 1979).

I do not wish to claim too much for Durkheim's theory of totemism. It may be enough to recognize that his was one of the first theories to show how totemic names and emblems were related to ritual and myth, to religious beliefs and sentiments, to language and the logic of classification, to cosmology, morality, and history, to social organization and the performing and practical arts. Whatever has been the fate of specific elements of Durkheim's emblem theory of totemism, it is a remarkable tribute to that theory to find that the major terms of discussion and debate are still couched in largely Durkheimian language and concepts. Raymond Firth's description of Durkheim's contribution, that "he focussed our attention upon the significance of a symbol for the corporate character of human conceptualization and sentiment," and his entire assessment of that contribution are worth quotation:

> Whether identified in nature or of human design and workmanship, the object chosen as symbol was regarded not as representing some cosmic principle or deity by direct reference, but as having been produced by and as having influenced the conduct of an association of *men*. Since this association, by implication, could be contrasted with other associations, and that symbol with other symbols, questions of defining characteristics, of boundaries, of structures, were foreshadowed, and stimulated more refined concepts and more precise field research. (Firth 1973:134)

When the object chosen as symbol was of human design (and for Durkheim it was usually so), it was a totemic *emblem*—painted, engraved, or carved images among the Indians of North America, while among the Australians, the sacred representations " . . . consist essentially of geometrical designs drawn upon the churinga, the nurtunga, rocks, the ground, or the human body . . . either straight or curved lines, painted in different ways, and the whole having only a conventional meaning" (Durkheim 1947:126–27).

Even when the object chosen as symbol is identified in nature—a species of plant or animal or a natural phenomenon—that object remains the object of a symbol, either as the member of a natural species symbolizing its own kind or as a totemic *emblem*. "It is the figurative representations of this plant or animal and the totemic emblems and symbols of every sort, which have the greatest sanctity; . . . thus the totem is before all a symbol, a material expression, of something else" (ibid.:206, 216).

The totemic animals represented by the emblems "become sacred because they resemble the totemic emblem," more so, perhaps, than human beings resemble the totemic emblems. This, for Durkheim, explains why the totemic animals are treated as an elder brother (ibid.:133, 139, 222).

Surrounded everywhere they turned by the signs of their totems, natural or constructed, the Australian totemists found in their totemic emblems "the permanent element of social life," which endured "after the assembly has been dissolved" and with the changing generations (ibid.:221; cf. Stanner 1965:227–28, 236–37; Munn 1973:215).

LATER CRITICISMS: RADCLIFFE-BROWN, LÉVI-STRAUSS, AND STANNER

Firth's characterization of Durkheim's contribution to the theory of totemism reflects some of the later criticisms and revisions, especially those of Radcliffe-Brown and Lévi-Strauss. It is interesting that both of these later theorists rejected the primary importance Durkheim assigned to the emblem theory. Recognizing with Durkheim that "the sentiments of attachment to a group shall be expressed in a formalized collective behavior having reference to an object that represents the group itself," Radcliffe-Brown nevertheless explained the choice of such objects to represent a group—whether the object be a flag, a king, a president, or a totemic emblem—in a manner very different from Durkheim (Radcliffe-Brown 1952:124–25). Radcliffe-Brown rejected Durkheim's explanation for the selection of natural species of plants and animals as emblems or representatives of clans and other social groups on the grounds that in Australia, at least, no totemic emblems could be found for sex totemism, moiety totemism, section totemism, or even clan totemism among many tribes. Where totemic designs are found, in Central and Northern Australia, the natural species are not sacred because they have been selected as representatives of social groups, or emblems, as Durkheim maintained. Radcliffe-Brown argued, on the contrary: ". . . that the natural species are selected as representatives of social groups, such as clans, because they are already objects of the ritual attitude on quite another basis, by virtue of the general law of the ritual expression of social values stated above" (ibid.:129).

The general law referred to is one that Radcliffe-Brown formulated when he studied the customs and beliefs of a nontotemic people, the Andaman Islanders: "Any object or event which has important effects upon the well-being (material or spiritual) of a society, or any thing which stands for or represents any such object or event, tends to become an object of the ritual attitude" (ibid.).

This is the reason, according to Radcliffe-Brown's first paper on totemism (1929), why the turtle in the Andamans, the salmon in Northwest Coast America, and the totemic species in Australia are "sacred," or objects of ritual attitudes. And any emblem or design that stands for or represents such a natural species will also tend to become an object of the ritual attitude or sacred.

Lévi-Strauss has called Radcliffe-Brown's generalized explanation for the selection of totemic species a form of naturalism, empiricism, and functionalism, and has contrasted it unfavorably with the explanation in Radcliffe-Brown's second paper on totemism (1958), in which Lévi-Strauss finds a structuralist analysis very similar to his own. In Radcliffe-Brown's second paper, "The animals in totemism cease to be solely or principally creatures which are feared, admired, or envied: their perceptible reality permits the embodiment of ideas and relations conceived by speculative thought on the basis of empirical observations. We can understand, too, that natural species are chosen not because they are 'good to eat' but because they are 'good to think'" (Lévi-Strauss 1963a:89).

The formulation in Radcliffe-Brown's second paper on totemism that so impressed Lévi-Strauss concerned the principle by which specific pairs of birds were selected to represent the moieties of a dual division. ". . . instead of asking 'why all these birds?' we can ask why particularly eagle-hawk and crow, and other pairs?" (ibid.:86). Radcliffe-Brown's answer, so surprising to Lévi-Strauss as an anticipation of his own structuralism, was that in all cases of exogamous moieties, the particular pairs of birds chosen to represent them, such as eagle-hawk and crow, are chosen because they are in a relation of "opposition"—in a double sense: as "friendly antagonists" and as "contraries by reason of their character" (ibid.:90).

For Lévi-Strauss, this answer is genuinely structuralist because it attempts to relate institutions, representations, and situations through their respective relations of opposition and correlation. In conformity with every anthropological undertaking, it asserts "a homology of structure between human thought in action and the human object to which it is applied" (ibid.:91). In other words, Radcliffe-Brown's second paper on totemism is for Lévi-Strauss but an example of his own conception of totemism as a coordination of two systems of differences, a natural series of animal and plant species, and a cultural series of human social units. This conception, Lévi-Strauss suggests, is a new one, deriving from structural linguistics and structural anthropology in the decade 1941–51, and represents a departure from Radcliffe-Brown's earlier empiricism, naturalism, and functionalism (ibid.:90).

Although Lévi-Strauss frequently refers to the "totemic illusion" and to "so-called totemism," his analysis constitutes a contribution to a positive theory of totemism, as Hiatt (1969) and others have pointed out. The heart of Lévi-Strauss's theory will be found in his postulate of a homology, or isomorphism, of structures between the two systems of differences, natural and social. In *The Savage Mind*, the postulate of homologous structures is combined with a theory of signs based on Saussure's conception of a sign as a dyadic relation of signifier and signified. This kind of structuralism in the analysis of superstructures presupposes functionalism, naturalism, and empiricism in the analysis of the "infrastructures" (Lévi-Strauss 1976:5–9; 1966:130–31).

Meyer Fortes has objected, in response to Lévi-Strauss's interpretation of Radcliffe-Brown's second paper on totemism, that neither he nor other anthropologists familiar with Radcliffe-Brown's work see any great departure from his earlier theories in the second paper (Fortes 1966). Fortes is probably justified in stressing the continuities in Radcliffe-Brown's work. Structuralist formulations can be found in earlier papers, just as empiricist, naturalist, and functionalist formulations persist into the later papers. However, there probably is a growing emphasis in Radcliffe-Brown's later papers during the 1940s on relational and structural analysis of social structure and kinship systems, joking and avoidance relations, and totemism. This emphasis probably derived from Radcliffe-Brown's interest in Russell's and Whitehead's philosophy of science based on events and relational structures rather than from structural linguistics or structural anthropology (Singer 1984).

Although Radcliffe-Brown in his later paper on totemism was turning toward a relational and structural analysis of both the natural and the cultural systems, and beginning to deemphasize naturalistic and functionalistic explanations, he did not reinstate Durkheim's emblem theory or develop an alternative symbolic analysis. Curiously, he formulates one of the general problems of totemism in Durkheimian terms in the second paper but then sets it aside without further explanation. In question is:

> . . . the problem of how social groups come to be identified by connection with some emblem, symbol, or object having symbolic or emblematic reference. A nation identified by its coat of arms, a particular congregation of a church identified by its relation to a particular saint, a clan identified by its relation to a totemic species; these are all so many examples of a single class of phenomena for which we have to look for a general theory. (Radcliffe-Brown 1958:113–14)

It is no accident that Radcliffe-Brown failed to develop a general theory of how particular social groups, or individuals, came to be identified by particular emblems. His desire to avoid particularistic historical studies and his emphasis on totems as natural objects rather than on constructed emblems is part of the explanation. A more important reason, I believe, is precisely his development of a structuralist analysis in his second paper on totemism. For structuralist analysis tends to abstract from individuals and individual collections of individuals. To deal with the individual objects of iconic signs, it is necessary, as Peirce pointed out, to have previous acquaintance with them and to employ indexical signs such as personal pronouns, demonstrative and relative pronouns, and "selectives," such as "any" and "some," for finding the objects (Peirce CP:8.181).

The problem is highlighted by Lévi-Strauss, who recognizes on the one hand that the series of natural objects are homologous to the series of social and cultural objects, yet rejects on the other both Peirce's indexical signs and Russell's "egocentric particulars" as devices for denoting the *particular* objects presupposed by the structural homologies (Lévi-Strauss 1966:214–26). This leaves only the gesture of pointing to bridge the gap between homologous structures and the social objects they signify, and also treats the individual as if it were a natural species. In our civilization, at least, "everything takes place as if . . . every individual's own personality were his totem: it is the signifier of his signified being" (ibid.:214).[3]

This statement takes us a long way from Durkheim's "individual totemism," with its insistence that the individual animal that represents an individual's totem and gives the individual its name and emblem is not the same as the animal species and its collective emblem (Durkheim 1947:160).

Stanner has tried to integrate the apparently disparate aspects of totemism—structural, symbolic, and substantive—by interpreting a collective totemic emblem as "an abstract symbol for the possible membership, over all space and time, of the sets of people symbolized by it—the dead, the living, the unborn. . . . Any particular instance of a totem at a place or point of time is, in the symbolic sense, an image of the whole indefinite family of sets." He reports that a thoughtful aboriginal once said to him: "There are Honey People all over the world" (Stanner 1965:229).

This interpretation stresses the structural and symbolic aspects of the concept but leaves the denotative aspects problematic: "Not *this* eaglehawk or *that* crow, but all and any eaglehawks or crows that were, are, or might be" (ibid.:228). Stanner's interpretation suggests a subtlety of thought not usually recognized for aboriginals, and a mathematical abstractness not included in Lévi-Strauss's "concrete logic." Perhaps, as Stanner says, although "totems may be associated only with primitive peoples, there is no primitivity in aboriginal totemic thought and imagery" (ibid:229).

Stanner's explanation of a collective totem as an abstract symbol seems to me logically similar to Peirce's explanation of an emblematic sign's *objective generality:* "A statue of a soldier on some village monument, in his overcoat and with his musket, is for each of a hundred families the image of its uncle, its sacrifice to the Union. That statue then, though it is itself single, represents any one man of whom a certain predicate may be true. It is *objectively* general" (Peirce 1955:263).

In Stanner's interpretation of totems as abstract symbols, the predicates are iconic signs, or, as he describes "the totemic idiom," "an imagery mimetic of vital or significant things in the environment" (1965:236). That imagery may seem exotic to Westerners but, "The fact that hunters and foragers developed a zoomorphic and phytomorphic imagery was as appropriate to men in the Australian environmennt as that nomadic shepherds developed a pastoral imagery in the environment of early Judea and Israel" (ibid.:237).

The problem of study for Stanner is not the particular kind of imagery, but rather Durkheim's problem—"how the associating of a totem with a collection of people was that which transformed them from just a collection into groups with a sign of unity" (ibid.). In dealing with this problem Stanner gives importance to history and the "irreducibly arbitrary" nature of the associations between totems and particular places and groups of people that have some features in common (ibid.:226). At the same time he emphasizes, more than Durkheim, that the totemic system symbolizes a link between cosmogony, cosmology, and ontology, as well as symbolizing aboriginal totemic groups as perennial corporations of a religious character.

The respect for totems, totem places, and insignia and emblems standing for persons indicates to Stanner the high value that the totemic system placed on the individual person, despite the iconic and generic character of totemic symbols. He sees this especially in the life-cycle rituals for males:

> Always a particular person, a very small group of equivalent persons, was thus honoured, and the community, not a clique or set, paid the honour. Each individual, at his due times was brought to the first place in public life. For days or weeks he was made the focus of elaborate efforts of the imaginative and material arts. . . . The effect was to dignify and in some sense sanctify each person so honoured. One is impelled to conclude that the rites had a plain meaning: man is of value in himself and for others. (Ibid.:216)

The movement of critical revision of Durkheim's emblem theory of totemism, which began with Radcliffe-Brown's 1929 "sociological theory" and culminated in 1962 (1966) with Lévi-Strauss's "postulate" of homology between systems of differences, natural and cultural, has raised new questions. One such question is whether the plants, animals, and natural objects selected as totems actually constitute "systems" of totemic symbols or are unsystematic and ad hoc. Citing the observations of Stanner, El-kins, Worsely, and Fortes, Hiatt finds that "the ethnographic record . . . points strongly to the conclusion that totemic symbolism is typically un-systematic" (Hiatt 1969:87). Hiatt nevertheless credits Lévi-Strauss with a positive conception of totemism as "a type of classification in which social groups are signified by natural species (as markers)" (ibid.:86). He believes that only a few cases, however, have been reported that verify Lévi-Strauss's homology hypothesis, namely, some instances of Australian moiety totemism (ibid.:89). Hiatt is also skeptical of Lévi-Strauss's at-tempt to explain the prevalence of unsystematic totemism by appealing to historical and demographic changes that may have dismantled previously existing totemic systems. Hiatt believes that the alternative explanation, that "the choice of totemic symbols has always proceeded unsystemati-cally," is as plausible as to suggest that "it began as a rational system and ended in ruins" (ibid.:90).

In the light of his criticisms of Lévi-Strauss, Hiatt urges a return to Durkheim's "assumption that, in general, group symbols signify both unity and difference, and are vitalized by affectivity." ("Sentiment, as Durkheim correctly saw, is the fuel of totemism, and not as Lévi-Strauss believes, a waste product that threatens to clog an alleged rationally con-ceived global system") (ibid.:90). Hiatt also reaffirms Goldenweiser's "sec-ond thoughts" on the reality of totemism as a distinctive and sharply defined institution of primitive society (ibid.:93).

Hiatt's call for a return to Durkheim and to Goldenweiser leaves the field open for a realistic and pluralist position, with a greater role for emotion and social action than seems to be provided by Lévi-Strauss. He pays a high price, however, for this position by abandoning structuralism and systematic totemic classification, and by denying a significant role to totemic emblems in defining and creating social identities. "We know that our own medical profession uses a representation of the staff and serpent of Aesculapius as an emblem. . . . But it would be curious to assert that the main point of the aboriginal medicine man's relationship with a snake species is that it provides him with a mark of identity" (ibid.:86). Ironi-cally, both Lévi-Strauss and Goldenweiser manage to retain a greater role for totemic classifications within an explanatory structuralist framework.

Although Lévi-Strauss is critical of Durkheim's emblem theory of to-temism, especially of his attempt to derive totems from graphic designs and the emotions associated with them (Lévi-Strauss 1962:93, 95–96; 1966:239), he recognizes that names and emblems, as well as food prohibi-tions, clothing, bodily paintings, and behavior, are some of the ways in which different clans signify their differences (1966:149–50). He even asserts that each clan "possesses 'a symbol of life'—a totem or divinity—whose name it adopts" (ibid.:147), and that the totemic animal "is not grasped as a biological entity but as a conceptual tool" (ibid.:148–49). For example, the inedible and distinctive parts of a totemic animal, such as the feathers, beaks, or teeth, may be "adopted as emblems by groups of men in order to do away with their own resemblances" (ibid.:106–108).

Goldenweiser's papers on totemism are not usually considered as presenting a structuralist interpretation. Indeed, one cannot find in them an explicit structuralist formulation comparable, say, to Radcliffe-Brown's second paper of 1951 or Lévi-Strauss's conception of the homologous two systems of differences. Yet there are some respects in which Goldenweiser anticipates both of these writers, others in which he goes beyond them.

In his linking of a totemic culture to a social organization, subdivided into functionally analogous or equivalent but separate social units, Goldenweiser is close to Radcliffe-Brown as well as to Durkheim. In such a community, "the first demand is for some kind of classifiers, perferably names, which would identify the separate units and yet signify their equivalence by belonging to one category." And, "all along, the classificatory aspect remains a fixed requirement, so whatever traits may develop in the social crucible appear as homologous traits" (Goldenweiser 1918:291).

Goldenweiser also stresses, as Lévi-Strauss does, that "things in nature," and particularly animals, are "constantly used for naming individuals, groups of all varieties, such as families, societies, clubs, game teams, political parties, houses, constellations" because they are homologous in structure to human social groups: "They are beautifully adjusted to the function of classifiers as names or otherwise, for they contain many individuals belonging to the same or to several wide categories, they are familiar, congenial to man, yet lie outside the circle of specifically human things and activities" (ibid.:293).

Perhaps even more than Radcliffe-Brown and Lévi-Strauss, Goldenweiser makes clear how these animals and "things in nature" serving as classifiers become "symbols of the social values of the group." "Their very objectivity as well as emotional significance lend themselves readily to artistic elaboration" (ibid.:291). Such objects are "early drawn into the domain of art—painted, tatooed, carved, woven, embroidered, dramatized in dances; they figure in all realistic as well as geometric representations, thus also rising into prominence as badges, signs and symbols" (ibid.:293; cf. Crane 1914).

Utilizing Boas's studies of Northwest Coast carving and painting, Goldenweiser points out that the distinctive parts of an animal or bird are selected for emphasis and become symbolic of that particular animal. These symbolic parts of animals appear when the whole animal is represented, but they may also be used when the animal form is dissected and reduced or disappears altogether. The carving of a beaver on a totem pole may be represented by protruding incisors, ears on top of the head, tail turned up in front, or a cross-hatching that represents the tail (Goldenweiser 1937:180–91; cf. Lévi-Strauss 1966:106–108).

In his explanation of the how and why of the process, Goldenweiser neither derives the totemic symbolism directly from the social organization, as he believed Durkheim tried to do, nor does he give primacy to the cognitive and intellectual factors. He postulates rather a mutual "fitness" of the social and cultural aspects of totemism, which are disparate but undergo a "mutual penetration" and "further elaboration" as they interact (1918:290). Through the operation of such a process of mutual adjustment, emotions, and attitudes, the totem's cultural content becomes "socialized" and the social groups that become associated with the symbols and objects of emotional value are "constituted as definite social units" (Goldenweiser 1910:275; 1918:290–91).

Along with Linton (1924) and Sapir (1949 [1927]:344–45), Goldenweiser found the tendencies and processes underlying totemism also operative in an attenuated form in modern society, where "equivalent social units are known to adopt as classifiers names, badges, pins, flags, tattoo marks, colors. One thinks of high school and college classes, baseball and football teams, political parties, the degrees of Elks and Masons, and the regiments of our armies" (1931:277). The totemic emblems and symbols so generated are "charged with potential emotions. Even the animal or bird mascots cultivated by military units become under appropriate conditions, such as war, immersed in a complex of attitudes and rites so exotic as to suggest an exaggerated analogy with totemism" (ibid.).

A full and detailed development of the analogy of modern society with totemic rites and beliefs was worked out in Warner's *The Living and the Dead*. This analogy had already become a topic for comment among some American anthropologists before Warner started his "Yankee City" research. It is also interesting to recall that Warner was trained at Berkeley in the Boas tradition under Lowie and Kroeber and was prepared to combine culture history and cultural psychology to arrive at conclusions about "cultural dynamics." That he eventually relegated these interests to an appendix of his Murngin book (1937: Appendix I) may be testimony to his encounter with Radcliffe-Brown and structuralism but does not entirely explain his return to Durkheim's emblem theory of totemism. That explanation will be found, I believe, in the fact that through the emblem concept Warner achieved a third kind of generalization, beyond the two kinds identified by Leach (1961b): Radcliffe-Brown's comparative method ("butterfly collecting") and Lévi-Strauss's structuralism ("inspired guesses at mathematical pattern"). The third kind of generalization is that of a semiotic anthropology, a kind that was not reached for by many other anthropologists until almost a decade later, but has by now become more popular, as Geertz has recently observed: "The move toward conceiving of social life in terms of symbols . . . whose meaning . . . we must grasp if we are to understand that organization and formulate its principles, has grown by now to formidable proportions. The woods are full of eager interpreters" (Geertz 1980a:167).

WARNER RETURNS TO DURKHEIM'S EMBLEM THEORY

After Durkheim's *Elementary Forms of the Religious Life* (1915), Warner's *Black Civilization* (1937) was the next serious effort to apply the emblem theory. Warner had based his monograph on three years of fieldwork in Northern Australia (1926–29), under the tutelage of Radcliffe-Brown. The totemic institutions and symbolism of the Murngin were of special interest, and he devoted a substantial portion of the monograph to their description and interpretation (Warner 1958 [1937]:chaps. 9–13). The roles of totemic emblems in funerals and in initiation rites were stressed, their relations to dances, songs, dramatic rites, and myths analyzed, and their social significance interpreted. Higher-rank emblems *(ranga)*, which could be seen only by the adult men and initiated young men, were distinguished from the lower-order emblems *(garma)*, which could also be seen by women. "When a *ranga* has been made by men of the clan for a ceremony and has been used during the nighttime, it is put back in the mud of the water hole so that the *wong* [or spirit of the totem] which is felt to be in the emblem may return to the well" (ibid.:21).

Warner lists *ranga* and *garma* totems for each of the Murngin clans, along with the water holes, by name, country, and moiety. The "sacred names" of the water holes and of the higher-order totems are in the Murngin "sacred language" (ibid.:39). In the initiation rites, the dancers and the boys are painted with human blood because the blood is now sacred and powerful, as if, say the natives, it were a totemic emblem itself (ibid.:281–82).

In a special appendix to *Black Civilization*, Warner describes the materials, measurements, and techniques of making the totemic emblems. Emblems of geometric design tend to be carved from wood and stone, while the naturalistic designs are made of bark.

Warner recognized in *Black Civilization* the need for a general theory of signs and symbols and began to apply Ogden and Richards's semantic triangle to his analysis of Murngin totemism (ibid.:247–48, 407–408). He did not however, formulate a method and theory for the study of "symbolic life" until his monograph on *The Living and the Dead* (1959:Part V). Although in this volume he said he followed the methods used in *Black Civilization* (1959:4), and he does in fact occasionally refer to Durkheim's conception of totemic emblems as collective representations, that conception is generalized to a semiotic analysis of signs and symbols. Emblems have become symbols and

> . . . the essential components of a symbol are the sign and its meaning, the former usually being the outward perceptible form which is culturally identifiable and recognizable, the latter being the interpretation of the sign, usually composed of concepts of what is being interpreted and the positive and negative values and feelings which "cluster about" the sign. The sign's meaning may refer to other objects or express and evoke feelings. The values and feelings may relate to the inner world of the person or be projected outward on the social and natural worlds beyond. (Ibid.)

It is striking how similar Warner's definition of a sign and its meaning is to Peirce's triadic conception of a sign, its object, and its interpretant. Peirce, however, defines "symbol" in a broader sense than Warner's usage or the popular one, to refer to any sign whose meaning depends on some kind of conventional agreement. Whether Peirce's semiotic theory was directly known to Warner is uncertain; more likely some of it filtered through Ogden and Richards, G. H. Mead, and C. W. Morris, all of whom are acknowledged, along with Sapir, Freud, Jung, Pareto, Levi and Frye, and Durkheim, Piaget, Radcliffe-Brown, Malinowski, Mauss and Kluckhohn, as contributors to symbolic theory (ibid.: 449–51).

Some influence of each of these theorists is evident in Warner's theory of symbolism. From Sapir comes the idea that each society has its own things—marks, colors, forms, actions and movements—that can be seen and identified, to which agreed-upon conscious and unconscious meanings have been attached and maintained through time. Each culture has its own sounds, noises, and silences, which arouse the attention of its members and have agreed-upon significance (ibid.:455).[4]

From the logicians and philosophers Warner accepted the proposition that "The meaning of a sign, however separately perceived, always involves and implies the meaning of other signs. The meaning of one sign can be understood only when related to the meanings of other signs; a sign is always a part of one or more sign systems" (ibid.:459, 484).

It was particularly the theorists of symbolism who stressed the social and psychological context of interpretation—Durkheim, G. H. Mead, Pareto, and Freud, among others—that were effectively incorporated by Warner: "All signs of definition are dependent for their existence on a community of interpreters implicating them—both signs and interpreters—in a system of meanings shared by those involved" (ibid.:455).

In fact, Warner's analysis of a dyadic exchange of signs between individuals in the context of social interaction is a neglected contribution to the theory of symbolic interactionism (ibid.: chap. 15). In the present

124 MAN'S GLASSY ESSENCEMAN'S GLASSY ESSENCE

chapter, however, we shall not deal primarily with Warner's general theory of symbolism as such; rather, we shall discuss how he applied that theory to the emblematic systems in Yankee City in the 1930s, and how these systems and the identities they symbolize were changing in the 1970s.

Warner frequently described his studies of Yankee City as being based on the same methods he had used in his earlier study (1925–29) of the Murngin tribe in Northeast Australia. In *The Living and the Dead*, the parallels between the two studies are especially explicit. Describing the preparations for the 1930 Tercentenary procession, Warner said that, "The arrangement of story and dramatic ceremony" provided "a close analogue to the historical myths and rites of a primitive society." And this, he said, made it possible for him "to study the collective rites of Yankee City by some of the same procedures used successfully on primitive peoples" (ibid.:116).[5] A footnotes cites the pages on Murngin totemism in Warner's book *Black Civilization*.

Again, his description of Yankee City Memorial Day ceremonies as "a cult of the dead organized around the community cemeteries" leads Warner to write that, "Just as the totemic symbol system of the Australians represents the idealized clan, and the African ancestral worship symbolizes the family and state, so the Memorial Day rites symbolize and express the sentiments of the people for the total community and the state" (ibid.:277).

Warner, no doubt, appreciated the shock value of describing the ways of the inhabitants of a modern community in terms of stone-age ritual and myths. But he had a more serious purpose than culture shock and social satire. He was also willing to read the parallel in the reverse direction and describe the Murngin rituals and myths in terms of drama and dance, recreation and play, and art, religion, and cosmology. This was the case not because he wished to flatter his Australian friends but because, following Radcliffe-Brown, he conceived of social anthropology as a generalizing science that, through the use of the comparative method, would develop a framework of concepts and methods for the study of all societies and cultures.

For Warner and for Radcliffe-Brown, the use of the comparative method to arrive at generalizations about all societies and cultures depends on the observation of differences as well as resemblances. Yankee City Memorial Day ceremonies and the Tercentenary procession suggested certain parallels to the totemic rituals and myths of the Murngin, but the description and analysis of these parallels would need to take account of the more complex culture and society of Yankee City, with its diversity of social groups and values and its background of written history. Its identity belongs to several different historical universes at one time and to ever-widening circles of identification: Massachusetts, New England, seaboard New England, the United States of America, Western culture, and the rest of the world. Yankee City's history has to be seen in the context of national and world events as well as in a local perspective (ibid.:115–16). It may very well be that Warner's use of the comparative method in his Yankee City studies yields a definition of collective representations and of their relations to the social structure that conforms to Durkheim's in the French sociologist's classic study of Australian totemism (Durkheim 1947 [1915]). Such a result cannot, however, be posited in drawing the parallel; it must be taken as a hypothesis for empirical inquiry.

YANKEE CITY AS A SHAKESPEAREAN WORLD

During our first visits to Yankee City, we were struck by the prominence given to emblems of identity and related visual and verbal symbols. A local guide pointed out "the Irish church," "the French church," "the Greek Orthodox church," "the synagogue," "the Unitarian church" with its handsome spire. Many participants and members of the audience in the annual Yankee Homecoming celebration were dressed in colonial costumes, as gentlemen and yeomen, patriots and redcoats. Officers and sailors of the Continental Navy marched in the "Jimmy Fund" parade in authentic costume, bearing muskets and led by a fife and drum corps and an honor guard carrying a colonial flag with thirteen stars. The partially restored buildings in Market Square were draped with flag bunting and marked with antique signs portraying occupations and products for sale. The early nineteenth-century buildings were fronted with colonial street lanterns and hitches for horses. The window of an antique store on one of the Market Square corners was so identified with "Antiques" and the name of the owner printed in Hebrew-like script.

Our initial impression was that we had come upon a Shakespearean world, in which religion, race, ethnicity, social class and rank, occupation, age, and sex were all visibly inscribed in dress and speech, in public and private architecture, in the façades of buildings and shops. This impression did not survive a closer acquaintance with the community, which has been undergoing changes that have blurred and practically effaced the colorful seventeenth- and eighteenth-century images of the city. Perhaps in the 1930s such a portrait retained enough verisimilitude to persuade the young social anthropologist Lloyd Warner that he had found a New England community with a sufficiently orderly social system, a long-enough standing cultural tradition, and enough of an old-family Yankee aristocracy to justify applying to that same New England city the social-anthropological methods he had used a few years earlier for a study of Australian aborigines.

At least one former inhabitant of Yankee City, John P. Marquand, the novelist, recalled that the old social order was still extant in the early 1930s when Warner and his staff came to study it. Nor was Marquand surprised by Warner's finding of six social classes in the town, although he drew some of his social satire in novels such as *Point of No Return* and *The Late George Apley* from the anthropologist's study and academic social classifications.

In 1960, when he published his revised biography of "Lord" Timothy Dexter, Marquand wrote that while the outlines of the society that so interested the Warner researchers were still extant, "it had been altered in many ways beyond recognition." The town was no longer an isolated community, High Street and its famous Federalist houses were no longer the same, and the Puritan and sophisticated traditions of the past were becoming replaced by "plastic motifs that give the most authentic part of State Street a jukebox air" (Marquand 1960:122). Noting that the last of Warner's Yankee City monographs, *The Living and the Dead*, had recently been published, Marquand suggested that "If Mr. Warner were to continue further with his Yankee City, another volume might be a very different saga" (ibid.:16–17).

Neither Marquand nor Warner wrote that different saga. The chiefly historical reconstruction of the life and career of the eighteenth-century eccentric merchant "Lord" Timothy Dexter was Marquand's last book about his home city. Warner revised and supplemented *The Living and the Dead* in *The Family of God* (1961) and also edited a condensed summary of his five-volume series in *Yankee City* (1963). Yet it was the kinds of changes that Marquand was beginning to discern in the early 1960s that had crystallized by the 1970s when we revisited the city. A careful reading of Warner's *The Living and the Dead* will find some anticipations of how the old order was beginning to change even in the days of "Biggy" Muldoon, Warner's epithet for the colorful populist mayor. That volume, however, can no longer be taken as an accurate ethnographic guide to Yankee City. In two other respects Warner's last monograph remains valid and highly valuable: as a base line for studying how the Yankee City of the 1930s has changed, and as a pioneering innovation in semiotic anthropology.

If, indeed, that New England urban community which Warner and his researchers studied in the 1930s by social-anthropological methods can no longer be represented by the traditional emblems of ethnicity, race, and religion—or of social class, occupation, age, and sex—why does it give visitors the impression that it is still a Shakespearan world? And how had these emblems of identity changed in the 1970s?

The historian Stephan Thernstrom has raised the question whether Lloyd Warner's portrait of Yankee City was already out of date by the middle of the nineteenth century. Thernstrom is particularly critical of what he regards as the ahistorical method of social anthropology and calls Warner's portrait a creation of his imagination and that of his upper-class informants (Thernstrom 1971:195). Even Thernstrom, however, excepts Warner's volume *The Living and the Dead* from this criticism, because Warner consulted historical sources in that study to distinguish the city's "mythical history" from its "actual history."

On our revisits to Yankee City, we met several inhabitants who spontaneously expressed their appreciation of Warner's account of Memorial Day celebrations in *The Living and the Dead* or *The Family of God*. They not only felt that the description was accurate, as they remembered the day from childhood, but they also believed Warner's account captured the occasion's spirit and what it meant to their families and the community. The contrast with contemporary Memorial Day celebrations heightened their appreciation, for these were no longer well-attended community-wide ceremonies.

Not many commented on Warner's comparison of Memorial Day with Australian totemism. Yet Warner's analogy to Australian totemism is easiest to trace, if not completely persuasive, in his description and interpretation of Memorial Day as an "American Sacred Ceremony." Chapter 8 ("The Symbolic Relations of the Dead and the Living") and chapter 9 ("The City of the Dead") in *The Living and the Dead* obviously correspond to chapters XII and XIII (on "Mortuary Rites" and their interpretation) in *Black Civilization*. Beyond this parallel, there is the deeper correspondence in the structure, organization, and functions of the rituals and ceremonies, the effect of which is to repair the injuries to the living inflicted by death and to restore the solidarity of the community weakened by loss of some of its members.

The basic outlines of this theory derive from Durkheim and Van Gennep, whom Warner acknowledged (Warner 1959:278, 303, 402). The detailed application of the theory to Memorial Day ceremonies is original to Warner and most ingenious in showing how varied social groups and associations, including ethnic groups who are otherwise excluded from participation in community activities, are incorporated into the Memorial Day ceremonies. The Memorial Day rites of Yankee City, and of other American towns, represent a modern "cult of the dead" that "dramatically expresses the sentiments of unity of all the living among themselves, of all the living with the dead, and of all the living and dead as a group with God" (ibid.:278–79). "Throughout the Memorial Day rites we see people who are religiously divided as Protestant, Catholic, Jewish, and Greek Orthodox participating in a common ritual in a graveyard with their common dead. Their sense of autonomy was present and expressed in the separate ceremonies, but the parade and unity of doing everything at one time emphasized the oneness of the total group" (ibid.:268).

In his detailed analysis of the Memorial Day ceremonies, Warner found that the graves of the dead were "the most powerful of the visible emblems" unifying all the groups of the community (ibid.:279). He interpreted the cemetery and its graves as both "a physical emblem" and "a social emblem." The several material symbols in the cemetery, such as the walks, fences, and hedges that marked its physical limits, the stone markers on individual graves with the surnames of those buried there, and the landscaping—all these constitute the cemetery as "an enduring physical emblem, a substantial and visible symbol of this agreement among men that they will not let each other die" (ibid.:285).

As a *social emblem*, the cemetery, according to Warner, provides for a number of social functions that are continuously renewed by the funerals and other rituals. These functions include disposal of the corpse and a firm and fixed social place for anchoring the disturbed sentiments about the dead, "where the living can symbolically maintain and express their kinship with the dead." The marked grave, Warner pointed out, is not merely a symbol that "refers generally and abstractly to all the dead," but is something that belongs to a separate personality.

The cemetery as a social emblem is thus "composed of many autonomous and separate individual symbols which give visible expression to our social relations, to the supernatural and to the pure realm of the spirit"; yet the cemetery as a sign is whole and entire (ibid.:286).

Warner's interpretation of the cemetery as a set of both physical and social emblems obviously generalizes the concept of emblems to embrace a variety of material symbols and their varied social functions. How such symbols become emblems of identity and whom or what they are emblematic of is explained by Warner in his analogy of the cemetery with "a city of the dead." This metaphorical designation he took from a hymn used during Memorial Day religious services, "City of Our Dead." Through intensive observations of several cemeteries and through interviews, he and his coworkers collected enough data to support his interpretation that the cemeteries are "the symbolic replica of the living community" (ibid.:286–87). "The social and status structures which organize the living community of Yankee City are vividly and impressively reflected and expressed in the outward forms and internal arrangements of the several cemeteries in the city" (ibid.:287).

The location of graves within a cemetery, the number, size, and location of headstones, and the kinds of stone borders, carvings, and inscriptions indicated to Warner and his staff the differences between elementary and extended families, the relatives status of members of a family according to age and sex, and the changing mobility of a family.

Ethnic, religious, and associational affiliations were also indicated by similar markers and by the use of distinctive emblems on the graves: the insignia of the American Legion, the Elks, and the Moose; the cross and lamb for Catholic Christians; and the greater use of the American flag for the graves of ethnic groups.

Warner noted the dual character of the symbolism on the ethnic graves in the cemeteries—inscriptions in English as well as in the ethnic language, headstones and wooden crosses on the same grave, an American flag together with a small replica of a house with wax flowers and a candle inside. He also observed that the dual symbolism was more prominent among the families of more recent immigrants.

FROM SACRED EMBLEMS TO SECULAR HISTORICAL MONUMENTS

Warner pointed out in *The Living and the Dead* that only six out of the eleven cemeteries were decorated on Memorial Day; the rest were neglected because their dead had no living representatives (ibid.:319). This observation leads him to suggest the interesting idea that cemeteries "die" and cease to exist as "sacred emblems" when members no longer bury their dead there and take care of the graves. Such cemeteries, however, become "historical monuments" over time. Their gravestones become "artifacts and symbols that refer to the past" (ibid.). They no longer symbolize a man's death, or evoke man's hope for immortality, but only show that he and others "once lived and constituted a way of life and a society" (ibid.). The living "lose their feelings for social continuity and the social character of the graveyard and its sacred character," although they may recognize it as an object of historical significance.

The "dead" cemeteries that have lost their sacred character and have become historical symbols still retain value for the community as collective representations expressing some feelings for the past and for the dead. In the 1970s, high-school students were recruited to work in one of these historic cemeteries, weeding, polishing and restoring the gravestones, marking boundaries, and the like. This project was not, however, undertaken to express respect for their own ancestors, for most of them were not buried in that cemetery. It was rather an effort to reduce vandalism and to help the students and others learn more about the community's history. The idea had been suggested by a sculptor who had organized a similar project in neighboring Gloucester as a first step toward involving (mostly "troubled") young high-school people in neighborhood community activities.

Warner's distinction between the "sacred emblems" of the living cemeteries and the "historical symbols" in the dead cemeteries is the key to the difference between his analysis of the Memorial Day ceremonies and his analysis of the celebration of the Tercentenary of the Massachusetts Bay Colony. The former deals largely with the sacred emblems, physical and social, of the dead, the past of the species, and the future of the individual, while the latter deals with largely secular symbols of the living, in the past and in the present. The polarity of the sacred and secular symbols also plays a role in Warner's interpretation of other calendrical and life-cycle rituals and in his discussion of religious beliefs and practices, but the contrast emerges most sharply when he compares Memorial Day with the Tercentenary (ibid.:5, 103). Warner even found it necessary to introduce in his analysis of the Tercentenary a concept of "secular ritualization" to parallel the ritual of sacred legitimation. Because in Yankee City "the souls of the ancestors cannot be called up ritually from the past to live in the present as they are in totemic rites of simpler peoples . . . something else needs to be done" (Warner 1961:104). That something else, for Warner, was a series of secular rituals appealing to the authority of scientific history and to the arts and crafts of historical reconstruction to legitimize the version of the past presented in the Tercentenary. "The people of Yankee City, mostly Protestant and all skeptics in that they live in a modern, science-based civilization, must settle for less— if not the souls of the ancestors, then at least images evoking for the living the spirit that animated the generations that embodied the power and glory of yesterday" (ibid.).

There is no question that the imagery of the Tercentenary, as Warner describes it (Warner 1959:Part II) and as independently checked by our own research, was evocative of the spirit of past power and glory. The paintings and pictures of sculptured models for the floats, the living actors in tableaux with historic costumes and settings, the representations of George Washington, Lafayette, and local "greats" produced on participants and audience alike just those sentiments which Durkheim said were inspired by "the glorious souvenirs" that are "made to live again before their eyes and with which they feel they have a kinship" (Durkheim 1947:37).

Historical markers on metal plaques describing the historic significance of over one hundred objects, placed by the Tercentenary Committee at selected houses, churches, cemeteries, historic spots on roads, rivers, the harbor, and public buildings, testified to the great interest in historical factuality and authenticity, which Warner pointed out and which still prevails.[6]

The need for "secular ritualization" in the Tercentenary may not have been as great as Warner supposed, for, as he himself pointed out, "a large proportion of the people are now ethnic, including Catholic Irish, Jews, French-Canadians, Greeks, Poles and others" (Warner 1959:151). Under these conditions neither iconoclasm nor skepticism was necessarily a dominant obstacle to belief and faith in the Tercentenary's historical images and symbols.

In the case of at least two Tercentenary floats, Warner tried to make a sharp distinction between the religious and the historical symbolism. About the float for Bishop Bass, the first Anglican bishop of Massachusetts and the minister of St. Paul's Church in Yankee City in 1752, Warner wrote that:

> Bishop Bass, as a symbol, is not the sacred representation of a saint often found in the community processions of Catholic Europe and Latin America, where they are offered to the faithful for their adoration and spiritual respect, but the image of a community ancestor whose presence today speaks of the power and glory of the period of greatness when the mercantile economic class and the social old-family class became the functional leaders and models for the whole society. (Ibid.:176)

Warner gave a similar interpretation of the float for the first Catholic bishop of Massachusetts, Bishop Cheverus:

> When the bishop rode forth among the people, he must be regarded not as one immersed in the close and intimate sacred mysteries that unite God and man and celebrate His eternal timelessness, but as a *man* who wore the proud regalia of a bishop and later the red robe of a cardinal. . . .
> The bishop's first duty as sign was to give secular status and high place in the community to the Irish, primarily, but also to other and later Catholic Americans. . . . (Ibid.:177).

It may have been that this kind of strict secular and historical interpretation of the two bishops' splendid images was intended by the organizing committee of the Tercentenary Procession, which was dominated, according to Warner, by members of old Yankee families, and possibly by some of the designers of the floats who had old Yankee names. It does not seem likely, however, that the religious interpretation of these images would have been set aside by the sponsors of the floats—the Episcopal Church for Bishop Bass and the "Irish church" for Bishop Cheverus—in Yankee City. Nor does it seem likely that Episcopalians and Catholics in the audience viewing the procession would have suppressed their religious reactions to the two images. At least, I have not been able to find any evidence in the contemporary 1930s accounts of the procession for such a strict separation between secular historical and sacred religious symbols and for a dominance of the secular symbols.

The official record of the Boston Tercentenary, which took place at about the same time as the Yankee City Tercentenary, contains some interesting comparative evidence (Curley 1931). Although Mayor James Curley was the chairman of the Boston Tercentenary and many more

"ethnics" were on its organizing committee than in the Yankee City Tercentenary, the Boston Tercentenary made no concentrated effort to feature religious events and floats. Its emphasis on historic and patriotic
themes through the dedication of tablets marking historic sites; the construction of colonial villages and period houses; dramas, pageants, and a
parade of floats, paralleled the Yankee city celebrations. On the other
hand, the Boston Tercentenary placed greater emphasis on two other
themes: (l) the cultural, educational, literary, and musical resources of the
city, along with the state's commercial and industrial development, and (2)
the diverse racial, religious, and service organizations.

The Art Exhibition that was held in Boston's Horticultural Hall from
July 7 to July 31, 1930, is a good example of the first kind of theme and
illustrates the wide range of historic and contemporary work, secular and
religious images. A special exhibition of portraits by American and British
painters of the eighteenth and early nineteenth centuries was held in the
R. C. Vose Galleries and was coordinated with the showing of a hundred
portraits by early American painters in the Boston Museum of Fine Arts.
In addition, the works of living painters, sculptors, architects, stained-
glass workers, wood-carvers, jewelers and other craftspeople, book-
binders, printers, and illuminators were exhibited in Horticultural Hall.
(The range of painters was limited and rather conservative, marked by
well-known Protestant names among both the choosers and the chosen.) A
small chapel was constructed with stained glass windows, ecclesiastical
wood carvings, decorations, and sculptures. Crosses of silver and gold
inlaid with jewels were displayed in the jewelry exhibit.

The Boston Tercentenary Racial Groups Committee organized a week
of events of "various European Racial Backgrounds." These included an
"Ancient Greek Tragedy: Oedipus Rex," a night program of Syrian music
and pageantry, and programs honoring Italian, Polish, German, Scandinavian, Armenian, Celtic, Lithuanian, Ukrainian, Negro, and Hebrew
descendants (Curley 1931:315–17).

Illustrations in the Tercentenary volume show some of these nightly
programs, as well as a delegation of Japanese businessmen, a group of
French aviators in the reviewing stand, Madame Ernestine Schumman-
Heink as a guest soloist, children of St. Mary's Polish School from South
Boston, the Order of Sons of Italy, a Negro Elks Lodge, Boston's Chi-
nese, and the Knights of Columbus in parade (ibid.:XI–XII).

The Honorable John F. Fitzgerald, LL.D., chairman of Boston's Tercentenary General Committee, probably struck the keynote of the celebrations when he said that: "The committees in charge of arrangement of
the full celebration and the whole citizenry cooperating with them
justified their claim to be true heirs, if not always (or indeed often) the
lineal descendants, of the early Bostonians by manifesting in the celebra-

tion itself the traditional qualities which have given Boston its peculiar standing" (ibid.:5). "Our people," he said, "are still middle class, upper or lower, as the case may be, but all essentially democratic in outlook." He agreed with James Russell Lowell that "we are all folks in New England" (ibid.:4).

The description of the Boston Tercentenary ball seemed to justify the Honorable Mr. Fitzgerald's characterization: "From all walks of life they assembled, colorful, picturesque, sheerly splendid and glittering; all eager to share in their last ceremony of celebration, and to be able to recall as long as memory shall last this 300th anniversary" (ibid.:270).

Before the dancing began, a "queen of the evening" was chosen from a parade of one hundred of Boston's most charming, beautiful, and youthful girls. Miss Gladys Norkunas was the winner. The first prize for "those of the racial group who participated in the march of one hundred odd costumed dancers" was won by Miss Arax Dinjian of Somerville wearing an Armenian costume (ibid.:271).

The glitter and euphoria of the Grand March itself evokes the 1976 Bicentennial celebrations, especially the parade of the Tall Ships in Boston Harbor and Arthur Fiedler's spectacular and well-attended Bicentennial Boston Pops Concert on the Charles River, as well as Yankee City's own 125th birthday party: "Figures in the civic and business life of the city, others active in social affairs, many dressed in powdered wigs and carrying with easy air staffs or swords . . . consuls of foreign countries, wearing their medals of honor and other insignia, all mingled and moved in and out of the milling crowd. Representatives of twenty-two nations shared in the march" (ibid.:270).

While members of the old Yankee families did not dominate the organization of Boston's Tercentenary, they were not entirely unrepresented: "On behalf of her work for the racial groups during earlier Tercentenary celebrations, Gustave A. Sandberg, chairman of the racial group, presented Mrs. William Lowell Putnam with a gold plaque topped by an eagle" (ibid.:272).

Clearly Boston's celebration of the Massachusetts Bay Tercentenary was an easy-going medley of ecclesiastical and secular symbolism, of native and ethnic cultural traditions. Yankee City's celebration of the Tercentenary might have been more self-consciously focused on a Yankee and Puritan past, as Warner suggests. Yet there is meager evidence for a strict separation between sacred and secular symbols in either celebration.

Warner's contention that the Yankee City Tercentenary procession was a secular ritual, in which patently religious symbols and figures were given a purely historical and secular interpretation, was maintained even for those floats that referred to Puritan fathers, among them Governor John Winthrop: "The symbols, officially and in fact, were referential;

their signs were marks that pointed to events of the Puritan past. But nowhere in the entire pageant was there any sacred sign which demanded an act of faith about a sacred world past. . . . The whole celebration was cast in rationalistic terms; all super-naturalism was suppressed" (Warner 1959:213).

Although the Puritans "in their own self-conceptions were a holy people directed by God in his Word, the Bible," Warner found that "the Bible, whose words carry different meanings for each of the churches, had no part in the general collectivity's pageant rites" (ibid.:215).

This passage is followed by a cryptic sentence, which may well hide significant exceptions to Warner's negative generalization: "Only in the sermons of the churches and a brief collective ceremony at a hill beyond the dwellings of the town after the celebration was over were the Bible and the sacred world allowed to enter the symbolism of the Tercentenary" (ibid.)

Judging from our observations in the 1970s, when some of the churches held ecumenical services before, during, and after historical reenactments such as the Battle of Bunker Hill, or the coming forth of volunteers in the Old South Church aisles in response to the historic minister's call to arms, it seems plausible to assume that the Bible and the sacred world were allowed to enter the Tercentenary's symbolism. It may have been true, as Warner explained, that the need for unity in a religiously diverse community "drove the markers and meanings of sacred life into the confined contexts of each church, and for some to the brief, unimportant ceremony on the hill" (ibid.). But the marks and meanings of these boundaries between religious and secular rites and symbols were probably not as sharply defined as Warner suggested.

Some indirect evidence resides in Warner's account for the proposition that the Catholic and other non-Protestant ethnic participants in the Tercentenary had no difficulty responding to religious and secular symbolism combined. This evidence comes from Warner's dichotomy between the visual symbolism of Catholic rituals and the verbal symbolism of Protestant rituals (ibid.: 306–308, 332–36). The visual symbols, said Warner, involve all the senses and the whole body; they consist of form, shape, color, texture, movement, and rhythm. Because they readily excite the emotions and the imagination, they are "non-logical" and tap deep organic and psychological needs. The verbal symbols of Protestant rites, chiefly the words of sermons, prayers, and hymns, Warner believed, reduced to "an arbitrary mechanical alphabet" the sacred and spiritual symbols of mental life. The poverty of symbolic expression, which is akin to "the cold, alien rationality of science," drives the "lower orders" to look for "compensatory substitutes" in "ecstatic emotional outbursts" for "the satisfactions they once felt in church rituals" (ibid.: 335–36).

The context of Warner's distinction between visual and verbal symbols is a discussion of sacred religious symbols and rites such as the Mass for Catholics and sermons, prayers, and hymns for Protestants. His analysis, however, of the response to visual symbolism should hold as well for the response to the pageantry, costumes, shapes, colors, and textures of the Tercentenary, even where symbols and figures of religious significance are excluded. And on the Protestant side, Warner himself points out that the laic liturgy has been changing in the direction of a greater recognition of the symbols of family, women, and organic needs and functions (ibid.: 391–95; 1961: 75). He interprets Mothers' Day, for example, as "a Return of the Woman and Her Family to the Protestant Pantheon" (Warner 1959:343).

Warner interpreted the trends of change in Protestant liturgy, which he or some members of his staff probably observed on a revisit to Yankee City in the 1950s, as a reversal of the alleged impoverishment of religious rites and symbolism by the Protestant revolt and Puritanism. In this respect, at least, the liturgical revival is also a return to the seventeenth century, which Mario Praz calls an age of emblems (an externalization of the image by plastic interpretation), an age of opera (when things were said and represented at the same time, according to Diderot), and an age of allegorical tableaux, when words were "made intelligible by being dia-grammatically related to one another—an age when a verbal culture was being transmuted into a visual culture" (Praz 1964:15). Praz cites an article by W. J. Ong, "From Allegory to the Diagram in the Renaissance Mind," published in 1959, as a source for his formulation.

WHERE HAVE ALL THE "YANKEES" AND THE "ETHNICS" GONE?

Warner's interpretation of the identities asserted by the display of flags and other emblems on Yankee City graves or by the wearing of colonial uniforms and insignia in the Tercentenary procession is at one level quite transparent, especially if the interpretation is based not only on the de-scription of isolated emblems but also on interviews with the participants in the ceremonies and an analysis of their social and cultural contexts. Given this kind of social and cultural context, as usually described in Warner's analysis, such distinctions as he makes between "physical em-blems" and "social emblems," or between "sacred emblems" and "secular symbols," become rather subtle but can be checked by other kinds of data. These distinctions depend on a constellation of factors—the graphic de-sign of the emblem, its context of use, the users' intentions, the observers' perceptions, local customs and social structure, etc. These are the kinds of considerations of which Warner took account when he wrote that ethnic graves displayed more American flags than "native" graves because the ethnic families wished to symbolize that their deceased relative was a citizen or intended to become one, while the custom among "native" families was to place flags only on the graves of soldiers.

In addition to such considerations that underlie Warner's and other anthropologists' interpretations of emblems, I believe there are usually some assumptions about the kind of social and cultural universe symbolized by a set of emblems, and about the different kinds of people whose identities are emblematized. For example, we recall that in our initial impression of Yankee City we tended to assume that it was a kind of Shakespearean world, in which individuals, families, social classes, and ethnic, religious, and social groups were clearly identified by distinctive emblems and names. These impressions were in part the afterglow, as Marquand observed, of that older social order that was still extant in Yankee City in the 1930s when Warner and his staff came to study it. That the old social order had begun to change beyond recognition by the early 1960s was not immediately reflected in the symbolism of emblems and names. In fact, it is astonishing to find so much of Yankee City's old order emblematized and identified in Warner's 1959 monograph, *The Living and the Dead:* the six social classes; the opposition between "Yankees" and "Ethnics"; the Federalist houses and gardens and associated streets and neighborhoods as status symbols; the superior prestige of "old families" who can trace their genealogies at least to the Federalist period of power and glory; the emphasis on the Protestant and Puritan revolt as a source of the city's long-established cultural and religious traditions.

That monograph opens with the story of "Biggy" Muldoon (actually "Bossy" Gillis), the colorful Irish mayor of the 1930s, whose dramatic assault on a Federalist house and garden and the Yankee establishment that it symbolized marked for many the opening blow against the old social order. Other evidences of change are also listed by Warner in his descriptions of how the "mobile elite" acquired houses with long-established "lineages," and of "a liturgical renaissance" among the Protestant churches, to cite two instances.

But such evidences of change, or those fictionalized in Marquand's novels, did not swamp Warner, because he believed he had found in the Memorial Day ceremonies, in the Tercentenary Procession, and in other sacred and secular rites evidences for the survival of the great tradition— its sacred dead, famous heroes, historic battles, sailing ships, grand houses, the faraway places and peoples with whom they traded. The symbolic representations of these events, objects, people, and places in the form of emblems, names, and other symbols were encapsulated in the cultural performances Warner observed and analyzed. The parallels he drew with the totemic rites and myths of Australian aborigines were not so much intended to demonstrate the primitiveness of a New England urban community; rather, the purpose of these parallels, for Warner as for Durkheim, was to suggest a method for discovering the values, cosmology, and history of an entire society and a culture.

During our revisits to Yankee City in the 1970s we found many of the same emblems, symbols, and themes Warner described for the 1930s. In the annual nine-day Yankee Homecoming events, in the Bicentennial celebrations of 1976, in the restoration of historic houses on High Street and on some of the side-streets, in church services and sermons, one could recognize visual and verbal, secular and sacred symbols from the Yankee City of the 1930s—eagles, flags, fifes and drums; colonial dress and uniforms, historic reenactments; prayers, hymns, sermons. There are some differences, to be sure, in the symbolism of the 1970s: for example, the restoration of the historic façades of Market Square's nineteenth-century commercial buildings had recently been completed, although the proposal for this project had been made as early as the late 1950s by William Perry, the local architect and restorer of Williamsburg, according to Marquand (1960:121–22).

Whatever other differences we may be able to adduce in the way of individual restorations or celebrations, the similarities are sufficiently numerous and striking to evoke the initial impression of a city that is still recognizably the same as the one Warner described. Can we conclude from our shock of recognition that Yankee City's constellation of emblems and symbols denotes or connotes the same identities—ethnic, racial, religious, social, national, and local—that Warner found in the 1930s? Such a conclusion seems doubtful, and I shall try to give some of the reasons for my doubts.

If our first impression of Yankee City was of a kind of Shakespearean world in which "Yankees" and "Ethnics" wore their emblems of identity on their houses, shops, and churches—if not on their clothes and tabards—it soon gave way to a second impression, haunted by the question, Where have all the "Yankees" and the "Ethnics" gone? In the Federalist and other old houses on High Street only one of the old Yankee families was still living in the ancestral house, and only about twenty Yankee families were living there at all. Death, moving away, and lack of children and grandchildren have decimated their numbers. They have been displaced by Irish, Greek, French-Canadian, Jewish, and Indian householders, doctors and prosperous young professionals. We even heard a candidate's failure to win an election being attributed to his having a High Street address.[7]

A similar shift in the relative composition of Yankees and Ethnics was also found in the organizing committees for Yankee Homecoming and Bicentennial activities, and in restoration, educational, and public-service groups. These organizations are no longer dominated by Yankees as they were in the 1930s, according to Warner, but rather by Ethnics or "former Ethnics." A sprinkling of ethnic surnames appeared even among the officers and membership lists of such citadels of Yankee tradition and family as the Historical Society and the Sons and Daughters of the First Settlers.

It was often pointed out to me during our visits that the city was run by an informal establishment that consisted of the then mayor, a newspaper editor, a banker, an insurance company director, and a lawyer. Only one of these five members of the establishment came from a local old Yankee family; the others came from second- or third-generation Ethnic families.

As significant as the changing relative statuses of Yankees and Ethnics are, the changes in the verbal categories and designations are perhaps more significant. Terms like "Yankees" and "Ethnics" are no longer popular or current. The city clerk reported that most people so vigorously resist answering questions about ethnicity, religion, race, income, and social class that he has had to drop these questions from the political registration cards. He was angered, along with other clerks, by a recent tendency for some parents to select surnames of choice for their children and for themselves. Although the State Supreme Judicial Court has ruled that this is a question of personal choice in matters of family life protected by the due-process clause, the clerk believed it would create "a colossal mess" in various types of records involving names. This new practice also tends to shake the heavy reliance people place on surnames as a source of information about ethnicity, religion, and race. Although such inferences from surnames are often guesswork, surnames are becoming the last surviving symbolism of the old social order.[8]

In these times even the popular designations of the churches are changing. The "Irish church" and the "French church" are beginning to lose their former interpretations. While a priest in charge of the "Irish church" acknowledged that about 90 percent of 6000 church members are Irish, he said he didn't like the name "the Irish church." "We like to say it is American or Catholic. The oldtimers still call it the Irish Church but we're all Americans here. . . . We're all Catholic, we're all Christians here" (interview, 1977, by D.G.).

The priest at the "French church" estimated that about half of his congregation of 350 families was French, and the other half was "no longer really French" but a mixture of French and either Irish, Yankee, or Polish. In the past four years, the priest said, with regret, he had conducted only two marriages in which both people were French. Now with the school gone, "There is no means to transmit the language. Everyone is typically American" (ibid.).

It is tempting to characterize the changing relative positions of Yankees and Ethnics, and the associated demographic and symbolic changes, as a transformation from a Yankee-dominated identity to an Ethnic-dominated identity with a persistence of the old emblems. Such a characterization, however, would run counter to several important groups of facts. First, many people feel unsure about their identities and are constantly looking for them through genealogical, historical, and archeological research. Their desire to validate their authenticity seems as obsessive as Warner says it was in the 1930s (Singer 1977). This is true of as many Yankees as it is of Ethnics. At the same time, the very categories of Yankee and Ethnic are becoming blurred in definition and use, while the old ethnic epithets are being strenuously avoided in public. A member of an authentic Yankee family, for example, said he would not consider his Polish immigrant farmer neighbor a "Yankee," but the locally born son of the farmer would qualify as one. On the other hand, a third-generation young man of Hungarian descent said that, while he would not call himself a Yankee, his young daughter was of that order because his wife was a Yankee. His wife disagreed, insisting that the daughter would be considered "Hungarian-American." She added that her own pedigree included some Irish and Scotch as well as Yankee.

There is a definite trend to broaden the definition of Yankee to anyone born in New England and to avoid such terms as "ethnic," "native," "foreigner," and the like. One local Yankee who was descended from English ancestors and was himself something of a historian, maintained that "Yankees" was what the French called the English and derived from *L'Anglais d'eau douce*. A second-generation ethnic ironically maintained that the only "natives" in the place were American Indians.

Amid the cross-currents of changing usage and shifting definitions, an appeal to statistics might be indicated. That the United States Census for 1970 reports that 76 percent of the population of Yankee City is "native of native parentage" is a justification for calling it a "Yankee City." And this figure might be compared to Warner's figures of 55 percent Yankee and 45 percent Ethnic. Such figures and comparisons have serious limitations, however. I interviewed a number of "natives of native parentage" who did not consider themselves Yankees and were not so called because they were of Ethnic descent. Warner's "Ethnics," on the other hand, included only 36 percent foreign born and 64 percent native born (42 percent in Yankee City, 20 percent in the rest of New England, and 2 percent in the rest of the United States). Of the "natives," 280, or about 8½ percent, were foreign born, mainly of English, North Irish, and Scottish descent (Warner 1963:2–4; 1941:220–21).

TWO SYSTEMS OF DIFFERENCES?

A trend that seems significant involves the usage of "native" and "outsider." While these are long-standing designations, I found that they are being used to mark a new kind of phenomenon. One family, for example, of seventeenth-century English descent, with one parent related to "old" and respected Boston Brahmins, well-known New England names, who had lived in Yankee City over forty years and had children born there, were still regarded as outsiders. In another family, on the other hand, considered to be natives, the father's parents had immigrated to Yankee City from Greece; they thus were by Warner's definition "Ethnics" and would have remained so for five or six generations. These contrasting usages, which were widespread, are significant not only because they indicate a speeding-up and, possibly, a reversal of Warner's predicted "time-table for assimilation" (Warner 1963:chap. 14; Warner and Srole 1945:chap. 10). They are perhaps even more significant in indicating the replacement or displacement of the older "Yankee-Ethnic" opposition. To paraphrase Lévi-Strauss, one system of differences, based on race, religion, ethnicity, and social class, is being transformed into another system of differences, based on local birth, duration of local residence, community acceptance, and lifestyle (cf. Schneider 1969, 1979).

Lifestyle is not defined in terms of Warner's social classes or of mobility within the system, but rather in terms of such polarities as "workingmen" and "intellectuals," "straights" and "Third World oriented." One leading banker in the city told me there were only two classes in the city, not six, and that he himself was a workingman. The city clerk described the intellectuals as coming from Harvard or Marblehead in their red MGs and trying to tell the natives how to run the city.

Some of the characterizations have been crystallized in recent years by disputes over urban renewal and restoration. The group pushing for conventional urban renewal, it turned out, were natives and workingmen, while those supporting restoration and preservation were outsiders and intellectuals.

Another group of outsiders are the arts and crafts people. These do not affiliate themselves with either the intellectuals or the workingmen, because they see their own lifestyle as distinctive. Without professional positions, incomes, permanent residences, or acceptance in the community, they regard themselves as an enclave of expatriates from the 1960s. Commenting on a midnight inspection tour by city officials of the loftlike craft studios in an old warehouse building where some of the craftsmen and their families also illegally resided, one of the craftspeople explained the "raid" as "a clash of lifestyles: crafting and artistry is opting for a lifestyle rather than an income level, and that right there separates people who are into a different reason for having jobs. . . . There's a communication gap right there, a little suspicion" (interview, 1977, by D.G.). (The official reason for the night inspection was fire prevention and ordinance enforcement.)

The suspicion, incidentally, is mutual, since most of the craftspeople and artists consider the other residents as "straight" and "non–Third

World oriented." With help from some of the older artists and craftsmen in the city and a Federal CETA grant, an effort was being made to close the communication gap and to integrate the craftspeople into the community.

Exhibitions of individual work have been held at a Craft Resources Center at the Public Library and at craft fairs in the YWCA Civic Center and in open sidewalk sales. The work is also on regular display in several special shops and galleries. Over 50 percent of the artists and craftspeople and the shop and gallery owners and managers are women.

The subjects of the arts and craft work are unusual in one respect: they tend to avoid the racial, religious, and ethnic typing and the historical portraits—so prominent in the Boston Art Exhibition of 1930. While nonrepresentational art is significantly represented, depictions of local scenes and historical and contemporary restorations are widely available in post cards, posters, signs, drawings, and paintings. One ceramic artist has constructed a series of porcelain "puzzle pictures" of city buildings and shops and has called them "A Touch of Gold," referring to the gilt edge outlining some of the pictures and probably a satirical comparison with Rockport and Gloucester. Her pictures have received national attention and have been called "very beautiful."

The passing of the old social order, in which the opposition between Yankees and Ethnics was the most salient symbolism, has been publicly recognized and discussed. In 1976, several features and editorials in the city's leading newspaper attributed the progress and influence of the ethnic groups to their abandonment of the crude confrontation tactics of a "Bossy" Gillis and to the "maturation" of the second and third generations. The grammar schools and high schools and their teachers, the baseball field, and the corner grocery store were singled out as important stimulators to the "maturational" process, through which the Ethnics became natives.

This picture was confirmed in my interviews with members of three-generation families, with allowances for individual, family, and other group variations. The older members of these families can still remember when Polish and Yiddish were spoken by many children starting out in the grammar school. They recall when an uncle volunteered to teach the immigrant boys to play baseball and remember the mixture of children that used to come into the corner grocery before the move was made from the old ethnic neighborhood to High Street. In reflection, the process of maturation was telescoped and smoothed out. From the seventy- or eighty-year careers of the three-generation families, many incidents of struggle, frustration, poverty, and discrimination were also remembered. (Compare T. H. White's similar recollections of his childhood in Boston [White 1978].) The overall picture described, however, was one of successful acculturation, moderate prosperity, and community acceptance.

The more articulate and thoughtful interviewees, including members of the establishment, also explained the smoothness of the maturational process by such factors as the traditional tolerance of a seaport city engaged in world trade, the relatively small numbers of most of the ethnic groups represented, and the more liberal and democratic attitudes that soldiers brought back from the Second World War and the Korean War.

Not everyone was carried away by the nostalgic euphoria of the Bicentennial. A local historian remembered the time American Nazis waited across the river in Salisbury to march into Yankee City when their leader was arrested. Another realist described a series of incidents in which the swastika and anti-Semitic and anti-black slogans were painted in front of someone's house. And one of the police officers recalled a burglary of a grocery store in which the Jewish store-owner was shot. Even for the realists, however, these incidents represented rare and ugly blemishes made by "madmen" in a distant past. During the Bicentennial, at least, the city's self-image was euphoric and serene. This mood was expressed in a page of photographs in the newspaper showing views from above restored buildings in Market Square, the Unitarian steeple, and the Merrimac River, under the description: "A city of renaissance through restoration, has maintained its charm of early American Yankee heritage. High above the city, from a seven-story vantage point, one can gaze upon the mighty Merrimac, the stately towering steeples, and the majestic brick Federalist buildings of the proud old Clipper ship town."

The maturation and acceptance of the different ethnic groups has not yet resulted in the complete disappearance of their ethnic identity. Many of these families have become quite acculturated, especially in the third generation, but they do not always feel completely assimilated. In our visits to their homes, we noted an interesting symbolic expression of this sense of persisting ethnic identity: emblems of their ethnic identity were usually displayed in a kind of counterpoint with emblems of their American identity. This dual symbolism seems reminiscent of that which Warner noticed in the 1930s cemeteries, but the domestic symbolism of the 1970s has a different meaning and function.

One family of Italian descent, at least three generations in Yankee City, displayed on the living-room walls two sets of portraits—one set of Bronzino-like drawings of a man and a woman, the other a set of painted portraits, probably early nineteenth century, of a man and a woman. Both the drawings and the paintings were bought in an antique shop.

A third-generation young man of Hungarian descent proudly displayed a crewel work made by his grandmother, with Hungarian lettering:

> Where there is faith, there is love;
> Where there is love, there is peace;

Where there is peace, there is blessing;
Where there is blessing, there is God;
Where there is God, there is no want.

An English Renaissance portrait symbolizing his wife's ancestry also hung on the wall.

In another home, a small segment of a genealogical chart tracing the wife's Yankee ancestry to 1620 was on the wall, while two Indian sculptures of Krishna and Buddha figures stood in the garden to symbolize her Indian husband's background.

A black couple showed us pictures of the husband's Mashpee Indian relatives in native American dress, together with pictures of a French forebear who married into the family in 1865 and gave the present patronym. They also displayed a Bicentennial certificate with the French surname printed on it and a coat of arms with the surname.

The grandfather of a prominent local family who emigrated from Greece had on his walls, beside family pictures of his Greek relatives and of his American son and grandchildren, a painting of the Church of Saint Sophia, a Greek Orthodox church calendar, and ceramic plates showing the Parthenon, ancient Greek soldiers, Dionysos' sailing boat, and dolphins.

Another member of a Greek-American family, in addition to many family pictures and Greek ceramics, had on her writing desk a picture of her parents next to a handsome nineteenth-century volume of Byron's poetry. A large needlepoint picture showing a Greek shepherd and shepherdess with a flock of sheep hung on one of her walls.

An Armenian grandfather displayed with his family pictures of children, grandchildren, and old-country relatives a striking picture, which he himself had painstakingly constructed from small pieces of wood inlay, of a well-known Armenian church.

In some of these homes—especially the Greek, Armenian, and French-Canadian—the number of family pictures is quite striking. The size of the families shows an obvious decrease from the first generation, which numbers from fifteen to twenty members, to the third generation, with four to five members. There is an increased stress on individual portraits of the grandchildren.

The dual or triple symbolism of the domestic emblems does not imply a conflict between an ethnic and an American identity. In our interviews we rarely found expressions of such a conflict, even among the most self-consciously ethnic families. The emblematic decorations seemed rather to be expressions of a desire to remind themselves of another identity, one that was almost forgotten or one that was being revived or newly acquired. The reminders usually came in the form of an artistic construction—a Chagall-like drawing or print of a reading rabbi with a pigeon overhead, a painting of a Scandinavian fisherman, the "house-lineage" and early picture of a famous Federalist mansion on High Street.

In the houses of some of the old Yankee families the dual symbolism is less obvious, although documents, portraits, and antiques showing English ancestry are in evidence. In one home, the framed documents on the walls included a 1773 sampler recording the birth in 1759 of a family member and a bill showing the business dealing of another family member with the eighteenth-century merchant Timothy Dexter. This is not quite equivalent to churinga stones, but for that family and many others in Yankee City, these are "glorious souvenirs," some of which they are also giving or loaning to the new Maritime Museum in an old Greek-revival customs building, with its "Marquand Room."

AN EMBLEM OF ULTIMATE IDENTIFICATION
AND COMPLETE BELONGINGNESS

In his monograph *The Living and the Dead*, Warner says of the Tercentenary procession: "The themes of the great ethnic migrations and their assimilation—the melting pot, the Promised Land, and the goddess of Liberty welcoming them—democracy for all and every kind of race and creed—such themes were nowhere present. Indeed those who conceived and presented the pageant saw themselves as teachers initiating the new peoples into the true significance of the nation" (Warner 1959:198). This statement may come as a surprise to those who recall Warner's emphasis on the aggregational and integrative functions of the Memorial Day and Tercentenary ceremonies, in which the diverse ethnic, religious, racial groups of the city were represented. The statement also seems inconsistent with the trends of change noted for the 1970s, especially the displacement of the Yankee-Ethnic opposition into a native-newcomer opposition, and the maturation of Ethnics into natives and even Yankees. The apparent conflicts can be resolved if we take account of some of Warner's assumptions and definitions. He assumed, in the first place, that Yankee City had a stable social order in the 1930s and a long-standing cultural tradition dominated by Yankees. Given such an assumption, it was quite plausible to assume, further, that integrative ceremonies such as Memorial Day and the Tercentenary would not change the social order or alter the dominant cultural traditions. To the extent that some changes deviated from the stable social order and cultural traditions—and Warner described at least one such change in "Biggy" Muldoon's attack on High Street and the Yankee establishment—the eventual result, Warner predicted, would be not a melting-pot fusion of the different ethnic groups but a gradual transmutation of ethnic elements into a system "almost homogeneous" with the American social system (Warner and Srole 1945:155).

The transmutation of ethnic groups resulted in a system not quite homogeneous with the American social system for three reasons, as I read Warner and Srole: (1) some ethnic groups became acculturated, lost their distinctive ethnic traits, and no longer participated in the ethnic life of their ancestors, yet were not completely accepted and assimilated; (2) those groups climbed the social ladder, beginning at the bottom, but never entered into the "upper upper" class; and (3) some retained their ethnic ways as a result of the influence of their parents and partly because they were not accepted (ibid.:32).

From these processes of adjustment and transmutation, Warner extrapolated "a time-table for assimilation" for the different ethnic groups, based on their affinity to the Yankees in race, religion, and nationality. Those groups similar to the white, Anglo-Saxon Protestants will assimilate in a generation or less, and those that are different will take as many as six or more generations, or will perhaps never assimilate (Warner 1963:chap. 14).

The ethnic group's structural place in the community and its social status and rank were not the only criteria, however, that determined the choice of a float to sponsor in the Tercentenary procession. There was also a problem in the "symbolic congruence" of the float's meanings to the sponsor and to others, and the "historical significance" of the symbol and the group (Warner 1959:198). Warner cites the Knights of Columbus's choice of the Columbus float as "multidetermined by several identifications": the identity of name, group, and hero. In spite of the fact that "there was no direct connection of the local association with the person for which the symbol stood," Columbus's standing as the "first" European to land in America and the prestige of the Knights of Columbus made the choice of float appropriate in terms of structural place, symbolic congruence, and historical significance.

A more problematic choice was made by two Jewish representatives on the procession's Central Committee. They first agreed to have the Jewish community sponsor a float for Benedict Arnold, who was a local hero, despite his later reputation as a traitor. This selection was considered inappropriate by the members of the Jewish community and was changed to sponsorship of Captain John Smith's float. Warner agreed that the Benedict Arnold float was an inappropriate choice for the Jewish community to sponsor. "The Jews could not really afford to sponsor such a symbol; their own self-regard and the respect and esteem they needed from others would not permit it" (ibid.:203). "Had one of the old Yankee organizations or one from the old-family upper class sponsored the float, the meaning of the *expedition* would have become paramount in the symbols and the meaning of Arnold, while prominent, would have been absorbed in the larger context" (ibid.).

That the float for "The First Class of Harvard" should have been sponsored by the local Harvard Club, or the floats for old-time shoemaking and early silversmiths by the modern representatives of those industries, Warner considered obvious and appropriate identifications. But it was in the sponsorship of the float for the landing of the first settlers by an historical association called "The Sons and Daughters of the First Settlers" that Warner found the greatest congruence between emblem and identity: "In terms of the ultimate identifications and belongingness, the Sons and Daughters of the First Settlers of old Yankee City who sponsored their own ancestors, the first founders, had a collective symbol to represent them to the whole collectivity which satisfied all the criteria. It said—and they and the community said—that they completely belonged, and they were so identified" (ibid.:199–200).

In the summer of 1976, a director of the Sons and Daughters of the First Settlers invited us to their forty-ninth annual gathering. We hesitated about going, especially after one of our local friends, a native, told us that since she was not a descendant of the early settlers, she would go only to the morning meeting and not to the lunch: she didn't want to interfere with the "mysteries." We finally gathered up enough courage to go to the afternoon program, an unveiling of a new bronze model of the *Mary and John*, the ship that brought the early settlers to America. The original model, which was dedicated in 1905, had "added an authentic fillip to the sturdy Ancestor Monument on the lower green" of Old Town. "Then in 1974, something happened. It was autumn, in time of low-land fogs along the coast. Natives of . . . went indoors early and closed up their houses against the thick night mist. It was in the morning that they discovered that the bronze replica of the ship Mary and John had been stolen during the night" ("Program," 1976).

The particular director of the society who had invited us to the meeting had recently organized a successful campaign to restore the ship's model and to secure it permanently to the granite monument. "The spirit of the ancestors lives on. Members and friends of the Sons and Daughters of the First Settlers . . . obliged in an honorable and generous manner: Noblesse Oblige" (ibid.).

The rededication program on the lower green was pleasant and marked by a spirit of friendliness and good feeling. Some of it, especially the group singing, evoked the assembly-hall gatherings in grammar school. It began with a medley of American folk music played on a small electric piano and included "When I First Came to This Land," "This Land is Your Land," and "Yankee Doodle." Then, after greetings from the president, introduction of platform guests, and a prayer of dedication, the bronze model of the *Mary and John* was unveiled by the sculptor and the oldest member of the society, a local amateur historian, traveler, and former banker in his nineties, who later made a short speech that began with Shakespeare's "There is a tide in the affairs of men." The model had been wrapped in a French tricolor for reasons not altogether clear. Someone explained that the president of the society had been to France during the summer and brought the flag back with him. (He also had a French name and was a teacher of French in the local high school.)

After the unveiling, there was group singing of the first two verses of "America the Beautiful," the presentation of the *Mary and John* to the town, and acknowledgment and acceptance. The ceremonies closed with group singing of the first three verses of "America," a benediction, and, as "Music to Leave by: Woody Guthrie's 'So Long, It's been Good to Know You.'"

As the gathering was beginning to break up, I spoke with several people. One man told me that he was not a member of the Sons and Daughters but that his wife had recently applied. He said that the society's requirements for genealogical proof of descent from early settlers were very rigorous and difficult to meet, since the early court records had been burned. There were some old apothecary records, but he doubted that these were sufficient to identify a descendant. He then began to ask me some questions. Did I have any ancestors in the area? When I told him no, that I was a visitor from the Midwest, he said, "Yes, but to which *local* family are you related? Everyone has to come to the United States by way of New England," he insisted. After I told him that my parents went directly to the Midwest through New York, he recalled that his wife's maternal relatives had also gone directly from New York to the West.

The printed program for the Sons and Daughters of the Early Settlers included two lists of members, one list of 43 "members" with the names of ancestors or of immediate relatives attached, and another list of 118 "members" without any ancestral names attached. A list of 59 "non-members," chiefly from the immediate area, was also included. The then president of the United States, Gerald Ford, was listed as an "honorary member," since the society's research had found him to be among the descendants of early settlers of the town and he had agreed to the listing.

The bronze model of the *Mary and John* is certainly an emblem of identity, a "collective representation" as well as a "condensation symbol." This is apparent not from the model alone but from the metal plaques on the granite pedestal. The inscription on the front pedestal reads: "To the Men and Women Who Settled . . . from 1635 to 1650 and Founded Its Municipal, Social and Religious Life this Monument is Dedicated 1905." The plaque on the back of the pedestal is inscribed with a list of the first settlers' names. If, as Warner said of the Tercentenary, the images and ceremonies will not call up the souls of the ancestors, "they will at least evoke for the living the spirit that animated the generations that embodied the power and glory of yesterday" (Warner 1961:104).

The restoration and dedication of "higher-rank emblems" such as the *Mary and John* model, I would suggest, do a bit more: they extend the collective identity they evoke beyond the lineal descendants of the early settlers to all those who through marriage, adoption of house lineages, residence, dramatic reeanctment, anthropological, archeological, and historical research, or other ways seek to identify with the great tradition symbolized by the emblems. And the identity may continue indefinitely into the future if it is maintained by the descendants of the present generation and adopted by future generations.

Whether in other forms, such as a model of the *Dreadnought* (Warner 1959:208), a colonial flag, or a sculptured eagle, emblems like the *Mary and John* model are signs with iconic, indexical, and symbolic features. Iconically they are replicas, or replicas of replicas, of historical objects; indexically they denote or connote such objects through proper names and other indices. Symbolically they address interpretants (and interpreters) in the form of a future self, descendants, and other persons addressed. The reference to the future is an essential component of the symbol, both because a self, a descendant, or other persons who interpret the emblem will continue or will come into being in the future, and because the interpretations themselves are tentative and fallible, subject to correction by future research, genealogical, historical, and anthropological. The authentic identity that the residents of Yankee City, and perhaps all Americans, are looking for will not be found in the past. It can only emerge in the dialogue of interpretations about the emblems constructed in the past and in the present, and about those that will be constructed in the future. Many of the emblems will be the same, although many will change. Warner's concluding interpretation of the Tercentenary applies as well to the end of the 1970s, if not to the Bicentennial years, and will probably continue to apply through the 1980s: "Time in the aftermath of glory has run down; it is a period of diminution, of loss of meaning, when life is less vital, men less significant, and heroes harder to find. Symbolically, Yankee City has changed her image of herself. She has become another symbolic collectivity, with new collective representations to tell her what she is and express what she is to others" (Warner 1959:208).

CONCLUSION

The development of a semiotics of emblems discussed in the preceding pages occurs in two distinct contexts—totemism among North American

Indians and Australian aborigines, and the memorial rites and celebrations of a modern New England urban community. Durkheim's *Elementary Forms of the Religious Life* (1912) was taken as a pioneer source for the first development and Warner's *The Living and the Dead* (1959) as a pioneer source for the second. That both developments involved a considerable interplay of ethnographic observation and speculative theory is obvious from the discussion. It may be useful to summarize more explicitly in this postscript some of the more problematic aspects of a semiotic theory of emblems in relation to the contexts in which it developed.

Durkheim's application of the analogy of totems with national flags and heraldic designs, brilliant and fruitful as it was, never transcended its context. That context included not only the ethnographic reports on North American and Australian totemism but also an acquaintance with flags and heraldry he shared with his contemporaries.

There is no doubt that to have regarded a totem as a flag of the clan, carved and engraved in graphic designs upon everyday objects, and having a sacred character related to the tribal religion and its cosmological and social systems of classification, brought an exotic realm of unfamiliar practices and beliefs into the realm of the familiar and comprehensible.

Durkheim also drew on the social-psychological theories of his time to speculate on why a soldier dies for his country's flag rather than for his country and on how assemblies of men need concrete, visual emblems to express and sustain their sentiments of social unity after the "effervescence" of their assemblies fades. He applied these theories to Australian totemism to argue that totemic emblems become the only permanent element of social life, since there are no other sources of unity in a clan.

The totemic emblems continues to bring to mind the experienced sentiments and evokes them

> even after the assembly has dissolved, for it survives the assembly, being carved upon the instruments of the cult, upon the sides of the rocks, upon bucklers, etc. . . . Since [the sentiments] are common to the group, they can be associated only with something that is frequently common to all. Now the totemic emblem is the only thing satisfying this condition. By definition it is common to all. . . . While generations change, it remains the same; it is the permanent element of social life. (Durkheim 1947 [1915]:221)

Having established the totemic emblem as the symbol of the clan and the source of its unifying sentiments, Durkheim invoked a principle of contagion to extend the sacredness of the emblem to the "concrete beings whose name the clan bears," since their material form resembles that of the emblem, then to the man, who resembles the totem less than do the totemic animals, and finally to the substances expressed by the primitive cosmological systems. "At last the whole world is divided among the totemic principles of each tribe" (ibid.: 223).

In spite of attributing so decisive a role to the totemic emblem as a symbol of the clan, and also recognizing that society consisted of "a vast symbolism," Durkheim was not always consistent in applying his symbolic theory of totemic emblems. When he appealed again in *The Elementary Forms* to the flag analogy to argue that the logic of modern science was born of the primitive logic of totemism, Durkheim interpreted the totemist's statement that man is a kangaroo as an identity statement, "like our saying that heat is a movement, or light is a vibration of the ether" (ibid.:238).

The comparison seems a bit recondite and not as apt as that suggested by Durkheim's own analysis of emblems as badges or insignia of membership in a social group. From this perspective the totemist's statement "I am a Kangaroo" and the modern lodge member's "I am a Lion" are probably exact parallels as identity statements. Both assert membership in a group whose totem, or mascot, is named in the statement; or so I would surmise.

An important implication of Durkheim's emblem theory of totemism is that the display of a graphic design (geometric or naturalistic) of the totemic animal, plant, or object can also make a statement of identity with the totem (the emblem's "manifest identity"), even in the absence of a verbal statement. Through such a statement of identity between the graphic design and the object it represents, the displayer asserts membership in the group whose emblem is displayed (the emblem's "latent identity").

Lévi-Strauss shares Durkheim's belief in the continuity between primitive and modern logic but disagrees with practically all the other features of Durkheim's theory of totemism—that totems are emblems that designate clans, that graphic totemic emblems are more sacred and real than "natural" totems and what they signify, that sacredness spreads by contagion to everything in the tribal universe to form a system of cosmic classification, and that all cosmic categories are social in origin. Lévi-Strauss's critical review of totemism in 1963 in fact echoes Goldenweiser's denial that totemism is a unitary and distinctive phenomenon and leads him to the conclusion that "so-called totemism" or the "totemic illusion" is simply a miscellaneous collection of traits that are differently emphasized in different societies and cultures.

There is, however, a more positive side to Lévi-Strauss's critique of totemism, as there also was to Goldenweiser's. For Lévi-Strauss, "so-called totemism" is made intelligible in a structuralist framework but cannot be understood within the older functionalist, empirical, and naturalistic framework. Viewing totemism as a complex set of relations between systems of social units and systems of natural species, Lévi-Strauss interprets it as a way of encoding the structural relations of social groups in the structural relations of natural species. The assumption that there is a similarity of structures between the two series, cultural and natural, is referred to by Lévi-Strauss as "the postulate of homology."

Recent criticism has questioned the validity of Lévi-Strauss's postulate as an empirical generalization. It cannot be denied, however, that taken as a hypothesis, Lévi-Strauss's postulate of homology has stimulated some fruitful discussion and research. It is also noteworthy that the structuralist interpretation of totemism is inconsistent neither with its being a unitary and distinctive phenomenon nor with functionalism. Radcliffe-Brown demonstrated this double compatibility in his second paper on totemism, and Goldenweiser foreshadowed the convergence in his later papers.

A problem that poses great difficulties for Lévi-Strauss's structuralist approach to totemism is to explain how particular social groups, or their individual members, come to be identified by some particular emblem or totem. This problem was already recognized by Radcliffe-Brown and clearly stated as in need of a general theory. We have suggested that Radcliffe-Brown's failure to develop such a theory is probably explained by his aversion to particularistic historical approaches and to the very structuralism of his second paper on totemism, which Lévi-Strauss applauded. A test of this suggested explanation is offered by the way Lévi-Strauss looks on history as a last resort. The problem is now more acute than for Radcliffe-Brown, because Lévi-Strauss rejects not only Durkheim's theory of "effervescence" and sentiments as causes but also Radcliffe-Brown's natural interest theory, according to which particular species are chosen as totems because they have already become objects of ritual attitudes for some practical reasons. Insisting that these species are chosen because they are "good to think" and not because they are "good to eat," Lévi-Strauss squarely confronts the challenge of showing how this postulate of homologous structures can account for the association of particular members of the natural series (species of plants and animals) with particular members of the cultural series (clans and other social groups). He displays impressive ingenuity on a wide range of ethnographic information to deal with this problem in his book on *The Savage Mind*. He even introduces a concept of "homological particularization" to derive a structural homology between the members of social groups and the members of species, from the structural homology between the social groups and the species (Lévi-Strauss 1966:169). He suggests, à la Radcliffe-Brown, that the categorical schemes of classification based on structural oppositions can, and do, absorb all sorts of social oppositions as well. In consequence, a society with a totemic cosmology "does not confine itself to abstract contemplation of a system of correspondence but rather furnishes the individual members of these segments with a pretext and sometimes even a provocation to distinguish themselves by their behavior" (ibid.:170).

In spite of this lucid presentation of the problem and his promising outline of its solution, Lévi-Strauss's detailed analysis is somewhat disappointing. He formulates the technical question in terms of whether proper names have any "meaning" or "signification" and argues, against the linguist Gardiner, that "the ultimate diversity of individual and collective beings" can be represented by systems of proper names that "always signify membership of an actual or virtual class, which must be either that of the person named or the person giving the name" (ibid.:185).

Lévi-Strauss's reduction of proper names to classes implies that totemic names are names of abstract concepts and not names of concrete individuals or collections of individuals. This implication is also drawn by Stanner on the basis of his intimate ethnographic acquaintance with Australian aborigines.

Lévi-Strauss's conclusion that primitives never name, that they always classify, and Stanner's Australian variant of this conclusion were probably motivated by a similar desire to do justice to the capacities of the "savage mind." But the conclusion is misguided, however laudable its motivation. At issue is not whether totemists classify or construct iconic images; that they do so has been recognized for a long time. The problematic question is how particular totems and totemic emblems come to denote particular individuals or social groups. And this question is not likely to find a satisfactory answer by reducing individuals to classes and the relations of individuals to structural homologies between the relations of classes and between the relations of relations.

Under the influence of Radcliffe-Brown's functional structuralism, Durkheim's emblem theory was eclipsed and the identity problem remained unsolved. The emblem theory was revived and significantly extended by Warner, almost unobstrusively in his Australian monograph on the Murngin (1937) and more fully in his last Yankee City monograph, *The Living and the Dead* (1959). Warner not only rehabilitated Durkheim's theory of totemic emblems; more importantly, he integrated the theory with a general analysis of symbols and symbol systems. With impressive empirical detail, especially in *The Living and the Dead*, he showed how particular emblems came historically to be identified with particular social groups and individuals, in sacred as well as in secular ritual contexts. The general theory of symbols that Warner used was derived, as he acknowledged, from Ogden and Richards, Freud, Jung, Pareto, Piaget, G. H. Mead, Sapir, and Charles Morris, among others. That the last three contributors were all at the University of Chicago just before or during the periods that Radcliffe-Brown and Warner taught there is a significant coincidence from the point of view of the development of a pragmatic, social, and semiotic anthropology.

Although Warner's symbolic analysis of emblems appears quite eclectic, it has a cohesiveness worthy of Peirce's general theory of signs or semiotic. While Peirce did not construct a semiotics of emblems, I have tried to show that much of Peirce's general theory of signs is relevant for a semiotics of emblems. It is precisely the manner in which Peirce's theory of signs enables us to show how the structural (or iconic) and the denotative (or indexical) features of signs and sign systems combine with one another and with verbal components that makes the theory applicable to a semiotics of emblems and the identity problem. (For a recent application to an Australian naming system, see Silverstein 1981.)

Warner's reversal of Durkheim's analogy, "the totem is the flag of the clan" to "the flag is the totem of Yankee City," was not only a tactic of cultural shock applied to the study of a modern American community; it was also a genuine, pioneering effort to find the collective and individual representations that form the enduring and permanent center of social life and evoke in a society's members the unifying sentiments of loyalty and identity.

In his Australian study Warner found such collective symbols of identity in the higher-rank totemic emblems and the local water holes where the ancestral spirits are invoked. Correspondingly, in his Yankee City study, he thought he found a collective symbol of "ultimate identification and belongingness" in the Society of Sons and Daughters of the First Settlers: "It said—and they and the community said—that they completely belonged, and they were so identified."

Since only a small fraction of Yankee City's residents can trace their ancestry over three hundred years to the first settlers, this symbol of identity is not common to all residents. In fairness to Warner, he did not interpret it as a symbol of the melting pot or of the American Dream. He regarded it rather as a standard of the ideal Yankee American identity by which to measure the hierarchical scale of ethnic approximations in a "time-table for assimilation."

In updating Warner's Yankee City study, I have found that the emblems of an American identity are probably closer to a melting-pot ideal now than they were at the time of Warner's original study. Paradoxically, the contemporary situation is also a closer parallel to the Australian model than was the case in the 1930s.

One of Yankee City's best known residents, John P. Marquand, conceded in one of his last books, published in 1960, that Warner's portrait of Yankee City's class system was still valid in the 1930s but had changed beyond recognition by the 1950s. On the whole Marquand disapproved of the trends of change and did not see much hope for the survival of the old social order. He may have been overly pessimistic.

Two trends of change have preserved emblems of Yankee City's past while bringing new groups and individuals under the emblems' latent identities. One of these trends concerns the way in which Ethnics and newcomers have matured into Yankees and natives after at least two generations of local birth and residence and adoption of a lifestyle acceptable to the community. The second trend is represented by the way in which the Society of Sons and Daughters has been expanding its membership and guest lists to include people who are not lineal descendants of first settlers. In both cases, the emblems, iconic and verbal, have preserved more or less the same manifest identities while their latent identities have expanded.

One might compare this situation in Yankee City to the aboriginal Australian one, as in fact Yengoyan recently suggested to me. There, too, the importance of a two-generation genealogy, a group-conforming life style, and myths of origin from the local water hole are associated with totemic emblems and their cults. Another and equally appropriate interpretation of Yankee City's emblems of identity is the one I have suggested in terms of a Peircean semiotic, as illustrated by the unveiling of the bronze model of the *Mary and John*.

I do not claim that a semiotics of emblems is the only possible method for interpreting emblems or that it is a method of studying symbols in anthropology that replaces functionalist, structuralist, and other possible approaches. A semiotic anthropology in any case includes functionalism and structuralism and is capable of embracing a fruitful competition of variant models, as the work of Geertz and Schneider, V. Turner and T. Turner, P. Friedrich, Sahlins, and Silverstein now attests.

6

On the Semiotics of Indian Identity

The concept of identity is notoriously vague and ambiguous. It has been used to refer to personal, social, and cultural identity; to ethnic, religious, and linguistic groups; to villages, cities, regions, nations, and to the planet earth. When applied to India the identity concept is no less ambiguous or elusive: it is perhaps more ambiguous than, say, that of American identity, because in addition to the existence of many sub-groups, as is the case in the United States, there are also Indian subcastes and a concept of ultimate reality with which everyone and everything is said to be identical. Yet in Indian scriptural tradition, ultimate reality cannot be positively described. Every attempt to describe it will be greeted with the refrain "not this, not that" *(neti, neti)*. There are only a few names that refer to this ultimate reality, such as "Nature," or the "It," "Brahman," "the All," and the demonstrative pronoun "that," as it occurs in the famous Sanskrit text of the Upanishads "You are that!" *(tat tvam asi)*. The meaning of this text has been a subject for exegesis by Indian and non-Indian scholars for hundreds of years.

Why a term such as "identity," with so wide a connotation and so ambiguous and vague a denotation, should be so popular in all fields of scholarship and should persist in spite of the failure to give it precise definition is an interesting puzzle. The explanation, apart from an appeal to Indian mysticism, I would guess, is that the denotation of the identity concept is the person or self, and that as long as it is difficult to give a precise delimitation of person and self, it will be difficult to pin down the denotation of "identity." This explanation implies that the boundary be-tween personal and social identity is vague and difficult to draw, an impli-cation that becomes more uncomfortable every day as we learn more about the "inwardness" of other peoples and of ourselves (Geertz 1974; Kakar 1978).

If my suggestion is correct, that we cling to an ambiguous and vague identity concept because we are more or less dimly aware that every kind of identity—ethnic, religious, linguistic, local, national—implicates the identity of a self, then we need to start looking at many fields—social, cultural, political—from the point of view of the self-axis—how their "identities" relate to selves and persons. Two intellectual strategies have conspired to occlude such an approach—the strategy of objectification and the strategy of subjectification. The objectification strategy tries to reduce phenomena to "scientific," objective criteria and measurement—all its identities are "things," including the identities of selves and persons. William James's insisting that a judgment of personal identity ("I am the same as I was") is not different from a judgment of the identity of a pen ("The pen is the same as it was yesterday") is a good example of the objectification strategy. James's extension of the approach to the self as an object, especially the social "me" ("everything he can call his own, his body and his psychic powers, . . . his clothes and his house, his wife and children, his ancestors and friends, his reputation and works, his lands and horses, and yacht and bank-account") was more fruitful, but left the self as "knower" (the "I") in a limbo of subjectivity (James 1961:44, 68).

The subjectification strategy relegates a certain class of phenomena to an "unscientific" and humanistic realm of feeling, intuition, and imagination, to be cultivated by sensitive poetic and artistic types. Its identities are all empathy and emotional identification, a strategy adopted by William's brother, Henry.

The inadequacies and failures of both strategies are too well known to need belaboring here. In one of the best possible cases, that of psychoanalysis, the failures are not only a matter of uncritical attempts to psychoanalyze whole societies and cultures without the necessary knowledge of the specifically cultural, social, and historical. The psychoanalyst sometimes does have such knowledge. The Indian analyst Kakar has knowledge of this kind, and he formulates a concept of identity that aims to do justice to the "outer" social realities as well as to the subjective side: "Identity, as used here, is meant to convey the process of synthesis between the inner life and outer social reality as well as the feeling of personal continuity and consistency within oneself" (Kakar 1978:2).

In his application of the identity concept to India, Kakar writes that:

> The concept is ideally suited to integrate the kinds of data—cultural, historical and psychological—which must be included in a description of the "Indianness" of Indians: the network of social roles, traditional values, caste customs and kinship regulations with which the threads of individual psychological development are interwoven. In this special sense, this book is also an exploration in Indian identity. (Ibid.)

The identity concept here announced is laudably comprehensive. How far does Kakar apply it? Does his book *The Inner World* integrate the different kinds of data one with another and with the feeling of personal continuity and consistency? Erikson's identity concepts and stages of life development provide Kakar his framework of analysis for Indian identity. Although Kakar concludes his book with the statement that "the prudent adult of psychoanalysis would be a welcome and compatible guest in the yoga schools of 'liberation,'" he does concede that psychoanalysis differs from the ancient Hindu image of the life cycle and the person on many points—infant sexuality, belief in rebirth, the idea of development. Erikson's own formulation of the difference between a psychoanalytic and a cultural definition of personal identity is also pertinent: "While the exact *age* of onset and the *length* of any stage of development as well as the *intensity* of the conflict experienced may all vary dramatically from one culture to another, the *order* and *sequence* of these stages remain fixed; for they are intrinsically related both to physiological stages and to the basic requirements of any social order" (Erikson in Kakar 1979:126; emphasis in original).

Ultimately, then, Erikson's psychoanalytical scheme insists on a fixed sequence of developmental stages that represents the psychoanalytic objectification of personal identity. Erikson does not deny this objectification even in his study of Gandhi, although he has based that study largely on interviews with Gandhi's friends and associates (Erikson 1969:33, 55).

Elaborating on Erikson's comparison of his life-cycle stages with the stages of life in the Hindu "world-image," Kakar finds the principles of fixed sequence and functional aggregation (Erikson's "epigenetic" principle) in both schemes (Kakar 1978:42–44). To base a concept of personal identity in India or elsewhere on Erikson's stages of life is to anchor it in phylogenetic and ontogenetic theories. In spite of this kind of objectification of the identity concept, Erikson and Kakar include in their respective studies illuminating observations and documentary materials that do not seem to require interpretation in terms of ontogenetic and phylogenetic sequences. Whether this material also demonstrates that the polar desires for separation and for fusion are "the essential psychological theme of Hindu culture" (ibid.:123–29) is a more problematic issue.

In this chapter I propose to develop an approach to Indian identity that is an alternative to the psychoanalytic approach. An alternative approach will be developed not only because I lack training and experience in psychoanalysis, but also because such an approach offers an alternative intellectual strategy to the two strategies of objectification and subjectification. The alternative strategy proposed derives from semiotic anthropology.

Peirce's general theory of signs bypasses the subjectification and the objectification strategies. The former strategy is avoided by denying that there is any intuitive and introspective knowledge of the self, and maintaining that all knowledge of the self depends on observation and inference from external facts. Such anti-Cartesianism (the label is Peirce's) does not result in objectification for at least two reasons—first, Peirce recognizes the existence of an immediate consciousness of feelings as they appear to the mind without respect to the existence of anything else, or to their truth or falsity. He refers to this as a *quale-consciousness* (a consciousness of the quality of feelings), which appears at a phenomenological level of cognition (CP:6.224–37). He does not, however, assume that we have such immediate consciousness of a self and ego: "Introspection is wholly a matter of inference. One is immediately conscious of his feelings, no doubt; but not that they are feelings of an *ego*. The *self* is only inferred" (CP:5.462).

A second reason why Peirce's anti-Cartesian semiotic avoids an objectification of identity is that it bases its analysis of the self-object relationship on an irreducibly triadic relation of sign, object, and interpretant, rather than on a dyadic relation of mechanical causality between stimulus and response, or between self and environment (CP:5.484). The triadic relation formulates a process of sign-action ("semiosis"), which includes dialogues between the utterer and interpreter of the sign, inner dialogues as well as outer dialogues.

Given Peirce's anti-Cartesian strategy, it is relatively easy to construct a theory of the self that is phenomenological, semiotic, social, and pragmatic. The fragments of such a construction are scattered through Peirce's writings. I have previously tried to collate various references and to integrate them into a consistent interpretation. In this chapter I shall summarize briefly those aspects of Peirce's theory of the self that are relevant for a semiotics of Indian identity.

Personal identity is defined in Peirce's theory of the self as consistency of feeling, of action, and of thought, and as a consistency of symbolization (CP:5.28, 29, 313, 315; chap. 3). The triad of feeling, action, and thought is neither random nor a bit of familiar nineteenth-century psychology. It illustrates an application of Peirce's three categories of being and of consciousness to the concept of the self. Together with his theory of signs, the application of the three categories—feeling as Firstness, action as Secondness, and thought as Thirdness—enabled Peirce to resist the reductionist psychophysics and psychophysiology that were beginning to take prominence in the new "scientific" psychology of his day.

This "new psychology" bifurcated the self-concept into an objective half, usually called "personality," and a subjective half labeled "self" or "personal identity" (for this usage, see *Baldwin's Dictionary of Philosophy and*

Psychology 2.282). Peirce made several contributions to psychophysics in his observations on stars and, with one of his students, Joseph Jastrow, on color discrimination (Peirce and Jastrow 1885; Lincourt and Olczak 1974). He insisted, however, on keeping this kind of psychology distinct from a more phenomenological self-concept, and on defining "personal identity" semiotically, independently of brain neurology and biochemistry (see chap. 3). The unity and continuity of the feeling-consciousness is logical and does not depend on the existence of a central brain cell (CP:6.229).

The consistency of symbolization is not spelled out in detail by Peirce. It includes both the consistency of individual signs and their expression as well as the consistency of language systems, for Peirce held that "my language is the sum total of my self" (CP:5.313–14).

In a semiotic anthropology, the consistency of language, and of sign systems generally, is not independent of and parallel to the consistency of feeling, of actions, and of thoughts, as if iconic, indexical, and symbolic signs, respectively, mirrored each of the psychological categories. The integration of the self is built up from an integration of feelings (including fear, anxiety, hope, and wonder), actions, and thoughts into "bundles of habits." A man is a "bundle of habits" with the unity of self-consciousness (CP:6.2281; 5.292). Peirce's concept of habit is that of a self-analyzing and self-correcting disposition to act in a certain way under given circumstances and motivations. A habit is for him the "final" or "logical" interpretant of a sign and, as such, gives Peirce's theory of signs an essentially pragmatic dimension. The making and remaking of habits, subject to self-control through muscular effort and "acts of imagination," constitute the chief means for the formation and growth of the self (see especially Peirce CP:5.486). A "bundle of habits" may include all kinds of signs or semiotic systems. Their specific constellations, structures, and meanings are matters for empirical investigation, as are the boundaries of the selves who are both subjects and objects of the semiotic systems.

A distinctive feature of Peirce's semiotic theory of the self is that personal identity is not confined to the body and the individual organism but may extend beyond these to include social and collective identities; personal identity is an "outreaching identity." The individual organism forms a kind of "natural" boundary and resting place for the integration of habit bundles of feelings, actions, and thoughts. Through sympathy, interaction, and conversation with others, the boundaries of the self and its identity are extended to embrace several individual organisms in a "loosely compacted person" (Peirce) and in a "community of interpretation" (Royce) of an entire society, culture, or civilization.

The nineteenth-century epistemological discussions about how a subjective self could know an objective world took on vitality and direction when first Peirce and then William James, Baldwin, Dewey, G. H. Mead, and Cooley translated the discussion into a problem in the use of personal pronouns in dialogues between the utterers and interpreters of "self-words" and of other signs of self. In this new semiotic and social context, thought was analyzed as an inner dialogue between an "I" and a "me," communication with others as an outer dialogue between "I" and "you," and corporate identity as a dialogue between "we" and "they" (chap. 4).

This development of a semiotic and social theory of identity in American pragmatism has served to counter the more egotistical and idistical tendencies in American life and to keep alive a tuistical spirit—defined by Peirce as the belief that all thought and conversation is addressed to a second person or to oneself as a second person.[1]

How can we apply Peirce's semiotic theory of the self to the problem of Indian identity? Some obvious possibilities suggest themselves. We might begin with a study of specific Indian signs and symbols—the name of the country, the flag and its emblems, verbal descriptions, perhaps some characteristic symbols in myths. To begin this way might eventually lead into the semiotics of Indian identity, but it would be neither a good semiotic nor a good anthropological starting point. Although Peirce defined his theory of signs as "quasi-formal," a theory of what *must* be true of all signs from the observation of some, he also believed that the application of semiotic to special fields requires travel, special experience, and knowledge—not only knowledge of special sign systems but acquaintance with the objects denoted by the signs (CP:3.414–24, 8.181, 183). The requirement for good semiotic procedure, in other words, calls for field experience with the use, context, and history of the sign systems to be studied and, not least, with the people whose dialogues communicate to one another, to themselves, and to the semiotic anthropologist the signs and meanings of their identity. In this chapter I shall draw upon ethnographic, textual, and historical studies of India, my own as well as those of others, for the materials to which to apply a Peircean semiotic of identity. It is essential to keep in mind in reading the chapter that a semiotics of Indian identity is not a logical deduction from Peirce's general theory of signs, but a conclusion to be achieved through an analysis and interpretation of specific symbols and sign-systems embedded in the contexts of specific observations and interviews. After reading the analysis and interpretations, the reader may wonder why there is such a good fit between Peirce's semiotic theory of the self and a semiotics of Indian identity. This question will be addressed in the concluding section of the chapter. Peirce's anti-Cartesian semiotics may not at first glance appear as a very promising path to an inner vision of Indian identity, but it provides an unexpected access to the inwardness of Indians and of Americans alike.

DISCOVERING THE PROBLEM OF INDIAN IDENTITY

I first encountered the problem of Indian identity in the early 1950s in Jawaharlal Nehru's *Discovery of India* (1946), which I read before visiting India. It was something of a surprise to find that a well-educated and articulate Indian leader should need to "discover" India and undertake a search for its identity. When I became more familiar with Nehru's biography and the fact that he was in prison for advocating Indian independence at the time he wrote the book, the reasons why he and other Indians should have an identity problem were more understandable. I think that the anthropological concept of a "traditional" society, well organized, with a coherent and unified culture, led me to suppose that Indians took their identity for granted. To learn, then, from Nehru's book that almost every aspect of Indian identity—the name of the country, its boundaries, history, political constitution, national emblems—was a matter of public debate and discussion presented a challenge to my preconceptions and to those then prevailing in the United States. Eventually, I came to realize that American identity was also problematic and needed to be discovered through travel, research, and discussion. This discovery was less startling than the comparable realization about Indian identity had been.

Superficially, the Indian and American identity problems resemble each other, particularly with regard to the role played by the British as colonial rulers and the resultant national movements for independence. Perhaps these resemblances are sufficiently close to justify a comparison of Crèvecoeur's asking, at the end of the eighteenth century, "What, then, is an American?" with Nehru's pressing Indian villagers to tell him who was this Mother India *(Bharat Mata)* beyond their patch of village land. While this kind of parallel can be drawn, it quickly recedes in the contrastive time perspectives of the two civilizations—over five thousand years for that of India, as against about five hundred years (to the present) for the civilization of the European settlers in the United States.

By regarding the civilization of the Europeans in America as a transplant from European civilization, or by assimilating the native American civilizations into that of the European settlers and later immigrants, the contrast in time perspectives can be reduced. Even so, one rarely encounters an American who feels about his civilization what Nehru and many other Indians discovered about theirs—that it has a unity and continuity across the full span of the civilization in space and time. To characterize this sense of cultural identity, as Nehru does in *The Discovery of India*, by claiming that any Indian would feel at home at any time and place within India, that the successions of invaders and immigrants in India have acquired a distinctive Indian culture, and that Indian emigrants have taken it with them to many other countries, may sound like political rhetoric and dramatic overstatement. But it must be taken seriously as a statement by a major political leader who traveled to all regions of India, read her history and some of her ancient literature in myths, legends, and epics, visited the old ruins and monuments, went to the great bathing festivals, and met and talked with ordinary villagers as well as with sophisticated intellectuals and scholars.

Nehru admitted that it was not easy to describe the character of the India he was looking for in his travels and studies, apart from her physical and geographical features. He was convinced, however, that there was "some depth of soul" that he could not fathom, like "some ancient palimpsest" on which many layers of thought and reverie had been inscribed and "had gone to build up the complex and mysterious personality of India" (Nehru 1946:47). Granting the outward diversity and infinite variety of people, he also found "a tremendous impress of oneness which held us together for ages past, whatever political fate or misfortune had befallen us" (ibid.). This felt unity of India was no longer a purely intellectual conception for Nehru but had become an emotional experience that overpowered him. Although India's "mysterious personality" remained elusive for him, Nehru did manage to convey something of its "spirit" and "soul" when he wrote that the "metaphysical democracy" of the Upanishads produced "that atmosphere of tolerance and reasonableness, that acceptance of free thought in matters of faith, that desire and capacity to live and let live, which are the dominant features of Indian culture, as they are of the Chinese. There was no totalitarian religion or culture, and they indicate an old and wise civilization with inexhaustible mental reserves" (ibid.:81–82).

Nehru's insight into the connection between Upanishadic metaphysics and social life came from "the realization that all things have the same essence." This realization "removes the barrier which separates us from them and produces a sense of unity with humanity and nature, a unity which underlies the diversity and manifoldness of the external world. . . . This all-embracing approach overrides all barriers of caste and class and every other external and internal difference" (ibid.:81).

It may sound incongruous for a science graduate of Cambridge University, a disciple of the Fabian socialists, and an admirer of the "new civilization" of the Soviet Union and its prophets Marx and Lenin, to quote the Upanishads much like a traditional Indian mystic: "He who sees the One Spirit in all and all in the One Spirit, henceforth can look with contempt on no creature" (ibid.).

While Nehru leaves no doubt about his faith in reason and science, he tempers his modernism with a recognition of their limitations. Throughout *The Discovery of India*, he is especially eloquent on the necessity of coming to terms with Indian traditional culture and what he calls the "burden of the past," as in the following passage:

> The roots of the present lay in the past and so I made voyages of discovery into the past, ever seeking a clue in it, if any such existed, to the understanding of the present. . . . If I felt occasionally that I belonged to the past, I felt also that the whole of the past belonged to me in the present. Past history merged into contemporary history; it became a living reality tied up with sensations of pain and pleasure. (Ibid.:11)

In the Epilogue to his book Nehru recognizes that his sense of intimacy with the past is both a generic Indian trait and a problematic hypothesis for further research: "The discovery of India—what have I discovered? It was presumptuous of me to imagine that I could unveil her and find out what she is today and what she was in the long past" (ibid.:575).

The "cultural unity amidst diversity" is there and binds together, as if by invisible threads, the "bundle of contradictions" that has the "elusive quality of a legend long ago . . . a myth and an idea, a dream and a vision, and yet very real and present and pervasive. . . . Shameful and repellent she is, occasionally perverse and obstinate, sometimes even a little hysteric, this lady with a past" (ibid.:576).

Nehru is also confident that despite India's "waking up to the present," "the old witchery will continue and hold the hearts of the people," maintaining a "true culture" that "derives its inspiration from every corner of the world" but is "home-grown and has to be based on the wide mass of the people."

Indians "do not have to go abroad in search of the past and the distant"; they already have them in abundance. If they go to foreign countries, "it is in search of the present. That search is necessary, for isolation from it means backwardness and decay." By seeking "wisdom and knowledge and friendship and comradeship" wherever they can find them, and cooperating with others in common tasks, but "not becoming supplicants for others' favors and patronage," Nehru believed that he and his countrymen would remain "true Indians and Asiatics, and become at the same time good internationalists and world citizens" (ibid.:579).

Nehru's characterization of Indian identity as both a "given" and an object of personal and collective search, as both traditional and modern, indigenous and cosmopolitan, metaphysical and scientific, a cultural unifier and a diversifier, intrigued me and stimulated my curiosity about the country and its people. I drew upon it for hypotheses to guide research when I began to apply to India Robert Redfield's idea of civilization as a compound structure of "great traditions" and "little traditions" (Redfield 1954, 1956, 1962). Nehru's book, to be sure, was not the only source for such hypotheses. There were other books and other people, especially as we started our visits to India in 1954.

Sitting on the ground, listening to Nehru lecture to a vast audience at Avadi outside Madras in 1955 on how to keep fit gave us a direct experience of that magical chemistry between him and crowds that he describes in his book. We also met on that visit, and on later visits, a number of Indians who shared Nehru's cosmopolitan outlook and exemplified many of the traits he attributes to an Indian identity. These individuals reinforced the preliminary paradigm of Indian identity suggested by Nehru's *Discovery of India*.

We did not suppose, then or now, that India's "complex and mysterious personality" could be summed up in the personality traits of a couple of dozen Indians, no matter how selected. We were even more staggered than Nehru was by the challenge of finding the distinctive Indian "spirit" amidst the millions of Indians living and dead. That challenge became manageable for Nehru because he was interested, predominantly if not exclusively, in India's identity as a culture and a civilization, persisting and changing over five thousand years of history. His travels, observations, and conversations, his literary and historical readings, served as grist for his mill because he was trying to construct a collective and holistic image of Indian civilization, not a statistical distribution of modal personality traits or the childrearing practices that presumably shape an Indian basic personality.[2] On a much smaller scale and with far less experience, knowledge, and insight than Nehru possessed, I tried to do something similar on our first trip to India. That task became practical for me only after it was focussed on the problem of "what happens to the great tradition of Sanskritic Hinduism[3] in a metropolitan center such as Madras City?" (Singer 1955, 1980b).

Because Redfield's operational concept of the "social organization of tradition" (Redfield 1955b, 1956) led directly to the "cultural specialists" who identified the domestic and temple rites and the corpus of scriptural texts, oral as well as written, it became possible through direct observation and interviews to devise a structure of Sanskritic Hinduism and an inventory of some of the processes of change that were adapting it to urban conditions. When I observed that these "cultural specialists," and ordinary people as well, took an active role in helping to locate, identify, exhibit, and explain many rites, ceremonies, and performances as representative encapsulations of their civilization, I came to the conclusion that these "cultural performances" were the minimum meaningful units of observation for both structural analysis and the study of trends of change in the structure.

When I first noticed the importance of cultural performances in Madras City for an understanding of Indian cultural configurations and Indian identity, I did not think of a cultural performance as an especially semiotic concept, nor did I try at that time to apply Peirce's general theory of signs. My preliminary framework for the analysis of cultural performances did not go very far beyond "concepts of observation." It included the *cultural performances* as concrete units of observation, the *cultural stage* on which the performance was enacted, the *performers* and *cultural specialists*, and the different kinds of *cultural media* used in the performance. Since my initial interest was to design an operational method for relating the cultural topography of an urban center to Redfield's more "cogitational concept" of a civilization as a compound and dynamic structure of great and little traditions, this seemed an appropriate level of analysis (Singer 1955).

As I observed and analyzed a variety of cultural performances in the Madras area, however, I noticed that the multimedia performances frequently included symbolic representations that referred to some aspect of Indian society, history, and cosmology. The significance of such symbolic representations for constructing the cultural configurations and identity of Indian civilization as a whole was, of course, obvious, but I did not possess a method for a symbolic level of analysis until I started to apply Peirce's general theory of signs to a semiotic anthropology. The need for such a level of analysis in the description and interpretation of cultural performances can be demonstrated with reference to a problem that arose in my original description and interpretation of the Radha-Krishna *bhajans* in Madras City.

THE CONSISTENCY OF FEELING: *BHAKTI YOGA*[4]

During our first trip to Madras, I was impressed by the friendly feelings expressed among participants and toward me at the Radha-Krishna *bhajan* sessions I attended. Because of this and the fact that at several points in the program of dances and songs the devotees embraced one another and rolled on the floor to take the dust from one another's feet, I interpreted the devotional *bhajan* groups in contemporary Madras as "a brotherhood now conceived in terms of modern democratic and equalitarian ideology." Generalizing my interpretation further, I wrote:

> The devotional movement in Madras City has become ecumenical, an expression of democratic aspirations within Hinduism. It links village and town, traditional and modern, the folk and classical, the sacred and secular spheres of culture. It brings together, at least within the religious and cultural sphere, different castes and sects, different linguistic and religious communities. (Singer 1980b:158)

While this interpretation was suggested by the two or three *bhajans* I had observed on the first trip, it had to be qualified in the light of later observations made during the second trip. At that time, I had an opportunity to observe and interview a much greater variety of *bhajan* groups, and I came to realize that they were not all democratic and equalitarian, in aspirations or in practice. Nor, after doing a study of the recent history of the Radha-Krishna *bhajans* and having a participating Sanskritist do a study of some of the scriptural texts, could I say that most of the *bhajan* forms and songs were of recent or modern origin.

T. K. Venkateswaran, who made a study of these Sanskrit texts from the point of view of nondualist theology and Krishna devotion, noted that such observed features of the contemporary *bhajans* as informal sociability, mutual prostration and embraces, singing, dancing, eating together, and the use of devotional songs in different languages all have specific scriptural sources and sanctions and may be interpreted in terms of appropriate theological doctrines (T. K. Venkateswaran in Singer 1968b:165–72). For example, the behavior of the devotees in embracing each other, taking the dust from one another's feet, and making mutual prostrations is sanctioned by references to instances of similar behavior in the *Bhagavata Purana* and in other Puranas cited in a treatise on *bhajanas* by the devotee Sadguruswami. The following stanza from the *Bhagavata* is quoted in this treatise: "By ignoring those who belong to oneself, those that mock at oneself, by giving up the sense of bodily conceit and shame, one [the devotee] should offer prostration [even] to the horse, the outcaste, the cow and the donkey" (quoted in Singer 1980b:231).

Had I been familiar on the first trip with the theology and history of the Krishna *bhajans* and how the devotees themselves interpreted them, I should not have been so quick to see in them a modern spirit of democracy and equality. The initial observations were accurate enough, but they were confined to what I could see and hear and left out the invisible and the imagined—especially Krishna. With the deeper perspective of the second visit, it became clear that many observed features of the *bhajans* that looked democratic and equalitarian to an American—examples are feeding the poor, friendliness, the singing of devotional songs, mutual prostrations—had other precedents and motives—in ritual requirements, the need for friends in a hostile large city, and the need for an "easier path to salvation" than strict ritual observance and meditation on the absolute spirit. The mutual prostrations at the *bhajans*, for example, were interpreted by many of the participants as expressions of humility and of respect to the element of divinity in other devotees. As one of these put it, "They do not prostrate to one another but to the Lord Krishna who is between them."

The realization that the devotees believed that they were addressing a divine being in their prostrations, songs, and other "attentions" to Krishna changed my interpretation of their gestures, acts, and words as well as my conception of the devotees' relations to one another. At first I was reminded of Sapir's statement that a "ceremonious bow is directed not so much to an actual person as to a status which that person happens to fill" (Sapir 1949b:564). This is not quite an exact analogue to a devotee's prostration to Krishna, because the bow, or curtsy to a royal figure, say, is not usually thought of in the West as addressing a being or quality separate from the person to whom the bow is addressed (except by social theorists). The devotees, on the other hand, imagine Krishna's presence among them in very concrete form and activities. G. H. Mead's (1922) ideas about how a "conversation of gestures" is transformed into significant communication when the actors respond to their own gestures as others respond to them is also relevant, although that interpretation cannot be applied until we know *which* gestures function as indexical signs to denote *which* significant "others." Saussure's comment that the Chinese bow is a conventional sign, in spite of some "natural" [iconic] features, because of the arbitrary number of bows required is also relevant (Saussure 1966 [1915]:68; cf. Firth 1973:299–327; Sebeok 1979).

Eventually I was able to put together an interpretation of the Radha-Krishna *bhajans* that does justice to its iconic, indexical, and symbolic components (for the details, see Singer 1980b:228–41). It may be useful here to spell out the semiotics of the devotee's statement that "they do not prostrate to one another but to the Lord Krishna who is between them" in the light of my observations. As I have noted, the initial assumption that the devotees' mutual prostrations were "natural" (iconic) expressions of mutual deference, respect, and a democratic spirit of equality had to be set aside as a result of the later observations and interviews. The presence of Krishna was never visible to me in the *bhajans*, nor was he visible to most of the devotees, by their own testimony. Some said they hoped to "see" him. During the *bhajans* the devotees invoked Krishna's presence in a ritual lamp, and in a lithograph of him, around which they danced and sang and *imagined* his presence in their "sports" *(lilas)* with him.

Underlying the songs and dances are two kinds of belief: first, that if the devotees enact the story of Krishna's "sports" with the milkmaids *(gopis)* as told in such scriptures as the *Bhagavata Purana*, they will experience Krishna just as the *gopis* did and so find their personal salvation. The scriptures thus provide a scenario for the *bhajans* subject to the improvisation of the devotees, who are free to imagine all sorts of "sports" with Krishna. A second set of beliefs includes such theological doctrines as that all men have female souls and only Krishna is male.

Without taking such beliefs into account, it is almost impossible to explain the behavior of the devotees at a Krishna *bhajan* no matter how detailed and accurate the ethnographic observations may be. With such beliefs, it becomes possible not only to explain the observed behavior at the *bhajans* but also to understand what the devotees mean when they say that "we do not bow to one another but to Krishna who is between us." They are acting out one of the sacred stories about Krishna and the *gopis*, sometimes following the scriptural text in literal detail, sometimes improvising on the text with songs, gestures, and dance steps considered appropriate for the milkmaids' "sports" with Krishna. Because the scriptural text says that Krishna multiplied himself in the forest dances so that there was a Krishna between every two milkmaids, the devotees have no difficulty in imagining that what happened to the milkmaids happens to them. And because many, if not all, of the devotees believe the theology and philosophy of the *bhajans*, which includes the doctrine that all souls are female and only Krishna is male, they have no difficulty in imagining themselves as milkmaids drawn to Krishna, believing he would save them as he saved the milkmaids (for similar doctrine and practice among the Vaishnavas of Bengal, see Dimock in Singer 1968b).

Neither the *gopis* nor the contemporary devotees who emulate them in the *bhajans* imagined themselves to be alone with Krishna. They sang together, danced together, and interacted, although Krishna chooses a favorite, Radha, at one point in the story. The *gopis'* relation to Krishna, in other words, did not exclude a mutual relation of sharing with one another, even if it entailed neglect of their own husbands and children. The devotees similarly stressed such mutual sharing, and not only during the *bhajans*. After the *bhajans* were over, they said they helped one another with advice, jobs, and money. Even if the participants do not bow to one another but to Krishna who is between them, the *bhajans* seem to engender and express a spirit of friendship and mutual respect that extends beyond the duration of a particular *bhajan*.

Was my initial impression, then—of the Radha-Krishna *bhajans* in Madras City as expressions of a spirit of democratic equality in social relations—correct after all? Obviously not, in any direct sense. If we think of the *bhajans* as indirectly mediating the social relations, we can see mild democratic tendencies associated with them. The mediation is indirect at two levels. At one level, the *bhajans* mediate the social relations of the devotees through the enactment of a sacred myth that calls for the intervention of a divine being in their midst. The enactment usually includes representations of the divine being in the form of lithographic, plastic, and metal images. At a second and more abstract level, the images and other symbolic representations of the divine symbolize social relations among the devotees. They symbolize not the *actual* social relations among them, for those are usually just the reverse of the relations during the *bhajans*, but *ideal* social relations that they would like to bring about with Krishna's timely intervention. This conception of the Radha-Krishna *bhajans* as a symbol of ideal social relations and of how they might be realized was eloquently and lucidly described by one of the devotees:

> The relation between devotees as one of complete equality is only their ideal. They wish to make it a matter of fact and a reality. But, at the same time, it does not replace the traditional respect of sons for fathers, of young for old, of the less devout for the more devout, of the lower castes for the higher castes, and so forth. Devotees fall at each other's feet and take the dust of the feet of each other and place it on their heads, embrace each other, and do other such things. It needs *constant* practice of these things so that they may become perfect equals. In actual life, the equality has not yet been achieved or realized. It is only the *ideal*, and devotees wish to reach this ideal sooner or later. It has not yet come, as I have said before. Fathers do think that they are superior to their sons, the elders do think that they are superior to youngsters, the more devout do think that they are superior to the less devout, the high-caste devotee thinks that he is superior to the low-caste devotee, and so forth. Thus they think one way and do another way when they exhibit equality or express democratic sentiments. There is no correlation between their mind and body. They do not act alike. They think one thing and do another thing. When by constant practice, their minds imbibe equality as their bodies express it, the ideal is reached by the harmony between mind and body. The two then act alike, and there is correlation between them. Until then there is no talk of complete equality as the body expresses equality and the mind does not. What the body expresses is thus only a gesture of the ideal to be attained, and constant gesture of this kind will bring about the ideal in its own good time. The body expressing equality and the mind expressing inequality produce insincerity in a person, a great sin in a devotee. (Quoted in Singer 1980b:231–32)

This devotee's lucid statement expresses both an ideal of social equality and a conception of how the *bhajans* may serve as a practical means for the realization of the ideal. The conception shows affinities with the ideas of some American pragmatists, especially James, Peirce, Dewey and G. H. Mead, about the formation and growth of the self through a dynamic process of making and unmaking habits—through a disciplined education of the emotions, bodily gestures in social interaction, and thought, and a harmonizing of the disciplines under the guidance of a practical ideal. While this particular devotee, who had been a mathematics teacher, may have heard about the pragmatists' ideas on education, it is not necessary to make this assumption, for similar ideas can be found in Indian sources. The organic harmony and interdependence of gesture, emotion, and thought, for example, are graphically described in *The Mirror of Gesture*, an ancient manual on classical dance: "The song should be sustained in the throat; its meaning must be shown by the hands; the mood [*bhāva*] must be shown by the glances; time [*tāla*] is marked by the feet. For wherever the hand moves, there the glances follow; where the glances go, the mind follows; where the mind goes, the mood follows; where the mood goes, there is the flavour [*rasa*]" (Coomaraswamy and Duggirala 1936:35).

Van Buitenen emphasizes in his interpretation of *bhakti* "the one-to-one relationship between God and each loyal follower, so that God can disclose his divinity gradually and to one at a time." One sees this aspect of *bhakti* still very much alive in India; in domestic and temple worship, the belief that each individual needs a God of his choice, his *ista devata*, is commonplace. And one also occasionally comes upon solitary devotees, in van Buitenen's words, "people who have withdrawn from the crowd to be with *their* god in solitude and privacy *(ekante)*, taking him aside and addressing him privately, as in the theatre one character may take aside another and whisper to him what the others should not hear" (1981:24–25).

The Radha-Krishna *bhajans* of Madras City emphasize another dimension of *bhakti*, the dimension of sharing—mutual choice and mutual loyalty—which is, according to van Buitenen, the root meaning of *bhakti*. The sharing, moreover, is not restricted to a one-to-one relation between God and devotee but embraces the loyalty of the devotees to each other as they act out their shared devotion to Krishna. *Bhakti* may be "a form of religiosity specifically Hindu in that it allows a religious man to create out of a social polytheism a personal montheism" (ibid.:25), but it also allows the devotees to create out of a social polytheism a *congregational* monotheism.

THE CONSISTENCY OF ACTION: *KARMA YOGA*

The Sanskrit word for action—*karman*—has a long history, in which its meaning changed in important respects. As J. A. B. van Buitenen points out in the introduction to his new translation of the *Bhagavat Gita*, these changes in the meaning of *karman* mark stages in the development of Indian religious and philosophical texts from the older Vedas to the Upanishads, and through the turning away from action in Buddhism and Jainism and the return to it in the *Bhagavat Gita*. In this historical perspective, Krishna's urging Arjuna to fight in the Mahabharata war against his own kinsmen appears as a two-forked argument. It aims, on the one hand, to counter the retreat from action and ritual that marked the previous historical period. But the argument also intends to bypass the older ritual action of the Vedic period, in which sacrificial rites served any purpose desired by an individual person and also became necessary conditions for the functioning of deities and the maintenance of the cosmos as a whole (van Buitenen 1981:14–21).

The *Gita*'s contribution was to prescribe action as a duty *(dharma)* and a path to salvation *(moksha)*, provided the action is disinterested, without desire for its fruits. "He is both a renouncer and a [*karma*] *yogin* who performs the task set for him without interest in its fruits" (ibid.:6.1).

While Krishna rejects both ritual and knowledge as ineffective by themselves, van Buitenen points out that for those whose practices include knowledge, "action culminates, finds its fulfillment, in the knowledge that accompanies the action. In other words . . . a *yoga* of knowledge is really part and parcel of a *yoga* of acting" (ibid.:22). And, we might add, a *yoga* of action also includes a *yoga* of devotion, or *bhakti*, for Krishna reveals himself to Arjuna as God, who promises shelter and release in return for devotion: "Only he comes to me, Arjuna, who acts for me, who holds me as the highest, who is devoted to me without self-interest and without any animosity against any creature" (ibid.:29). Thus the *Gita* represents a synthesis of a *yoga* of action *(karma yoga)*, a *yoga* of devotion *(bhakti yoga)*, and a *yoga* of knowledge *(jnana yoga)* (cf. O'Flaherty 1980).

Although he was aware of it, van Buitenen does not discuss the relevance of the *Gita*'s doctrine of action for modern times—war, politics, or social and economic reform. In a passage that seems to echo Oppenheimer's quotation from the *Gita* when he watched the first nuclear explosion at Los Alamos, van Buitenen refers to the *Gita* and adds a laconic comment: "Arjuna's vision of God turns from the awed contemplation of God in his majesty (11.15–24) to the horrifying sight of God as war, devouring the warriors who like moths fly into his flaming mouths (11.25–31). God identifies himself as Time, which is death" (ibid.).[5]

The *Gita* doctrine of disinterested action that is motivated not by a personal desire for specific results but by some religious aim that transcends individual personality, has had a significant influence on modern reform movements in India. Some of the leading reformers have written translations of and commentaries on the *Gita* that emphasize a dynamic and activist interpretation. The most widely known figure is Mahatma Gandhi, who not only wrote a commentary on the *Gita* but, through his habits of personal asceticism and his lifelong nonviolent campaigns on behalf of untouchables, cottage industries, and Indian independence, also acquired a reputation as a modern *karma yogin* and saint who practiced the *yoga* of action. With loincloth and walking stick he came to symbolize, in India and throughout the world, the compatibility of traditional Indian spirituality with modern reform. Gandhi himself agreed with this interpretation by arguing that in applying the *Gita* to the modern age it was necessary to recognize that each age demanded a special form of sacrifice. The sacrifice required in this age was "body labor" in the service of others (Singer 1956:85–86, 1980b:31–39; Desai 1946).[6]

Gandhian "body labor" was not restricted to spinning thread on the *charkha,* or even to manual labor. It included any activity in the service of others *(sarvodaya),* carried on by nonviolent means. In India today Gandhian "workers" work in this spirit at special centers and ashrams. In every walk of life, however—government administration, the professions, agriculture, industry—one meets people who use the words of the *Gita,* and Gandhi's interpretation, to describe their attitudes toward their work. They do not necessarily consider themselves Gandhians and they are probably a minority in every field, but they are a significant indication of how the *Gita* doctrine of action provides a philosophy and motivation for work in modern times.

On our second visit to India, in 1960–61, I met a successful industrialist in Madras who told me that he took an ascetic attitude toward his work, since he worked very hard and put in more than he took out. Further interviews with him and some of his associates, as well as observation of his activities, convinced me that his self-description and his reputation were well deserved. He was acquainted with Gandhi's interpretation of the *Gita* and had introduced a health-care center for employees and several progressive management practices such as quality control and safety codes. This industrialist reminded me of Weber's description of the seventeenth-century Puritan capitalists' "this-worldly asceticism." Yet he was a Brahman, considered himself a good Hindu, and supported traditional Hindu institutions and functionaries and was supported by them. Because he was so different from the stereotype of the Indian businessman prevalent in India and in the West, I decided on our third trip to do a study of the top industrial leaders in Madras to find out how they adapt their cultural and religious traditions to their economic activities and vice versa. A major interest of the study was to test Weber's prediction: "It could not have occurred to a Hindu to see the economic success he had attained through devotion to his calling as a sign of his salvation. And what is more important, it could not have occurred to a Hindu to prize the rational transformation of the world in accordance with matter-of-fact considerations, to undertake such a transformation as an act of obedience to a Divine Will" (Bendix 1960:206).

The study found that the Brahman industrialist mentioned above was typical of an observed group of nineteen successful industrial leaders in the city. Nine of them were, in fact, Brahmans, seven were Hindu non-Brahmans, two were Muslims, and one was a Syrian Christian. Not only was the practical ethic of the Hindu industrialists compatible with the spirit of capitalism (and of socialism), but the successful Muslim and Syrian Christian industrialists had a very similar work ethic (see Singer 1980b:273–380).

It *did* occur to some of these industrial leaders to consider their devotion to their calling a "sign" of their salvation and to undertake a rational transformation of the world as an act of obedience to a Divine Will. Although not claiming to be *karma yogis* of Gandhi's stature, they did look on industrial leadership as their fate *(karma)* and felt it was a moral duty *(dharma)* to provide jobs and products for all. The profits, power, and pleasures of industry were no doubt incentives for them but were not dominant values for most. This may be a *kali yuga* (dark age) of disorder and moral decline, but they had no doubt that Indian industry has made much progress since 1949 and that this progress is irreversible and is not an illusion. While they did not expect to gain ultimate release *(moksha)* from the cycle of rebirths by means of their industrial career, it was a *corridor* through which they passed on the road to enlightenment and salvation.

Several spiritual leaders of orthodox Hinduism support the industrialists in their belief that one can be a good Hindu, even a good Brahman, and follow a career in industry. Although unhappy about the industrialists' lapses from strict ritual observance and family discipline, the spiritual leaders interpret the ancient *varna* doctrine of castes for modern times: "Some are born to make money, others to rule and protect, and still others to be workers and scholars. 'Kings and rich men' are expected to make money in ethical ways and to perform works of charity. 'Rulers and the business class' need luxuries as an incentive to develop the 'arts' " (Singer 1980b:341).

Weber has written that "the *karma* doctrine has transformed the world into a strictly rational, ethically-determined cosmos; it represents the most consistent theodicy ever produced in history" (Weber 1958:21).

Whether it is the *most* consistent theodicy will probably not be determined until many more comparative studies of theodicies become available. But there is no doubt that the doctrine of *karma* and rebirth *is* impressively consistent. The context of Weber's assertion is the question of an individual's ability to leave the caste into which he was born as a result of his actions *(karma)* in a previous life. Weber's answer is an emphatic "No!": "In this life there is no escape from the caste, at least no way to move up in the caste order. The inescapable on-rolling *karma* causality is in harmony with the eternity of the world, of life, and above all of the caste order" (ibid.:121). "Anyone who wished to emancipate himself from this world and the inescapable cycle of recurrent births and deaths had to leave it altogether to set out for that unreal realm to which Hindu 'salvation' leads" (ibid.:123).

Most of the Madras industrial leaders (fifteen out of nineteen) believed in the *karma* doctrine, but they did not think of themselves as prisoners of an "iron law" of caste and *karma*. They recognized that the caste system was changing and that caste ritual was declining in their factories and offices. However, they saw the *karma* doctrine as a way of explaining inequalities. One of them said that even after the caste system disappeared, he would still believe in the doctrine of *karma* and rebirth as the best way to explain and justify the remaining gross inequalities.

Nor did the industrial leaders look upon the doctrine of *karma* and rebirth as a fatalism that dooms all effort, foresight, and intelligent planning.

> As one of them put it, "Without God's will nothing can move, but if you think God is going to give you everything on a platter, you are a fool." His thought was echoed by the other leaders; effort, hard work, time spent on thinking about a project, knowledge, and genius are considered essential ingredients in success—and so is luck. Sometimes luck is interpreted as opportunity, and sometimes as just a fortuitous breeze that "blows the falling leaf in one direction rather than in another." It was not always clear how many of these ingredients were also included in one's personal fate as determined by past actions, that is, in one's *karma*. Some were inclined to include everything in *karma;* most left the issue open, beyond suggesting that ability, intelligence and will power were inherited from one's parents and grandparents. Acutely conscious that "one's ego is always there, always claiming that it has done this, it has done that," they nevertheless believe that "I am not doing anything; somebody or something else is directing me." (Singer 1980b:337)

While they have not renounced all the fruits of their industrial activities and become true *karma yogins*, these men and others like them in various fields are giving a new meaning to the *yoga* of action that may turn out to be as significant a change in the concept of *karma* as the change from Vedic ritual sacrifice to the *Gita* doctrine of disinterested worldly action. Their interpretation and application of the doctrine of *karma* and rebirth is changing it from a consistent theodicy of a caste system to a consistent theodicy for an industrial system.

THE CONSISTENCY OF THOUGHT: *JNANA YOGA*

Discussing the doctrine of the *yuga* cycles in cosmic history, one of the Madras industrialists commented that people think that "the past is always golden." As far as he was concerned, he believed that the *Advaita* philosophy of the Upanishads reconciles the transitory and the eternal. He then recited in his office with great zest an Upanishadic passage, first in Sanskrit and then in a free English translation: "I am that truth. You are that truth. The entire universe is that truth. Everything is that truth. That truth, that energy which is in the sun is in you. *That* is one universal brotherhood."

When I asked my Sanskritist colleague van Buitenen to identify the textual source of this passage, he thought that it might have come from several different Upanishads, but that the core passage seemed to be the famous text "That thou art" *(tat tvam asi)* from the Chandogya Upanishad. Van Buitenen preferred the more colloquial English translation, "You are that."

This is the same text that was quoted by Nehru in his *Discovery of India* as an answer to the question "What is the soul?" Nehru wrote, "It cannot be defined or described except negatively: 'It is not this, not this.' Or, in a way, positively: 'That thou art!' The individual soul is like a spark thrown out and reabsorbed by the blazoning fire of the Absolute Soul" (Nehru 1946:81).

Nehru's interpretation of the Upanishadic text and the industrialist's use of it indicate that in India speculative thought has a status and textual tradition of its own, quite apart from its association with the *yogas* of action and devotion. In the introduction to his *Gita* translation, van Buitenen points out that this tradition of philosophical and religious speculation centered on a homology between, on the one hand, the microcosm of the human person and his vital force *(atman)* and, on the other, the universe and its motive force *(brahman)*. Historically, these homologies between microcosm and macrocosm were then followed by perceptions of such identities as "I am *brahman*" *(aham brahamasmi)* and "You are that" *(tat tvam asi)*. One outcome of this line of speculation was that the "divine," the cosmic force, was also perceived as spirit, immanent in the human person.

In spite of the many refinements in this conceptual scheme, and the apparent irreconcilability between the position that individual souls are but reflections and components of one cosmic soul and the position that they are monads, together constituting the order of the cosmic person, van Buitenen believed that the "final positions remained in a continuum of thought that took off from the two forms of the one *brahman*." The Buddha "broke the continuum by refusing to care about the soul in order to go on with the task of alleviating sorrow." In any case, van Buitenen concludes that "all these labors of thought hardly prepared the soil for a hardy thriving theism [of the *Gita*]" (van Buitenen 1981:26).

The breaking of the continuum of thought by Buddhism and the later theistic movements of devotion *(bhakti)* did not end the Upanishadic speculative tradition. That was vigorously continued by a long line of commentators and original thinkers, two of the best known of whom, Sankara and Ramanuja, wrote commentaries on the Upanishadic text *tat tvam asi*. These are subtle pieces of semiotic analysis, diametrically opposed in their ultimate interpretations.

The Upanishadic text "You are that" is frequently interpreted as a direct expression of a spiritual and mystical truth:

> The consubstantiality of the spirit in man and God is the conviction fundamental to all spiritual wisdom. It is not a matter of inference only.

In the spiritual experience itself, the barriers between the self and ultimate reality drop away. . . . We belong to the real and the real is
mirrored in us. The great text of the Upanisad affirms it—*Tat tvam asi*
(That art Thou). It is a simple statement of an experienced fact. (Radhakrishnan and Moore 1957:626)

In contrast, the classical commentators on this text seemed to feel that
such an assertion of identity between the individual self and ultimate
reality needed intensive analysis and explanation. What puzzled them,
and still puzzles many of us today, was how an identity could be asserted
between two objects so apparently different—one very near in space and
time to the speaker, one remote; one highly concentrated in individual
persons, the other dispersed through the universe; one accessible to direct
experience, the other imagined.

The answers suggested by the commentators follow an essentially
semiotic analysis of the Upanishadic text, which is interpreted as asserting
that the object denoted by "you" is identical with the object denoted by
"that," without necessarily implying that the connotations of "you" and
"that" are also identical. Up to a point, the analysis of the assertion appeals
to analogous everyday assertions such as "This is that Devadatta." The
analogy with the colloquial sentence ceases to be exact when the semiotic
analysis is extended from the everyday example to such transcendental
sentences as "I am *brahman*." In the latter case, the denotations of "I" and
"*brahman*" are not unambiguously identical visible objects but suggest all-
pervasive spiritual forces that cannot be positively characterized. To
maintain the analogy with the sentence "This is that Devadatta," it becomes necessary to introduce special semiotic interpretations into the exegesis. Sankara is quite explicit about this and about the semiotic
interpretations he uses to maintain the analogy with "This is that Devadatta": ". . . the word *tat* has the meaning of interior self, the word *tvam*
has the meaning of the word *tat;* both words drop part of their meaning,
tvam that of empirical ego, *tat* that of non-self" (quoted in van Buitenen
1956:63). In other words, if the interpretation of "you" as the empirical
ego is dropped, then the interpretation of "you" as the transcendental
interior self remains; and if the empirical interpretation of "that" as nôt-
self is dropped, then its transcendental interpretation as the absolute
brahman remains.

Sadananda, one of the post-Sankara commentators, summarizes the
entire analogy in detail:

Therefore, as the sentence, "This is that Devadatta," or its meaning,
on account of the contradictions involved in one part of their import,
viz., Devadatta as existing in the past and in the present, implies, by
abandoning the conflicting portion which has reference to time, only the
non-conflicting portion, viz., the man Devadatta,—similarly, the sen-

tence, "Thou art That," or its meaning, on account of the contradictions involved in one part of their import, viz., Consciousness characterized by remoteness and immediacy, implies, by abandoning the conflicting portion which has relation to remoteness, immediacy, etc., only Absolute Pure Consciousness which is common to both "Thou" and "That." (Deutsch and van Buitenen 1971:300)

The same commentator then described the state of mind that results from the use of the analogy:

When the teacher in this way clears the meaning of the words "That" and "Thou" by the removal of superimpositions, and makes the qualified student grasp the import of the sentence, "Thou art That," which is Absolute Unity, there arises in his mind a state of absolute Oneness in which he feels that he is Brahman, by nature eternal, pure, self-illumined, free, real, supremely blissful, infinite and one without a second. (Ibid.:300–301)

The commentators did not always agree in their interpretation of "You are that." Ramanuja, according to van Buitenen, did not believe it was necessary to assume a metaphorical implication to explain the identity of "this here and now" *(ayam)* and "that there and then" *(tat)*. " 'This is that Devadatta' means nothing but 'Our Devadatta here was, at some previous time, somewhere else, he is the same person who was there at the time' " (van Buitenen 1956:64).

Although Ramanuja's use of the everyday example has the same aim as Sankara's, namely to illustrate "an analogy of the intuition of a non-differentiated brahman," van Buitenen believes that their use of the analogy leads them to "diametrically opposed views of how to approximate the Absolute in its transcendence":

Whereas for Sankara *brahman* is the *Other*, and he goes even farther in the way of excluding from its concept all that is related to the world, to the point of denying the reality of the world in the final analysis, Rāmānuja worships a God that is verily *Supreme* and includes in his concept all that is of this world, to the point of affirming this world just because it is related to God. (Ibid.:65)

Which interpretation of *brahman* attracts van Buitenen's sympathies is pretty clear from the following characterization of Ramanuja:

Devout Vaisnava if ever there was one, his vision can be understood. Visnu, the god of incarnations *par excellence*, who in every age takes personally a hand in the direction of the world's affairs, god of preservation and maintenance, who pervades the Universe, the Visvarupa and omnipresent one, will lead his devotee to a very different conception of

Absolute and World from that to which Siva would inspire, the god of annihilation, who represents yogic renunciation and systematic abnegation. (Ibid.:65–66)

After Sankara and Ramanuja, the continuum of Indian thought developed still other interpretations of "You are that" and a crystallization of the theistic and nontheistic systems. This is not the place to trace that history further; it is in any case beyond my competence to do so. It may be illuminating, however, to consider that the double interpretation of "You are that" as an assertion of an identity both between an empirical ego and some empirical other and between a transcendental ego and a transcendental absolute first appeared in the Upanishads. The sage Uddalaka instructs his son Svetaketu in a series of dialogues, in each of which he describes some concrete everyday phenomenon that becomes so refined that it turns invisible and pervasive. The father concludes each dialogue with the same refrain: "This is the very fineness which ensouls all this world, it is the true one, it is the soul. *You are that*, Svetaketu."
One of the sixteen dialogues will give the flavor:

> "Bring me a banyan fruit."
> "Here it is, sir."
> "Split it."
> "It is split, sir."
> "What do you see inside it?"
> "A number of rather fine seeds, sir."
> "Well, split one of them."
> "It is split, sir."
> "What do you see inside it?"
> "Nothing, sir."
> He said to him, "This very fineness that you no longer can make out, it is by virtue of this fineness that this banyan tree stands so big.
> "Believe me, my son. It is this very fineness which ensouls all this world, it is the true one, it is the soul. *You are that*, Svetaketu."
> "Instruct me further, sir."
> "So I will, my son," he said. (Deutsch and van Buitenen 1971:15)

In the context of such a dialogue, even a transcendental interpretation of "You are that" is a bit easier to understand. The father, addressing his son with the pronoun "you," is telling him that just as the splitting of the banyan seeds has resulted in an invisible and pervasive "fineness" that produces the banyan trees, so this fineness pervades the world and is the soul. Consequently, when the father tells the son, "You are that," "that" as a demonstratitive pronoun refers to a double analogy—first to the specific "fineness" of the concrete phenomenon described in the particular dialogue, and second to the "fineness" which ensouls all this world.

By the first analogy, Svetaketu should be able to understand how he becomes a person through a process that refines gross into subtle, invisible materials. It would be far more difficult for him to comprehend how the refining process of different kinds of things all produce the one true kind of "fineness" that is the soul of the world and of himself. If Svetaketu asked a question about this, his father would probably have called his attention to how "Just as the bees prepare honey by collecting the juices of all manner of trees and bring the juice to one unity, and just as the juices no longer distinctly know that the one hails from this tree, the other from that one, likewise, my son, all these creatures have merged with the Existent they do not know, realizing only that they have merged with the Existent" (ibid.:14).

The aggregation of all refining processes, in other words, is itself represented by an analogy of aggregation. One of the most popular metaphors for aggregation, one still very much alive in India today, is that of rivers flowing into the ocean. Uddalaka describes it concisely to Svetaketu:

> "The rivers of the east, my son, flow eastward, the rivers of the west flow westward. From ocean they merge into ocean, it becomes the same ocean. Just as they no longer know that they are this river or that one, just so all these creatures, my son, know no more, realizing only when having come to the Existent that they have come to the Existent. Whatever they are here on earth, tiger, lion, wolf, bear, worm, fly, gnat or mosquito, they become that.
> "It is this very fineness which ensouls all this world, it is the true one, it is the soul. *You are that*, Svetaketu."
> "Instruct me further, sir."
> "So I will, my son," he said. (Ibid.)

When, on our first trip to Madras, I observed the restrictive legislation then being directed against temples and ashrams, I was surprised to find that many of the Brahmans remained detached and serene in the face of disturbing changes. One of them used the oceanic metaphor to express their cosmic perspective: "Many of the temples and *Mathas* are only 700 or 800 years old. They have been destroyed before and revived. New values must be admitted. Life will grow, if old values are not destroyed. Life is one huge, infinite ocean in movement" (Singer 1980b:195–96).

ON THE CONVERGENCE OF INDIAN
AND AMERICAN SEMIOTICS

When I first began a comparative study of Indian and American identities in the early 1970s, the contrast between them seemed most apparent. As a hypothesis I formulated the contrast in terms of differing attitudes toward the relation between tradition and innovation. Indians, the formulation went, were maintaining their identity by selectively adding modern innovations to a changing accumulation of traditional culture, while Americans were maintaining their identity by seeing their past as a frontier for innovation. This formulation was suggested in part by my studies in India (Singer 1980b, esp. chap. 9). A preliminary exploration of the American side of the hypothesis, through visits to some shrines to American innovators—Henry Ford's Greenfield Village in Dearborn, Michigan; the Shelbourne Village Museum in Vermont, initiated by Electra Havemeyer Webb, with its three centuries of American "ingenious products"; the Hammond Museum in Gloucester, Massachusetts; the Lewis Comfort Tiffany Collection of Hugh McKean and his wife in Winter Park, Florida; and some West Coast museums—was encouraging.

About 1974 the study took two new turns: it began to concentrate on the series of revisits to Lloyd Warner's "Yankee City" described in chapter 5, and it also began a systematic application of Peirce's general theory of signs to anthropology. These new directions of the study reinforced each other, since at least one of Warner's "Yankee City" monographs, *The Living and the Dead* (1959), not only dealt with the city's attitude toward its and America's past, but used a method of analysis that made the monograph in effect a pioneering study in semiotic anthropology. The book's subtitle was *A Study of the Symbolic Life of Americans.*

As we have noted, Warner's method and general theory of symbolic analysis did not directly and explicitly use Peirce's theory of signs. His point of departure was Durkheim's emblem theory of totemism (Warner, 1958 [1937]). Indirectly, he did make use of a semiotic analysis through his acknowledged use of Ogden and Richards, G. H. Mead, Sapir, and C. W. Morris, among others (Warner 1959:450–51). One effect, in any case, of combining Warner's last book on the city with Peirce's semiotic in the "Yankee City" restudies was to provide a needed baseline for contemporary observations of a New England city as a symbolic focus for an American identity (Singer 1977, 1982a). Another and unexpected effect was to put my Indian studies in a different perspective, a perspective in which Indian identity appears more similar to American identity than it did in the first formulation of the hypothesis about tradition and innovation. The similarities, in fact, were so extensive that the new question might well be raised whether the original hypothesis has, in fact, been falsified.

The similarities between Indian and American identity referred to are not the kind of parallel occasionally mentioned or observed by others—that both Indians and Americans have a problem of building a national unity amid a diversity of religious, linguistic, social and racial groups. A reviewer of Myron Weiner's book *Sons of the Soil: Ethnic Conflict in India* was so impressed with the American parallels that he recommended that the sections on internal migration be read "in conjunction with recent scholarship on the opening of the American frontier and other frontiers where settled populations already existed" (Cohen 1981:416). One wonders, however, whether comparative reading of such parallels would also support Weiner's conclusion that the ethnic conflicts and narrative movements are not economic in source: "Given a choice, people prefer to hate others because of their religion, or race, caste or tribe, rather than because of their wealth" (ibid.; Weiner 1978:173). Would the reviewer still maintain that changes in "casteism" or regionalism depend on changing expectations about employment opportunities and economic growth? "If the pie is thought to be of fixed size, it is not surprising that regions, states, and subregions—when confronted with migrants who seek a share of the pie (although they may in fact increase its size)—pass legislation providing for reservations, quotas, or other exclusionist measures" (Cohen 1981:416).

   The American parallels to these kinds of ethnic conflicts and nativistic movements in India are not difficult to find, but they are not the kinds of parallels between Indian and American identity suggested by this chapter. It is, rather, similarities in the symbolic and historic structures in the identity of Americans and Indians that the chapter implies. Although only the semiotics of Indian identity is explicitly discussed, the symbolic and historic structure of American identity has been discussed previously (Singer 1977; chap. 5).

   Since Peirce's general theory of signs provides a common framework for the specific empirical studies of both American and Indian identity, the structural parallels in the two cases should not be overly surprising. Peirce's definition of a man's identity as the consistency of what he feels, does, and thinks, including further his explanation of consistency as the consistency of symbolization, the "intellectual character of a thing, that is its expressing something" (CP:5.315), provided a framework for describing and analyzing Indian identity. The scheme used in this chapter takes *bhakti yoga* to represent Peirce's category of feeling, *karma yoga* to represent his category of action, and *jnana yoga* to represent his category of thought and knowledge. This selection of Indian categories was made not only because it establishes a formal correspondence with Peirce's categories, but also because it offers a scheme for describing the structure and organization of Indian identity that fits the ethnographic facts. Together with the correspondence in the general categories, this "fit" to the ethnography gives considerable assurance that the selection of the framework was not arbitrary or based on purely formal parallels in definition and translations of individual terms. The Sanskritist's definition and explanation of *yoga*, for example (as "self-yoked," "discipline," "commitment," van Buitenen 1981:17–18), suggest parallels with the ideas of self-consistency in the organization of feeling, action, and thought, but such formal parallels are not sufficient until they can be used in ethnographic descriptions of particular people at specific times and places. The chapter has shown how this can be done by using observations in Madras for descriptions of a *yoga* of feeling in the Radha-Krishna *bhajans*, of a *yoga* of action practiced by successful Madras industrial leaders, and a *yoga* of thought or meditation practiced by these laymen as well as by a miscellaneous selection of "cultural specialists," sannyasis, and saints. In each case, the ethnographic observations were supplemented by relevant historical and textual studies that were made available by colleagues or personal archival research. The use of such diverse sources makes the construction of an integrated interpretation of the materials more difficult than it would be for a synchronic small-community study. At the same time, their use makes possible interpretations of much greater scope and depth than would be likely for the small-community study.

In what sense is the ethnographic description semiotic and in what sense does it show a consistency of symbolization in Indian identity? The organization of the description in terms of verbal categories such as *bhakti yoga, karma yoga*, and *jnana yoga* is semiotic in an obvious sense, as are the references to images, pictures, gestures, dress, and the like. In a less obvious sense, the descriptions are semiotic because they concentrate on the analysis and interpretation of several symbolic representations that emerged as significant and problematic in the course of the field studies, for example, the mutual prostrations of devotees to each other in the Radha-Krishna *bhajans*, the industrialists' belief in *karman* and rebirth and other major tenets of Hinduism, and the contemporary use of the Upanishadic text "you are that" *(tat tvam asi)*. The interpretations of these symbolic representations are not merely syntactic or semantic but are fully semiotic in the sense that they try to take full account of the contexts of use and of the dialogues between the utterers and interpreters of the signs.

Do the semiotic interpretations of these several symbolic representations add up to a portrait of Indian identity? Considering the limited nature of the selection and the small numbers of people observed or interviewed, the data base for generalization is very fragmentary. However, if we think of the problem of extrapolation not as one of statistical generalization from a sample, but rather, as Peirce did, as a problem in drawing inferences from the fragments of a system, then the possibilities for sketching a generalized portrait of Indian identity are more encouraging. The major clue to these possibilities derives from the fact that Indians themselves have already selected symbols and performances to represent aspects of their culture and society in encapsulated forms, which they regard as self-images of their identity. When I first became aware of such selected and enacted self-images, I called them "cultural performances." With the help of a Peircean semiotic analysis, we can now see that these cultural performances provide the names and forms, the images and diagrams, the songs, dances, and stories in a moving tableau of a self, not just of a self burdened with an ancient past, but of an ideal self just coming into being. Indian identity is an "outreaching identity" of a self that reaches out to other people through personal devotion to a personal deity, that aspires to the general welfare through disinterested action, and, finally, that seeks a vision of ultimate cosmic reality in meditation.

The structural parallels and similarities between a semiotics of Indian identity and a semiotics of American identity are not the artifact of imposing the latter on the former, but the result of a genuine convergence of the two. An explanation of the convergence as an arbitrary imposition of Peirce's semiotic concepts and theory on the Indian case is not valid because the categories used to organize the description of Indian identity—the *yogas* of *bhakti, karma,* and *jnana*—and the concepts of their structures and interrelations are all indigenous and "native categories." They are used by many Indians in everyday conversation and have also been recognized and expounded as leading ideas of the Indian world view by Indian and non-Indian scholars (Raghavan 1955, 1966; Edgerton 1942; Brown 1966; Heimann 1964; van Buitenen 1981; Dumont 1970, 1980; Marriott 1976, 1977).

In her interesting studies of Indian thought, Betty Heimann, a Sanskritist, has described a number of distinctive facets of the Indian world view in the fields of metaphysics and theology, physics and mathematics, grammar and rhetoric, psychology, politics, and anthropology. She tends to emphasize not only that these features are distinctively Indian but also that many of them are directly contrary to the Western world view. Some of these contrasts are familiar as the staples in Western characterizations of Indian world view in the works of Weber, Schweitzer, and other scholars: nondualistic metaphysics of matter and spirit, a vague mysticism about cosmic unity, the identity of the world spirit with the individual, an otherwordly ethic of inaction beyond good and evil, a cyclical conception of time and of cosmic creation and description, and a predilection for fiction, fantasy, and myth in preference to empirical realities. On behalf of Heimann, it should be said that her characterizations of Indian thought rarely fall into stereotypes; they are concise, lucid, and precise about the textual sources and always illuminating. It is her contrasts of Indian with Western thought that raise questions, especially for anyone familiar with Peirce's writings.

If we use Heimann's contrasts as a standard, Peirce's world view is much closer to the Indian than to the Western! His emphasis on the productive value of vagueness and generality, even to the point of violating the principles of contradiction and the exluded middle—"anything is *general* in so far as the principle of excluded middle does not apply to it and it is *vague* in so far as the principle of contradiction does not apply to it" (CP:5.448, 5.505); his belief that matter and mind are but two aspects of the same stuff; his attachment of a greater reality to generality and continuity, even if only at the level of imagination, than to observed empirical existence, are some of the striking points of coincidence with Indian thought. Beyond these, there are many details of Peirce's thought that seem to echo features of Indian thought as described by Heimann, for example, his fondness for trichotomies (a "triadmania," he once called it ironically), especially in the family (father, mother, and son) and in the general categories of being and of consciousness (passion, inertial resistance, and mediation between the first and second), as well as in numerical and linguistic tripartitions (Heimann 1964:95–96; also see chap. 4, pp. 83–86). Peirce's concept of a *quale-consciousness* of the instantaneous present (a "now-consciousness"), severed from past and future, seems very similar to the Indian conception of the present as a kind of zero-point from which the past and future extend indifferently (Peirce CP:6.251; Heimann 1964:103).

Do these coincidences suggest that Peirce may have been influenced by Indian thought? That seems to me a more plausible explanation than the hypothesis of the structural unity of the human mind. That hypothesis may well be valid, but even if it is, it would not explain similarities in the mental outlook of people from different cultures, say Peirce and Ramanuja, or differences in people from the same culture, say Ramanuja and Sankara. The Indian influence on Peirce was probably not direct, through his own knowledge of Indian texts, but was indirectly transmitted through his knowledge of American transcendentalists and post-transcendentalists, especially Emerson and Royce, and of German transcendentalists and related thinkers—Kant, Schiller, Schelling, and Hegel are most often mentioned by Peirce.

The possibility of an indirect transmission of Indian thought through American sources is described by Peirce himself somewhat ironically in his 1892 cosmological paper on "The Law of Mind":

> I may mention, for the benefit of those who are curious in studying mental biographies, that I was reared in Cambridge—at the time when Emerson, Hedge and their friends were disseminating the ideas they had caught from Schelling, and Schelling from Plotinus, from Boehm, and from God knows what minds stricken with the monstrous mysticism of the East. But the atmosphere of Cambridge held many an antiseptic against Concord transcendentalism; and I am not conscious of having contracted any of the virus. Nevertheless it is probable that some cultural bacilli, some benignant form of the disease was implanted in my soul, unawares, and that now, after long incubation, it comes to the surface,

modified by mathematical conceptions and by training in physical investigations. (Peirce 1955:339; CP:6.102)

Whatever specific historical and biographical studies may turn up about an Indian influence on Peirce, there is not much doubt about the existence of close parallels between Peircean semiotics and Indian semiotics. Nor is there much doubt that India has a long-established, indigenous development of semiotic analysis, the similarities of which to Western developments have been noted in several recent studies (Piatagorsky and Zilberman 1976; Staal 1966; Ingalls 1951; Nagatomi 1980; Matilal 1977).

The probability that Peirce's "infection" with the mysticism of the East took, and produced an American *yogi*, is intriguing and needs to be fully explored. In spite of the many similarities between his own and Indian thought, Peirce was resolutely determined to avoid the Indian conceptions of a transcendental self and a transcendental absolute. Yet Peirce's conception of ultimate reality as the object of those beliefs destined to be accepted by an unlimited community of investigators shares some of the indefiniteness and productive ambiguity of the Indian outlook. In any case, his friend William James approached both Peirce's and the Indian conception of ultimate reality asymptotically, in the distinction between knowledge by acquaintance and knowledge by description, as expressed by a grammatical sentence:

> Its "subject" stands for an object of acquaintance which, by the addition of the predicate, is to get something known about it. . . . We may already know a good deal, when we hear the subject named—its name may have rich connotations. . . . The minimum of grammatical subject, of objective presence, of reality known about, the mere beginning of knowledge, must be named by the word that says the least. Such a word is the interjection, as *lo! there! ecco! voila!* or the article or demonstrative pronoun introducing the sentence, as *the, it, that.* (James 1904:1.22)

SUMMARY

At a national level, the signs of Indian identity are easy to describe and interpret. They can be found in any encyclopedia—the name of the country; the national flag, with its white, green, and saffron bars and Asoka's wheel in the center; a coat of arms with a three-headed lion capital from the Buddhist stupa at Sarnath; and a national anthem, *Jana-gana-mana,* "The Mind of the Multitudes of People," based on a poem by Tagore. The deeper meaning of these emblems and symbols is more ambiguous and elusive, for they also stand for hundreds of millions of people, a vast subcontinent from the Himalayas to Cape Comorin, and the complex history of a civilization, composed of great and little traditions in changing structures of interaction. To find the principles of continuity and unity of an Indian identity is a staggering challenge even for a highly educated and widely traveled Indian, as Jawarhalal Nehru's *The Discovery of India* tells us.

To approach the problem of Indian identity from the point of view of what India means to particular individuals and groups is equally staggering, and not only because there are so many, the land is so vast, and the social and cultural history is so long and complex. These are indeed formidable obstacles to any research effort. Another major obstacle has been the absence of an adequate theory of personal and social identity from the point of view of the self. The concept of personal identity tends to get reduced to the identity of "things" by "scientific" psychology, or to the identification of quivering emotions by introspective empathy. I have tried to avoid both kinds of reductionism by drawing on Charles Peirce's semiotic theory of the self and of personal identity.

For Peirce the self is a "bundle of habits," with the unity of self-consciousness. Its identity is neither physiological nor psychological but consists in the logical consistency of its feelings, actions, and thoughts, which is also a consistency of symbolization: "My language is the sum total of my self."

As a "bundle of habits," dispositions to act in certain ways in the future under given conditions and motivation, a self grows and changes. The making and remaking of habits is a process subject to self-control by voluntary muscular efforts exerted on the body and its environment, and by the "inner" acts of imagination. Peirce does not restrict personal identity to the consciousness of an individual organism ("carnal consciousness"); he extends it to embrace, under certain conditions, a consciousness of other living persons ("social consciousness" of a "loosely compacted person") as well as a consciousness of the persons no longer living ("spiritual consciousness"). Through interaction and conversation with others, a child acquires a self and a personal identity; these are not immediate data of consciousness; they are inferred from the experience of social interactions and dialogues—the inner dialogues of "I" and "me," the outer dialogues of "I" and "you," as well as the collective dialogues of "we" and "they." The semiotics of personal identity is to be found in a self that is both an object and an interlocutor in such dialogues.

An application of Peirce's semiotic theory of the self and of personal identity to the problem of Indian identity requires some empirical data; it is not a purely logical deduction from the theory. The empirical data used in this chapter are chiefly the author's observations and interviews in Madras and in other parts of India made during visits in 1954–55, 1960–61, and 1964. These data have been supplemented by archival research and correspondence and by the study of textual and historical studies done by other scholars.

One major result of the application is the finding that Sanskritized Indians categorize their identities in terms very similar to those used in Peirce's semiotic theory—a consistency of feelings in *bhakti yoga*, a consistency of action in *karma yoga*, and a consistency of thought or knowledge in *jnana yoga*. These categories are long established alternative categories in India; they are not only used as verbal labels but refer to disciplines, or scripturally sanctioned *paths* to personal salvation and enlightenment. These paths are practiced by individuals and groups according to their "degree of spiritual evolution." The path of *bhakti yoga*, for example, followed by devotees in the Radha-Krishna *bhajans*, includes regular meetings with prayers, singing of hymns, and dances in which male devotees reenact the story of Krishna's "sports" with the milkmaids in the hope that they too will "see" Krishna. Such multimedia enactments were called "cultural performances" in my original Madras studies, referring to their role of encapsulating a self-image of some aspect of Indian culture and society for Indians as well as for outsiders. A semiotic analysis of some of the symbolic representations in the *bhajans*, for example, the mutual prostrations of the devotees, reveals that the devotees are not only exhibiting and enacting some aspect of their culture. They are also trying to change some of their own habits of feeling, acting, and thinking—their selves, in short—to bring body and mind into greater harmony, and thus closer to an ideal of social equality.

A similar semiotic analysis of the Madras industrial leaders and of the various "cultural specialists" and guides—domestic and temple priests, gurus, pundits, and saints—indicates not only how Indians, in following the paths of *karma yoga, jnana yoga*, or *bhakti yoga*, are reinterpreting and restructuring ancient cultural categories—of *bhakti, karma, dharma, yugas, moksha*, etc.—to accommodate modern innovations. A semiotic interpretation shows, in addition, that these activities of reinterpreting and restructuring old signs and symbols of Indian identity are the activities of growing and changing selves, whose identities are reaching out to the future as well as to the past, to the foreign as well as the native. These Indians are trying to become *that* by "seeing everything in the self and the self in everything." We in the United States are looking for our identities in a similar way. If Gandhi found inspiration for his idea of nonviolent resistance *(satyagraha)* in the ancient Indian ideals of noninjury *(ahimsa)*, truth and love *(satya)*, and firmness *(agraha)*, and confirmation in the Sermon on the Mount, in Thoreau's "On Civil Disobedience," and in Tolstoy, Martin Luther King chose Gandhi's *satyagraha* as a path to the American dream of freedom, equal opportunity, and justice for all.

Now is the time for Americans, Indians, and all people to disarm the "pseudo-species mentality" by developing the wider and more inclusive identities needed to preserve themselves and the planet earth from nuclear holocaust (Erikson 1969:431–33). This urgent task calls for the cooperative efforts of many different kinds of specialists—Freudian psychohistorians, to lift the burdens of past guilt to a conscious level of recognition; Gandhian *karma yogis*, to teach us by their example the new nonviolent self-sacrifices necessary to assure the world's welfare; and Peircean semiotic anthropologists, to discern the signs and symbols of the new identities, whose interpretants and "cominterpretants" will appear in the remade habits of our future selves and of our descendants.

NOTES

1. Introduction

1. A critical edition of Peirce's papers, published and unpublished, is now in preparation under the general editorship of Max Fisch at Indiana University–Purdue University, Indianapolis. Twenty volumes are contemplated, in a single chronological order. Volume I (1982) covers the years 1857–66 and includes the whole series of the 1866 Lowell Lectures.

Until the new critical edition becomes available, the most complete published collection of Peirce's papers is that published by Harvard University Press in eight volumes. Volumes 1–6 were edited by Hartshorne and Weiss (1931–35), and volumes 7–8 by Burks (1958). These are cited as *Collected Papers* or CP, with volume and paragraph number.

The most useful and available one-volume selection of Peirce's papers was edited by Justus Buchler, published by Dover. I cite it under Peirce 1955 with page numbers. The Peirce-Welby correspondence, edited by Charles Hardwick, has been published by the Indiana University Press (1977).

2. Lévi-Strauss discussed the relationship of his structural anthropology to mathematical and logical conceptions of structure in his 1952 paper on "Social Structure" (Lévi-Strauss 1963a). What the unnamed mathematician told Lévi-Strauss sounds like a concrete illustration of Bertrand Russell's general formulation that the structure of a relation does not depend on the particular nature of the terms that make up the field of the relation (Russell 1971 [1921]:60–61). Since Lévi-Strauss had not read Russell (Singer 1984), it seems likely, as Boon has suggested, that the unnamed mathematician was André Weil, who contributed the appendix "on the algebraic study of certain types of marriage laws (Murngin System)" to Lévi-Strauss's *Elementary Structures of Kinship*. Neither Weil nor Russell ever denied, however, that the terms in the field of a relation may have all sorts of nonstructural properties, even in the most organic social systems. To forget this important fact is to commit the fallacy of "misplaced abstractness."

3. Leach's characterization of Radcliffe-Brown as a "butterfly collector" is challenged in Singer 1984.

4. Dumont also credited Evans-Pritchard's *The Nuer* (1940) with an independent discovery of the notion of structure (Dumont 1980:chap. 2, §23). More recent discussions of Dumont's structural interpretation of Indian society will be found in *Contributions to Indian Society* V (1971); and in Barnett, Fruzetti, and Ostor 1976 and Marriott 1976.

5. Lévi-Strauss has denied that his position is mentalist or idealist: "Structural analysis can take shape in the mind because its model already exists in the body."

> As a matter of fact, even the more abstract ideological constructs (such as those included under the label of "mythology") which to a greater extent than other

aspects of social life, seem to enjoy an unlimited freedom in respect to both ecology and technology, cannot be successfully handled without paying the closest attention to the ecology and to the various manners in which each culture reacts to its specific environment. (Lévi-Strauss 1972:14)

6. The impossibility proved by Goedel is relative to the conditions stipulated by Hilbert, namely, that the consistency and completeness of classical mathematics need to be proved by "finite" methods that are not "richer" than those of classical mathematics. In a more positive sense, Goedel's proof can be interpreted as proving that our capacity to make meaningful and true statements about mathematics always outruns our capacity to formalize the proof of such statements (cf. Carnap 1937; Nagel and Newman 1964 [1958]; Quine 1981:143–47).

7. For a more detailed historical discussion of these developments, see Quine 1981:148–55, and Kleene 1952. Although Hilbert was one of the first to formulate and develop the idea of taking mathematical proofs as special structures of "meaningless strings of marks" for scientific investigation in a *metamathematics*, the practice of formalization was accepted by many logicians and mathematicians before him. Whitehead's *Treatise on Universal Algebra* (1898), for example, explained "formal reasoning" in mathematics "in the sense that the meaning of propositions forms no part of the investigation" (1898:vi). He quoted with approval the psychologist Stout's distinction between words and "substitute signs": "A word is an instrument for thinking about the meaning which it expresses; a substitute sign is a means of not thinking about the meaning which it symbolizes" (ibid.:4). Peirce was a contributor to these early developments and explicitly formulated the language-metalanguage distinction as early as 1906 (quoted in chap. 3, note 8, below).

8. Compare Murdock 1971 and Leaf 1979 for contrasting views of anthropology's interdisciplinary past.

3. Signs of the Self

1. Hallowell and Redfield combined "subjective" and "objective" points of view (Hallowell 1955:79–80; Redfield 1955a:78–82).

2. For a critical review of the "personality and culture" movement, see Singer 1961 and also Singer in Piers and Singer 1973. Opler's presidential address to the American Anthropological Association in the 1960s was still complaining of the neglect by anthropologists of the individual as a cultural and human being (Opler 1964).

3. Peirce believed he had succeeded in reducing the traditional lists of categories to three phenomenological categories, which he called Firstness, Secondness, and Thirdness. He regarded these three categories both as modes of being and as states of consciousness; the modes of being are also *phanerons*—that is, all that is "in any way or in any sense present to the mind, quite regardless of whether it corresponds to any real thing or not." Qualities of feeling, brute interaction with external facts, and meaningful continuity are frequently cited by Peirce as respective illustrations of Firstness, Secondness, and Thirdness. Peirce's conception of feeling as a quality is not that of a psychological event or experience, but that of a possible state or may-be: "I can imagine a consciousness whose whole life, alike when wide awake and when drowsy or dreaming, should consist in nothing at all but a violet colour or a stink of rotten cabbage. It is purely a question of what I can imagine and not of

what psychological laws permit" (Peirce 1955:81). The many other ideas with which Peirce illustrates his three categories have been collected and discussed by Freeman (1934).

4. The conception of the self as a "stream of consciousness" (or "stream of thoughts") whose unity is functional rather than substantial was being developed at the time by William James, Peirce's contemporary and friend. James did not interpret the "stream of thoughts" as Peirce did, in terms of a stream of signs, although his "I"-"me" dialogue eventually received a semiotic formulation (James 1961 [1891]:18ff.; Baldwin 1957:604).

5. Peirce does not use the designation "semiotic system" or even "symbol system." He was, however, quite familiar with the concept of system as distinct from that of class and saw its use as an important innovation in the logic of relations: "When ordinary logic talks of classes the logic of relatives talks of *systems*. A *system* is a set of objects comprising all that stand to one another in a group of connected relations." Peirce also drew the methodological consequences of this system-concept for making inferences: "Induction according to ordinary logic rises from the contemplation of a sample or a class to that of the whole class; but according to the logic of relatives it rises from the contemplation of a fragment of a system to the envisagement of the complete system" (CP:4.5). Only in the perspective of such a system-concept can we understand Peirce's emphasis on the relational character of the sign-function, on thinking as a chain of inferences from signs, on signs as meaningless in isolation, and on the self as constituent, product, and agent of semiosis.

A conception of system based on the logic of relations entered social anthropology through Radcliffe-Brown's definitions of "social system," "social structure," and "social personality" (1952). He was probably led to this conception by Whitehead and Russell, not by Peirce (Radcliffe-Brown 1957:21–22; Singer 1984).

I have applied the relational concept of system to the study of a cultural system in *When a Great Tradition Modernizes* (Singer 1980b: 78–80).

6. Peirce notes "a regular progression of one, two, three in the three orders of signs, Icon, Index, Symbol" (Peirce 1955:114). In effect, this indicates that his trichotomy of signs is coordinated with his three categories.

7. "Taking sign in its broadest sense, its interpretant is not necessarily a sign. Any concept is a sign, of course . . . But we may take a sign in so broad a sense that the interpretant of it is not a thought, but an action or experience, or we may even so enlarge the meaning of a sign that its interpretant is a mere quality of feeling" (CP:8.332).

Peirce's best discussion of habit and habit-change, especially in relation to semiosis, is found in his essay on "Pragmatism in Retrospect: A Last Formulation" (Peirce 1955:269–89). He makes it clear in that essay that the veritable and final logical interpretant of a concept "is the deliberately formed, self-analyzing habit," and concludes that "the most perfect account of a concept that words can convey will consist in a description of the habit which that concept is calculated to produce. But how otherwise can a habit be described than by a description of the kind of action to which it gives rise, with the specification of the conditions and of the motive?" (ibid.:286).

8. The word "metalanguage" does not, as far as I know, occur in Peirce's writings. It was introduced, I believe, in the 1930s by the logicians Tarski and Carnap, generalizing Hilbert's distinction between metamathematics (Kleene 1952:55, 59–65), the informal discussion of a mathematical system, and the formal

mathematical symbolism (Tarski 1956:167; Carnap 1937:9, 325; 1942:3–4; 1955 [1939]: 147). Peirce, however, explicitly made this distinction and recognized its importance:

> The language employed in discoursing to the reader, and the language employed to express the thought to which the discourse relates should be kept distinct and each should be selected for its peculiar fitness for the purpose it was to serve. For the discoursing language I would use English which has special merits for the treatment of logic. For the language discoursed about, I would use the system of Existential Graphs throughout, which has no equal for this purpose. (Peirce 1977:195–96)

> . . . when we investigate the language of a formalized deductive science, we must always distinguish clearly between the language *about* which we speak and the language *in* which we speak, as well as between the science which is the object of our investigation and the science in which the investigation is carried out. The names of the expressions of the first language, and of the relations between them, belong to the second language, called the metalanguage (which may contain the first as a part). (Tarski 1956:167)

9. For Benveniste (1971:225) the polarity of the "I" and "you" is the condition of language and of dialogue and constitutes person, for it implies reversal of roles. "*I* becomes *you* in the address of the one who in his turn designates himself as *I*. Because of this, *I* posits another person, the one who, being as he is, completely exterior to *me*, becomes my echo to whom I say *you* who says *you* to me." G. H. Mead analyzed this polarity in behavioristic terms as "taking the role of the other" and regarded it as an objective condition for the development of significant communication and of the self as a social object (Mead 1922, 1925). Cooley's more introspective analysis made both the "I-me" dialogue and the "I-you" dialogue parts of the inner self and thus blurred the inner-outer distinction (Cooley 1929, 1922). Mead himself noted this difference between Cooley's theory of the self and his own (Mead 1930a:703–704).

4. Personal and Social Identity in Dialogue

1. These discussions were held at the Center and were attended by Maya Hickmann, Benjamin Lee, Addison Stone, Bernard Weissbourd, and James Wertsch.

2. The social and dialogical nature of hermeneutic interpretation is emphasized in Royce's application of Peirce's semiotic. Royce, however, seems to have identified the sign to be interpreted with the object (Royce 1913:240–45, 286–91). See also: "Psychologically, interpretation differs from perception and from conception by the fact that it is, in its intent, an essentially social process. It accompanies every intelligent conversation. . . . It is used whenever we acknowledge the being and the inner life of our fellowmen. It transforms our own inner life into conscious interior conversation wherein we interpret ourselves" (Ibid.:159). "Two individuals trying to share experiences do not so much imitate each other's responses to things as they attempt to interpret one another, through the medium of conversation, what they see, feel and think in regard to such objects" (Ibid.:120).

3. "We may take it for certain that the human race will ultimately be extirpated."

4. Michael Silverstein comments on this issue as follows: "so-called 'honorific pronouns' are really *triplex* (at least) indexicals. The German *Sie*, for example, referring to second person interlocutor, combines its referentiality, Tu-ism, and

honorific marking in a way that is not isomorphic to its surface form or categories." He would also distinguish the level of speaking interpersonally ('I'/'Me' speaks to 'You,' the *pragmatic* level) with the development of *intention to speak interpersonally* through the *inner* dialogue of 'I' with 'Me' ('I' discusses with 'Me' how to speak to a 'You,' the *metapragmatic* level). For further discussion of these two levels of analysis and related functions, see Silverstein 1979, 1976.

5. Porter's analysis of *Richard II* finds that the first person dominates Richard's speech, even his use of the royal plural (1979:21). This finding is not a confirmation of Lyons's *egocentricity* principle, but, as Porter says, "a characteristic of Richard's mind noticed by many readers of the play, one having much to do with his apparent tendency toward solipsism" (ibid.:24), and toward soliloquy and isolation, but directed toward a general non-specific public (ibid.:40).

Porter's interpretation of Richard's egocentricity seems correct: ". . . in Richard's pronouns and presumably in his mind, *person* is a single feature, . . . there is for him only *one* person, with its negation—that *ego is the simple negation of other*, and vice versa" (ibid.:23–24; italics in original). Porter makes it clear, however, that Richard's egocentric speech is the peculiarity of one king, not characteristic of all kings, let alone of all speakers in the dramaturgy of speech acts (ibid.:42–47).

6. In his Lowell Lectures Peirce compared his "divine trinity" of object, interpretant and ground with the Christian Trinity—the object as the Father, the interpretant the Son, and the sign the Mother [*sic*]. Fisch points out that although Peirce was brought up a Unitarian, he was converted to Episcopalianism in 1862 through the influence of his first wife, and adopted her feminist interpretation of the Trinity (Fisch in Peirce 1982:xxx–xxxii).

7. William James wrote in one of his notebooks in 1862: "The *thou* idea, as Peirce calls it, dominates an entire realm of mental phenomena, embracing poetry, all direct intuition of nature, scientific instincts, relations of man to man, morality, etc. *All analysis* must be into a triad; *me* and *it* require the complement of *thou*" (quoted by Fisch in Peirce 1982:xxix).

8. See, for example, Lee 1982; Lyons 1977; Porter 1979; Silverstein 1976; Bean 1978; Fillmore 1972.

9. James usually wrote the pronouns in italics or in capitals as names of the different aspects of the self, as well as names for the linguistic expressions, a practice also followed by Peirce and most of the later symbolic interactionists. Cooley was one of the first to write the pronouns with quotation marks as names for linguistic expressions.

10. Mead found in Dewey, "the philosopher of America," the culmination of that movement of thought that began with Peirce's "laboratory habit of mind" (Mead 1930b:225) and James's biological and psychological individualism (ibid.:227), a movement that eliminated an antecedent social and natural universe as precondition for the moral act and the cognitive act: "As it is shown in the former that it is in social participation that the peculiar character of the moral appears, so in the latter it is through the participation that is involved in communication, and hence in thought itself, that meaning arises" (ibid.:229).

In both cases, a method is developed for eliciting the intelligence "implicit in the mind of the American community" by stating ends in terms of means and their social consequences (ibid.:231).

11. The use of pronoun pairs as units of analysis that affect the meaning of the constituent pronouns was noted by Buber: "There is no 'I' as such but only the 'I' of the basic word 'I'-'you' and the 'I' of the basic word 'I'-'it'." (1970:54).

5. Emblems of Identity from Durkheim to Warner

1. Nadel includes, in his discussion of types of consistency in "symbolic behavior," both the manifest identity ("as when the sculptured representation of an animal serves as the emblem of a totemic group" [1964:261]) and the latent identity ("the emblems and badges of group membership are undoubtedly also adequate means for the practical requirement that group membership should be rendered conspicuous" ([ibid.:263]). He does not seem to have brought his analysis of "symbolic behavior" to the point of integrating the iconic, indexical, and conventional features of an emblem. Compare Umiker-Sebeok and Sebeok for the semiotics of aboriginal sign languages (1976:Introduction).

2. Durkheim's quotation from Schoolcraft stresses the role of the totem as an emblem of *family* identity: "The totem is in fact a design which corresponds to the heraldic emblems of civilized nations, and each person is authorized to bear it as proof of the identity of the family to which it belongs" (Durkheim 1947:113). The immediately preceding passage in Schoolcraft also emphasizes *individual* and *clan* totems: "The greatest stress appears to be laid throughout upon the totem of the individuals, while there is no device or sign to denote their personal names. The totem is employed as the evidence of the identity of the family and of the clan" (Schoolcraft 1851:1.420). In a related passage Schoolcraft adds that "no person is permitted to change or alter his totem," and he interprets this as "a consequence of the importance attached to the ancient family tie" (ibid.).

Gibbon the historian refers to a kinsman, John Gibbon, who had a passion for heraldry and who observed an Indian war dance in Virginia between 1659 and 1661 in which the dancers carried bark shields, and their naked bodies were painted "with the colors and symbols of his favorite science" (Wagner 1978:7)

3. Lévi-Strauss has argued that with increasing technical complexity and social differentiation, the homology to the system of social classification is found not in the "external model" of natural species but in the differentiation of occupations, services, and cultural products, as in the Indian caste system (1963b). Schwartz (1975) has generalized this possibility by suggesting a "cultural totemism," in which "the perceived similarities and differences among human cultures themselves, the ethnic groupings conceived of by men as if those groupings were species," be added as a third model to Durkheim's social model and to Lévi-Strauss's natural model for the formation of ethnic and individual identities, in primitive as well as in modern society (1975:107). Boon and Schneider (1974) have shown that Lévi-Strauss's structural method is applied differently to the analysis of myth than it is to the analysis of kinship. Boon (1979) has tried to deal with the problem of cultural differences wholly within Lévi-Strauss's structuralist and semiological framework.

4. In 1928 Sapir replied to a request from W. F. Ogburn for advice on the symbolism for the new Social Science building that he was "not in favor of having either names of scientists, mottoes, or dates put on the building. I do not think that lettering is at all beautiful in the great majority of cases. My preference is for strictly plastic features which work in well with architectural design" (Sapir to Ogburn, October 25, 1928). Sapir added that he would be in favor of "purely descriptive symbols" such as Ogburn suggested in his letter, for example, "the red cross which is used on the Russell Sage Foundation Building in New York" and the retort on the Chemical building. Ogburn's "Committee on Symbolism" took Sapir's advice and recommended nine conventional emblems to be placed on the outside of the building on the fourth floor, where they are seldom noticed. The

only exception to this was Lord Kelvin's famous dictum about the necessity of measurement for knowledge, which was placed on the entry to the building.

5. In Yankee City's public library, my wife found a scrapbook of the 1930 Tercentenary procession compiled by one of the organizing chairmen that contained a graphic record of the procession: the story of each historical episode dramatized by a float was clipped from the local newspaper and pasted on a page of the scrapbook, and a painting and a photograph of the same float were pasted on a facing page. It is possible that Warner's inspection of such a scrapbook may have suggested as well as confirmed "the close analogue to the historical myths and rites of a primitive society."

6. Warner refers to many of these objects identified by the historical markers as "symbols" or "emblems." See especially his discussion of the historic cemeteries (1959:265–70, 280–87); the old houses and furnishings, paintings, and gardens (ibid.:44–50, 114, 151–55); and the sailing ships (ibid.:48–49, 140–42, 208). In Warner's interpretation, possession of "old" objects—dating back to Yankee City's period of power and glory, 1790–1815—symbolizes a claim to upper-class social status. But the validation of the claim depends on more than the possession of old objects: "Only when a house encloses a style of existence that conforms to its outward form, and when its inner way of life has been recognized and accepted through the intimate participation of its owners with the top group, does it cease to be no more than a claim to upper-class status and become a symbol of the actually achieved status of a family" (ibid.:47).

Warner's distinction between a "good house" as a symbol of a *claim* to upper-class status and a symbol of *actually achieved* status is introduced as a criticism of Veblen's theory of "conspicuous expenditure." The "form and manner in which conspicuous expenditure is made," not conspicuous expenditure per se, "determine its efficacy for advancement in status" (ibid.). Although Warner agreed with Veblen that the highly competitive gift-exchange in contemporary American society justified the analogy with the Northwest Coast potlach that Boas described (ibid.:241), he did not discuss Veblen's theory of how the "trophies of exploit" develop with increases in population density, and more complex and elaborate social relations, into "a system of rank, titles, degrees and insignia, typical examples of which are heraldic devices, medals, and honorary decorations," or Veblen's view of manners as in large part an "expression of the relation of status—a symbolic pantomime of mastery on the one hand and of subservience on the other" (Veblen 1965 [1899]:44, 47).

7. Warner did not give a statistical count of the historic houses in the High Street area. In one reference he estimated that there were about fifty houses on which Tercentenary markers were placed (1959:114) and added that "the present people who occupy them belonged largely to the upper class; most are owned and occupied by the old-family aristocracy" (ibid.:152). In another reference to a book on Yankee City houses that was used as a source for the historical markers, he estimated that approximately 90 percent were in the High Street area and that a fourth of the houses are now owned and occupied by those who trace family ownership back to the Great Period or to an earlier period, the seventeenth century (ibid.:154). To this estimate he adds: "We know enough about the past owners [whom Warner defines as a 'lineage' for a house] to say that most were in the upper-class at all periods of the history of the houses; some were moving hopefully into that class when they purchased or built them; a few occupants, present and past, have not achieved upper-class position" (ibid.).

In the 1930s and in his last monograph on Yankee City, Warner believed the historical houses were the most important symbol of the upper class and the channel for transmitting their values. These houses "gave shelter and grace to generations of families whose parents and children with marriages into similar families transmitted the values and beliefs and other products and symbols of superior status down through the years" (ibid.).

8. Marquand confessed in his attempt to reconstruct the old social order of Federalist Yankee City in terms of Warners' six social classes that he was "bewildered by exactly how the lines were drawn and attributes of lineage and wealth were required to create a Colonial Gentleman" (1960:58). He added that it was pointed out to him in his youth that "there were only two families from England that could be classed as gentry. . . . This limiting assertion may be startling to many families of Boston, Salem, and elsewhere, who have been able to secure coats of arms . . . but it is doubtful whether the College of Heralds would have confirmed most of [Yankee City's] armory" (ibid.). The "pathetic desire in the eighteenth century for an enclave of gentry" and the often self-styled additions of honorific titles such as "gentleman" or "lord" to a name "appealed to the risibility of some sections of the community" (ibid.:59).

The subject of Marquand's biography, "Lord" Timothy Dexter, is perhaps the most picturesque example of the "ancestor worship and status strivings" Marquand describes. Dexter surrounded his famous mansion on High Street with about forty carved wooden statutes of former presidents, Napoleon, and other "greats," animals and goddesses, and a statue of himself incribed "I am the first in the East, the first in the West, and the greatest Philosopher in the Western World" (ibid.:265).

6. On the Semiotics of Indian Identity

1. The triad "egotistical, tuistical, and idistical" formed from the Latin first-, second-, and third-person pronouns, was probably coined by Coleridge but was used by Peirce to characterize the ethos of historical eras as well as of individual personalities (chap. 4, pp. 85–86; Fisch in Peirce 1982).

2. For a discussion of "basic personality" and "modal personality" in culture and personality studies, see Singer 1961.

3. "Sanskritic Hinduism" was introduced into Indian studies by the social anthropologist M. N. Srinivas to designate a concept of all-India Hindu beliefs and practices that are sanctioned by Sanskritic scriptures. Srinivas also described a process he termed "Sanskritization," whereby lower castes tried to move up in the hierarchy by adopting the rituals and beliefs of Sanskritic Hinduism (Srinivas 1952; 1962, esp. chap. 2; 1966, chap. 1). The Indians in the study are "Sanskritized" in the sense that they participate in Sanskritic Hindu rituals and are familiar with some Sanskritic terms, such as *bhakti, karma,* and *yoga.* They are not, however, "Sanskritized" in the sense that they all know Sanskrit, or are all of Hindu descent. For further discussion, see references to M. N. Srinivas in Singer 1980b [1972].

4. The usual English gloss for *bhakti* is "devotion" to a deity, less frequently "love." The derivation, according to van Buitenen (1981:24) is from the root *bhaj-* ("sharing") and from one line of evolution from this meaning, "a loyal choice." Madras devotees (Singer 1980b:156–58) considered *bhakti yoga* "an easier path to salvation" than *karma yoga,* the path of strict ritual observance, or *jnana yoga,* the path of knowledge and meditation. In this context, the usual gloss for *yoga* is "discipline," especially "self-discipline," but as van Buitenen points out, the connotation of *yoga* (from *yuj-,* "to yoke") includes the notion of a person making a

commitment to something or someone for a purpose (van Buitenen 1981:17–18). The *yogas* of feeling, action, and thought may thus be interpreted as three alternative *paths* to which one may commit oneself in order to seek salvation and enlightenment. For further discussion, see Raghavan (1955) and Edgerton (1942).

5. That van Buitenen saw the connection of this passage with Oppenheimer's use of the *Gita* is quite likely. When I showed him part of the Oppenheimer quotation from *Gita* 11.12, he gave me an alternative translation for it (Singer 1980b:36).

6. For interpretations of Gandhi along these lines, see Rolland 1924, Sheean 1949, Bondurant 1965, and Iyer 1973.

REFERENCES

Bailey, F. G. 1959. "For a Sociology of India?" *Contributions to Indian Sociology* 3:88–101; 4:82–89.

Baldwin, J. M., ed. 1957. *Dictionary of Philosophy and Psychology*. Gloucester: Peter Smith. (Originally published 1901–1905.)

Barnett, S., L. Fruzetti, and A. Ostor. 1976. "Hierarchy Purified: Notes on Dumont and His Critics." *Journal of Asian Studies* 35(4):627–46.

Barthes, R. 1970 [1963]. *Elements of Semiology*. Boston: Beacon Press.

Bateson, G. 1958 [1936]. *Naven*. Stanford: Stanford University Press.

———. 1972. *Steps to an Ecology of Mind*. New York: Ballantine Books.

Bateson, G., and M. Mead. 1942. *Balinese Character: A Photographic Analysis*. New York: New York Academy of Sciences.

Bateson, G., and J. Ruesch. 1968 [1951]. *Communication: The Social Matrix of Psychiatry*. New York: Norton.

Baxtin, M. 1973. *Problems of Dostoevsky's Poetics*. Ann Arbor: University of Michigan Press.

Bean, S. S. 1978. *Symbolic and Pragmatic Semantics: A Kannada System of Address*. Chicago: University of Chicago Press.

Beckett, S. 1974. *That Time*. New York: Grove Press.

Bendix, R. 1960. *Max Weber; An Intellectual Portrait*. Garden City, N.Y.: Doubleday.

Benedict, R. 1934. *Patterns of Culture*. Boston: Houghton Mifflin.

Benveniste, E. 1971 [1966]. *Problems in General Linguistics*. "Saussure after Half a Century," 29–40. "The Nature of the Linguistic Sign," 43–48. "The Nature of Pronouns," 217–22. "Subjectivity in Language," 223–30. Coral Gables, Fla.: University of Miami Press.

Beteille, A., and T. N. Madan, eds. 1975. *Encounter and Experience: Personal Accounts of Fieldwork*. Honolulu: University Press of Hawaii.

Bhagavata Purana, The Wisdom of God. 1947. Trans. Swami Prabhavananda. Mylapore, Madras: Sri Ramakrishna Math.

Boas, F. 1911a. "Introduction." *Handbook of American Indian Languages*, Pt. I. B.A.E. Bull. 40. Washington, D.C.: U.S. Govt. Printing Office. Reprinted in Hymes 1964.

———. 1911b. *The Mind of Primitive Man*. New York: Macmillan Co.

———. 1974. *The Shaping of American Anthropology, 1883–1911. A Franz Boas Reader*, ed. G. W. Stocking, Jr. New York: Basic Books, Inc.

Bondurant, J. 1965. *Conquest of Violence*. Berkeley: University of California Press.

Boon, J. A. 1972. *From Symbolism to Structuralism*. New York: Harper & Row.

———. 1983. *Other Tribes, Other Scribes: Symbolic Anthropology in the Comparative Study of Cultures, Histories, Religions and Texts*. Cambridge: Cambridge University Press.

Boon, J. A., and D. M. Schneider. 1974. "Kinship *vis-à-vis* Myth: Contrasts in Lévi-Strauss' Approaches to Cross-Cultural Comparison." *American Anthropologist* 76(4):799–817.
Börgstrom, B. E. 1980. "The Best of Two Worlds: Rhetoric of Autocracy and Democracy in Nepal." *Contributions to Indian Sociology*, n.s. 14:35–50.
Brown, R. W., and A. Gilman. 1960. "The Pronouns of Power and Solidarity." In *Aspects of Style in Language*, ed T. A. Sebeok. New York: John Wiley & Sons.
Brown, W. N. 1966. *Man in the Universe: Some Continuities in Indian Thought.* Berkeley: University of California Press.
Buber, M. 1970 [1923]. *I and Thou.* A New Translation with a Prologue and Notes. New York: Charles Scribner's Sons.
Burke, K. 1966. *Language as Symbolic Action.* Berkeley: University of California Press.
Burks, A. W. 1948–49. "Icon, Index, and Symbol." *Philosophy and Phenomenological Research* 9:673–89.
Carnap, R. 1937. *The Logical Syntax of Language.* New York: Harcourt, Brace.
———. 1939. *Foundations of Logic and Mathematics.* International Encyclopedia of Unified Science. Vol. 1, Part 1. Chicago: University of Chicago Press.
———. 1942. *Introduction to Semantics.* Cambridge: Harvard University Press.
———. 1943. *Formalization of Logic.* Cambridge: Harvard University Press.
———. 1956 [1947]. *Meaning and Necessity, A Study in Semantics and Modal Logic.* Chicago: University of Chicago Press.
Cassirer, E. 1953. *Philosophy of Symbolic Forms.* 3 vols. New Haven: Yale University Press.
———. 1976 [1944]. *An Essay on Man.* New Haven: Yale University Press.
Cherry, C. 1966. *On Human Communication.* 2d ed. Cambridge: MIT Press.
Chomsky, N. 1968. *Language and Mind.* New York: Harcourt, Brace.
Cohen, A. 1974. *Two Dimensional Man.* Berkeley: University of California Press.
Cohen, S. 1981. Review of Weiner 1978. *Journal of Asian Studies* 40:415–17.
Colby, B. N., J. W. Fernandez, and D. B. Kronenfeld. 1981. "Toward a Convergence of Cognitive and Symbolic Anthropology." *American Ethnologist* 8:422–50.
Cooley, C. H. 1908. "A Study of the Early Use of Self-Words by a Child." *Psychological Review*, n.s. XV:6.
———. 1922. *Human Nature and the Social Order.* New York: Charles Scribner's Sons.
———. 1929 [1919]. *Social Organization: A Study of the Larger Mind.* New York: Charles Scribner's Sons.
Coomaraswamy, A., and G. K. Duggirala. 1936. *The Mirror of Gesture.* New Delhi: Munishiram Manoharlal.
Crane, W. 1912. "Art and Character." In *Character and Life, A Symposium*, ed. P. C. Parker. London: Williams and Norgate.
———. 1914 [1898]. *The Bases of Design.* London: G. Bell and Sons.
Curley, James M. 1931. *Tercentenary of the Founding of Boston.* Boston City Council.
Davidson, D. and G. Harman, eds. 1972. *Semantics of Natural Language.* New York: Humanities.
De Laguna, G. A. 1927. *Speech, Its Function and Development.* New Haven: Yale University Press.
Derrida, J. 1973. *Speech and Phenomena and Other Essays on Husserl's Theory of Signs.* Evanston: Northwestern University Press.

Desai, M., ed. 1946. *The Gita According to Gandhi*. Ahmedabad: Navajivam.

Deutsch, E., and J. A. B. van Buitenen, eds. 1971. *A Source Book of Advaita Vedanta*. Honolulu: University Press of Hawaii.

Devereux, G. 1976. *Dreams in Greek Tragedy: An Ethno-psycho-analytical Study*. Berkeley: University of California Press.

Dewey, J. 1925. *Experience and Nature*. Chicago: Open Court.

———. 1930 [1922]. *Human Nature and Conduct*. Modern Library.

———. 1946. "Peirce's Theory of Linguistic Signs, Thought and Meaning." *Journal of Philosophy* 43:85–95.

Dolgin, J. L., D. S. Kemnitzer, and D. M. Schneider, eds. 1977. *Symbolic Anthropology: A Reader in the Study of Symbols and Meanings*. New York: Columbia University Press.

Douglas, M. 1966. *Purity and Danger: An Analysis of Concepts of Pollution and Taboo*. London: Routledge & Kegan Paul.

———. 1973 [1970]. *Natural Symbols*. New York: Pantheon.

Dumont, L. 1957. "For a Sociology of India." *Contributions to Indian Sociology*. Reprinted in Dumont 1970.

———. 1970. *Religion/Politics and History in India: Collected Papers in Indian Sociology*. Paris/The Hague: Mouton.

———. 1980 [1966]. *Homo Hierarchicus, The Caste System and Its Implications*. Chicago: University of Chicago Press.

Durbin, M. 1974. "Comments to George Mounin's 'Lévi-Strauss' Use of Linguistics.'" In Rossi 1974.

Durkheim, E. 1947 [1915]. *The Elementary Forms of the Religious Life*. Glencoe, Ill.: Free Press.

Durkheim, E., and M. Mauss. 1963 [1903]. *Primitive Classification*. Trans. R. Needham. Chicago: University of Chicago Press.

Eco, U. 1976. *A Theory of Semiotics*. Bloomington: Indiana University Press.

Edgerton, F. 1942. "Dominant Ideas in the Formation of Indian Culture." *Journal of the American Oriental Society* 62:151–56.

Eggan, F., ed. 1955. *Social Anthropology of the North American Tribes*. Chicago: University of Chicago Press.

———. 1966. *The American Indian*. Chicago: Aldine.

———. 1968. "Kinship Systems." *International Encyclopedia of the Social Sciences* 8:396.

———. 1974. "Among the Anthropologists." In *Annual Review of Anthropology*, vol. 3. Stanford: Stanford University Press.

Erikson, E. H. 1969. *Gandhi's Truth: On the Origins of Militant Nonviolence*. New York: Norton.

Evans-Pritchard, E. 1951. *Social Anthropology*. London: Cohen and West.

Filliozat, J. 1970. "Scientific Thought in Ancient Asia." *East and West* 6:285–92.

Fillmore, C. J. 1972. "Toward a Theory of Deixis." Mimeo.

Firth, J. R. 1957. "Ethnographic Analysis and Language with Reference to Malinowski's Views." In R. Firth 1957.

Firth, R., ed. 1957. *Man and Culture: An Evaluation of the Work of Bronislaw Malinowski*. London: Routledge & Kegan Paul.

———. 1963 [1951]. *Elements of Social Organization*. Boston: Beacon Press.

———. 1973. *Symbols: Public and Private*. Ithaca: Cornell University Press.

Fisch, M. H. 1978. "Peirce's General Theory of Signs." In *Sight, Sound, and Sense*, ed. T.A. Sebeok. Bloomington: Indiana University Press.

———. 1979. Presidential address to the Semiotic Society of America. Bloomington, Indiana, October 6, 1979.

———. N.d. Preface to the Edition as a whole (draft).

———. N.d. Introduction to Volume I (1857–1866) (draft).

———. 1981. "Peirce as Scientist, Mathematician, Historian, Logician, and Philosopher." In Ketner et al. 1981.

———. 1982. "The Range of Peirce's Relevance, Part II." *The Monist* 65:123–41.

Flannery, K. V. 1982. "The Golden Marshalltown: A Parable for the Archaeology of the 1980s." *American Anthropologist* 84(2):265–78.

Fortes, M. 1966. "Totem and Taboo." *Proceedings of the Royal Anthropological Institute*, 1966.

Fortes, M., and G. Dieterlen, eds. 1965. *African Systems of Thought*. Oxford: Oxford University Press.

Freeman, E. 1934. *The Categories of Charles S. Peirce*. Chicago: Open Court.

Freud, S. 1927. *The Ego and the Id*. London: Hogarth Press.

———. 1938. "The Interpretation of Dreams." In *The Basic Writings of Sigmund Freud*, trans. and ed. Dr. A. A. Brill. New York: Modern Library (condensation: 320–36, 653–55).

———. 1949 [1922]. *Group Psychology and the Analysis of the Ego*. Trans. J. Strachey. New York: Liveright.

———. 1953 [1930]. *Civilization and Its Discontents*. London: Hogarth Press.

Friedrich, P. 1977. "Sanity and the Myth of Honor: The Problem of Achilles." *Ethos* 5:281–395.

———. 1978. *The Meaning of Aphrodite*. Chicago: University of Chicago Press.

———. 1979. *Language, Context and the Imagination*. Ed. A. S. Dil. Stanford: Stanford University Press. Includes "Structural Implications of Russian Pronominal Usage" (1966); "Speech as a Personality Symbol: The Case of Achilles" (1978); "The Symbol and Its Relative Non-Arbitrariness" (1978).

Friedrich, P., and J. Redfield. 1978. "Speech as a Personality Symbol: The Case of Achilles." *Language* 54:263–89.

Fuss, P. 1965. *The Moral Philosophy of Josiah Royce*. Cambridge: Harvard University Press.

Gallie, W. B. 1966. *Peirce and Pragmatism*. New York: Dover.

Geertz, C., ed. 1971. *Myth, Symbol and Culture*. New York: Norton.

———. 1973. *The Interpretation of Cultures*. New York: Basic Books. Includes "Person, Time, and Conduct in Bali: An Essay in Cultural Analysis" (1966a); "Religion as a Cultural System" (1966b); "The Cerebral Savage" (1967); "Thick Description: Toward an Interpretive Theory of Culture" (1973).

———. 1974. "From the Natives' Point of View: On the Nature of Anthropological Understanding." *Bulletin of The American Academy of Arts and Sciences* 28 (no. 1).

———. 1976. "Art as a Cultural System." *MLN* 91:1473–99.

———. 1980a. "Blurred Genres: The Refiguration of Social Thought." *The American Scholar* 49:165–79.

———. 1980b. *Negara, the Theatre State in Nineteenth-Century Bali*. Princeton: Princeton University Press.

Goldenweiser, A. 1910. "Totemism: An Analytical Study." *Journal of American Folklore* 23:179–293.

———. 1918. "Form and Content in Totemism." *American Anthropologist* 20:280–95.

———. 1931. "Totemism: An Essay on Religion and Society." In *The Making of*

Man, ed. V. F. Calverton. New York: Modern Library. Reprinted in abridged form in *Reader in Comparative Religion,* ed. W. A. Lessa and E. Z. Vogt. New York: Harper & Row, 1965.

———. 1937. *Anthropology, An Introduction to Primitive Culture.* New York: F. S. Crofts & Co.

Goodenough, W. H. 1956. "Componential Analysis and the Study of Meaning." *Language* 32:195–216.

———. 1965. "Yankee Kinship Terminology: A Problem in Componential Analysis." In *Formal Semantic Analysis,* ed. E. A. Hammel. *American Anthropologist* 67(5), pt. 2.

———. 1970. *Description and Comparison in Cultural Anthropology.* Chicago: Aldine.

———. 1974. "Culture, Language, and Society." In *Addison-Wesley Module in Anthropology,* No. 7. Reading, Mass.: Addison-Wesley.

Goudge, T. A. 1959. *The Thought of C. S. Peirce.* Toronto: University of Toronto Press.

Grabes, H. 1975. *Speculum, Mirror und Looking-Glass.* Tubingen: Max Niemeyer Verlag.

Granet, M. 1973 [1933]. "Right and Left in China." In *Right and Left, Essays on Dual Symbolic Classification.* Chicago: University of Chicago Press.

Greenberg, J. H. 1957. *Essays in Linguistics.* Chicago: University of Chicago Press.

———, ed. 1963. *Universals in Language.* Cambridge: MIT Press.

———. 1964 [1948]. "Linguistics and Ethnology." In Hymes 1964:27–31.

Griaule, M. 1965. *Conversations with Ogotêmmli: An Introduction to Dogon Religious Ideas.* Oxford: International African Institute.

Groddeck, G., M.D. 1961 [1923]. *The Book of the It.* New York: New American Library.

Grossman, C. M., and S. Grossman. 1965. *The Wild Analyst: The Life and Work of George Groddeck.* New York: Braziller.

Hallowell, A. I. 1955. "The Self and Its Behavioral Environment." In *Culture and Experience.* Philadelphia: University of Pennsylvania Press.

Heimann, B. 1964. *Some Aspects of Indian Thought.* London: Allen & Unwin Ltd.

Hiatt, L. R. 1969. "Totemism Tomorrow: The Future of an Illusion." *Mankind* 7:83–93.

Hoijer, H., ed. 1954. *Language in Culture.* Chicago: University of Chicago Press. Includes Hoijer, "The Sapir-Whorf Hypothesis."

Hymes, D. 1961. "Linguistic Aspects of Cross-Cultural Personality Study." In *Studying Personality Cross-Culturally,* ed. B. Kaplan. Evanston, Ill.: Row, Peterson.

———, ed. 1964. *Language in Culture and Society.* Foreword by A. L. Kroeber. New York: Harper & Row.

———. 1971. "Sociolinguistics and the Ethnography of Speaking." In *Social Anthropology and Language,* ed. E. Ardener. London: Tavistock.

Hymes, D., and J. J. Gumperz, eds. 1970. *Directions in Sociolinguistics: The Ethnography of Speaking.* New York: Holt, Rinehart, & Winston.

Ingalls, D. H. H. 1951. *Materials for the Study of Navya-Nyāya Logic.* Cambridge: Harvard University Press.

Iyer, R. 1973. *The Moral and Political Thought of Mahatma Gandhi.* New York: Oxford University Press.

Jakobson, R. 1971. *Selected Writings II.* The Hague: Mouton. Especially "Linguistics and Communication Theory" (1961); "Linguistics in Relation to Other Sciences" (1967); "Language in Relation to Other Communication Systems" (1968); and "Visual and Auditory Signs" (1971).

———. 1973. "The Place of Linguistics Among the Sciences of Man." In *Main Trends in the Science of Language*, ed. R. Jakobson. London: George Allen & Unwin Ltd., New York: Harper & Row.

———. 1975. "Coup d'oeil sur le development de la semiotique." Bloomington, Ind.: Research Center for Language and Semiotic Studies.

———. 1978 [1940]. *Six Lectures on Sound and Meaning*, with a preface by Claude Lévi-Strauss. Cambridge: MIT Press.

James, W. 1904. *The Principles of Psychology*. 2 vols. New York: Henry Holt.

———. 1961 [1891]. *Psychology: The Briefer Course*, ed. with an intro. by Gordon Allport. New York: Harper Torchbooks.

Kakar, S. 1978. *The Inner World: A Psycho-analytic Study of Childhood and Society in India*. Delhi, Oxford, New York: Oxford University Press.

———. 1979a. *Identity and Adulthood*. Delhi: Oxford University Press.

———. 1979b. *Indian Childhood: Cultural Ideals and Social Reality*. Delhi: Oxford University Press.

Kant, I. 1855 [1787]. *Critique of Pure Reason*. Trans. J. M. D. Meiklejohn. London: G. Bohn.

Kaplan, B. 1968. "The Method of the Study of Persons." In *The Study of Personality*, ed. E. Norbeck et al. New York: Holt, Rinehart, & Winston.

Keesing, R. M. 1974. "Theories of Culture." In *Annual Review of Anthropology*, Vol. 3.

Ketner, K. L., et al. 1981. *Proceedings of the C. S. Peirce Bicentennial International Congress*. Lubbock, Tex.: Texas Tech. Press.

Kleene, S. C. 1952. *Introduction to Metamathematics*. Princeton: Van Nostrand.

Kloesel, C. J. W. 1981. "Speculative Grammar from Duns Scotus to Charles Peirce." In Ketner et al. 1981.

Kohut, H. 1977. *The Restoration of the Self*. New York: International Universities Press.

Krader, L. 1974. "Beyond Structuralism: The Dialectics of the Diachronic and Synchronic Methods in the Human Sciences." In Rossi 1974.

Kristeva, J. 1973. "The System and the Speaking Subject." *Times Literary Supplement*, 12 October 1973.

Kristeva, J., J. Rey-Debove, and D. J. Umiker. 1971. *Essays in Semiotics*. The Hague: Mouton.

Kroeber, A. L. 1944. *Configurations of Culture Growth*. Berkeley: University of California Press.

———. 1948 [1923]. *Anthropology: Race, Language, Culture, Psychology, Prehistory*. New York: Harcourt, Brace.

———. 1952. *The Nature of Culture*. Chicago: University of Chicago Press.

———, ed. 1953. *Anthropology Today: An Encyclopedic Inventory*. Chicago: University of Chicago Press.

———. 1957. *Style and Civilizations*. Ithaca: Cornell University Press.

———. 1963. *An Anthropologist Looks at History*, ed. T. Kroeber. Berkeley: University of California Press.

Kroeber, A. L., and C. Kluckhohn. 1963. *Culture: A Critical Review of Concepts and Definitions*. New York: Vintage.

Kroeber, A. L., and T. Parsons. 1958. "The Concepts of Culture and of Social System." *American Sociological Review* 23:582–83.

Kroeber, T. 1970. *Alfred Kroeber, A Personal Configuration*. Berkeley: University of California Press.

References

Krois, J. M. 1981. "Peirce and Cassirer: The Philosophical Importance of a Theory of Signs." In Ketner et al. 1981.

Lacan, J. 1968. *Language of the Self.* Baltimore: Johns Hopkins University Press.

Langer, S. 1942. *Philosophy in a New Key.* Cambridge: Harvard University Press.

Leach, E. 1957. "The Epistemological Background to Malinowski's Empiricism." In R. Firth 1957.

————. 1961a. "Lévi-Strauss in the Garden of Eden." *Trans. of the New York Academy of Sciences* 23:386–96.

————. 1961b. "Rethinking Anthropology." In *Rethinking Anthropology.* London: University of London, Athlone Press.

————, ed. 1967. *The Structural Study of Myth and Totemism.* London: Tavistock.

————. 1970. *Claude Lévi-Strauss.* New York: Viking Press.

————. 1976. *Culture and Communication.* Cambridge: Cambridge University Press.

Leaf, M. J. 1979. *Man, Mind and Science: A History of Anthropology.* New York: Columbia University Press.

Lee, B., ed. 1982. *Psychosocial Theories of the Self.* New York: Plenum.

Lévi-Strauss, C. 1958. *Tristes Tropiques.* New York: Atheneum.

————. 1963a. *Totemism.* Boston: Beacon Press. First published in France in 1962.

————. 1963b. "The Bear and the Barber." *Journal of the Royal Anthropological Institute* XCIII:1–11.

————. 1966. *The Savage Mind.* London: Weidenfeld & Nicholson. First published in France in 1962.

————. 1970 [1964]. *The Raw and the Cooked. Introduction to a Science of Mythology,* Volume I. New York: Harper & Row.

————. 1971. *Mythologique IV: L'Homme Nu.* Paris: Plon.

————. 1972. "Structuralism and Ecology." New York: Barnard College.

————. 1976. *Structural Anthropology,* vol. 2 (vol. 1, 1963). New York: Basic Books.

Lincourt, J. M., and P. H. Hare. 1973. "Neglected American Philosophers in the History of Symbolic Interactionism." *Journal of the History of the Behavioral Sciences* 9:333–38.

Lincourt, J. M., and P. V. Olczak. 1974. "C. S. Peirce and H. S. Sullivan on the Human Self." *Psychiatry* 37:78–87.

Linton, R. 1924. "Totemism and the A.E.F." *American Anthropologist* XXVI: 296–300. Reprinted in *Reader in Comparative Religion,* ed. W. Lessa and E. Z. Vogt. New York: Harper & Row, 1965.

Lyons, J. 1977. *Semantics.* 2 Vols. Cambridge: Cambridge University Press.

Mackesey, R., and E. Donato. 1970. *The Language of Criticism and the Sciences of Man: The Structuralism Controversy.* Baltimore: Johns Hopkins University Press.

McNeill, D. 1979. *The Conceptual Basis of Language.* Halsted.

McQuown, N. A. 1972. "The Nature of Culture." In *Studies in Linguistics in Honor of George L. Trager,* ed. M. E. Smith. The Hague: Mouton.

Malinowski, B. 1946 [1923]. "The Problem of Meaning in Primitive Languages." In Ogden and Richards 1946.

————. 1965 [1935]. *The Language of Magic and Gardening.* Bloomington: Indiana University Press.

Maquet, J. 1974. "Isomorphism and Symbolism as 'Explanations' in the Analysis of Myths." In Rossi 1974.

Marquand, J. P. 1960. *Timothy Dexter Revisited.* Boston: Little, Brown & Co.

Marriott, M., ed. 1955. *Village India*. Chicago: University of Chicago Press.
———. 1976a. "Interpreting Indian Society: A Monistic Alternative to Dumont's Dualism." *Journal of Asian Studies* 36(1):189–95.
———. 1976b. "Hindu Transactions: Diversity Without Dualism." In *Transaction and Meaning*, ed. B. Kapferer. Philadelphia: Institute for the Study of Human Issues.
———. 1977. [Remarks]. In *The New Wind: Changing Identities in South Asia*, ed. K. A. David. The Hague: Mouton; Chicago: Aldine.
Matejka, L. 1973. "On the First Russian Prolegomena to Semiotics." Appendix I. In *Marxism and the Philosophy of Language*, ed. V. N. Volosinov. New York: Seminar Press.
Matilal, B. 1977. *The Logical Illumination of Indian Mysticism*. Oxford: Clarendon Press.
Mead, G. H. 1922. "A Behavioristic Account of the Significant Symbol." *Journal of Philosophy* 19:157–63.
———. 1925. "The Genesis of the Self and Social Control." *International Journal of Ethics* 35:251–77.
———. 1929. "National Mindedness and International-Mindedness." *International Journal of Ethics* 39:385–407.
———. 1930a. "Cooley's Contribution to American Social Thought." *American Journal of Sociology* 35:693–705.
———. 1930b. "The Philosophies of Royce, James and Dewey in Their American Setting." *International Journal of Ethics* 40:211–31.
———. 1934. *Mind, Self, and Society*. Ed. C. W. Morris. Chicago: University of Chicago Press.
———. 1977 [1956]. *Selected Papers on Social Psychology*. Ed. A. Strauss. Chicago: University of Chicago Press.
Mead, M. 1939 [1928, 1930, 1935]. *From the South Seas: Studies of Adolescence and Sex in Primitive Societies*. New York: Morrow.
———, ed. 1959. *An Anthropologist at Work: Writings of Ruth Benedict*. Boston: Houghton Mifflin.
———. 1962. "Retrospect and Prospect." In *Anthropology and Human Behavior*. Washington, D.C.: Anthropological Society of Washington.
———. 1972. *Blackberry Winter: My Earlier Years*. New York: Morrow.
Mead, M., and R. Metraux, eds. 1953. *The Study of Culture at a Distance*. Chicago: University of Chicago Press.
Meissner, W. W. 1978. "Theories of Personality." In *The Harvard Guide to Modern Psychiatry*, ed. A. M. Nicoli, Jr. Cambridge: Harvard University Press.
Merleau-Ponty, M. 1964. *Signs*. Evanston: Northwestern University Press.
Miller, D. L. 1973. *George Herbert Mead: Self, Language and the World*. Austin: University of Texas Press.
Miller, D. R. 1961. "Personality and Social Interaction." In *Studying Personality Cross-Culturally*, ed. B. Kaplan, 271–300. Evanston, Ill.: Row, Peterson.
Montague, R. 1974. *Formal Philosophy*. New Haven: Yale University Press.
Morris, C. W. 1948–49. "Signs about Signs about Signs." *Philosophy and Phenomenological Research* 9:124–27.
———. 1955a [1938]. *Foundations of the Theory of Signs*. Chicago: University of Chicago Press.
———. 1955b [1946]. *Signs, Language and Behavior*. New York: Braziller.
———. 1964. *Signification and Significance: A Study of the Relations of Signs and Values*. Cambridge: MIT Press.

————. 1970. *The Pragmatic Movement in American Philosophy*. New York: Braziller.

————. 1971. *Writings on the General Theory of Signs*. The Hague: Mouton.

Munn, N.D. 1973. *Walbiri Iconography*. Ithaca: Cornell University Press.

Murdock, G. P. 1971. "Anthropology's Mythology." Huxley Memorial Lecture, *Proceedings of Royal Anthropological Institute, 1971*.

Murphey, M. G. 1961. *The Development of Peirce's Philosophy*. Cambridge: Harvard University Press.

Musée Guimet. 1964. *Emblèmes Totems Blasons*. Paris: Ministère D'Etat Affaires Culturelles.

Nadel, S. F. 1964 [1951]. *The Foundations of Social Anthropology*. New York: The Free Press of Glencoe.

Nagatomi, M., et al., eds. 1980. *Sanskrit and Indian Studies: Essays in Honor of Daniel H. H. Ingalls*. Boston: Kluwer.

Nagel, E., and J. R. Newman. 1964 [1958]. *Gödel's Proof*. New York: New York University Press.

Natanson, M. 1956. *The Social Dynamics of George Herbert Mead*. Washington, D.C.: Public Affairs Press.

Needham, R. 1972. *Belief, Language, and Experience*. Chicago: University of Chicago Press.

————. 1973. "Introduction." In *Right and Left: Essays on Dual Symbolic Classification*, ed. R. Needham. Chicago: University of Chicago Press.

Nehru, J. 1946. *The Discovery of India*. New York: John Day.

Nida, E. A. 1964 [1945]. "Linguistics and Ethnology in Translation Problems." In Hymes 1964.

O'Flaherty, W., ed. 1980. *Karma and Rebirth in Classical Traditions*. Berkeley and Los Angeles: University of California Press.

Ogden, C. K. and I. A. Richards, eds. 1946 [1923]. *The Meaning of Meaning: A Study of the Influence of Language upon Thought and of the Science of Symbolism*. New York: Harcourt, Brace & World.

Ong, W. J. 1959. "From Allegory to the Diagram in the Renaissance Mind." *Journal of Esthetics and Art Criticism* XVII, no. 4 [June 1959].

Opler, M. E. 1964. "The Human Being in Culture Theory." *American Anthropologist* 66:507–28.

Ortiz, A. 1969. *The Tewa World: Space, Time, Being and Becoming in a Pueblo Society*. Chicago: University of Chicago Press.

Ortner, S. B. 1973. "On Key Symbols." *American Anthropologist* 75:1338–46.

Parsons, T. 1957. "Malinowski and the Theory of Social Systems." In R. Firth 1957.

————. 1968. "Social Interaction." In *International Encyclopedia of Social Sciences* 7:429–41.

————. 1970. "On Building Social System Theory: A Personal History." *Daedalus* 99:826–81.

————. 1972. "Culture and Social System Revisited." *Social Science Quarterly* 53:253–66.

Peacock, J. L. 1975. *Consciousness and Change*. New York: Wiley & Sons.

Peirce, C. S. 1931–58. *Collected Papers*, vols. 1–6, ed. C. Hartshorne and P. Weiss; vols. 7–8, ed. A. W. Burks. Cambridge: Harvard University Press.

————. 1955 [1940]. *Philosophical Writings of Peirce*. Ed. J. Buchler. New York: Dover Publications.

————. 1974. *The New Elements of Mathematics* III (Pt. 1). Ed. C. Eisele. The Hague: Mouton.

————. 1977. *Semiotic and Significs: The Correspondence of Charles S. Peirce and Victoria Lady Welby*. Ed. C. S. Hardwick. Bloomington: Indiana University Press.

————. 1978. "Ideas, Stray or Stolen, about Scientific Writing." *Philosophy and Rhetoric* 2:147–55. With a bibliographic note by J. M. Krois.

————. 1982. *Writings of Charles S. Peirce*. A Chronological Edition. Volume I, 1857–1866. Bloomington: Indiana University Press.

Peirce, C. S., and J. Jastrow. 1885. "On Small Differences in Sensation." Washington, D.C.: National Academy of Sciences.

Perry, R. B. 1926. *General Theory of Value*. New York: Longmans, Green.

Piaget, J. 1971. *Structuralism*. New York: Harper & Row.

Piatagorsky, A., and D. Zilberman. 1976. "The Emergence of Semiotics in India." *Semiotica* 17:255–65.

Piers, G., and M. Singer. 1973 [1953]. *Shame and Guilt: A Psychoanalytic and a Cultural Study*. New York: Norton.

Popper, K. R., and J. C. Eccles. 1977. *The Self and Its Brain*. Berlin: Springer International.

Porter, J. A. 1979. *The Drama of Speech Acts*. Berkeley: University of California Press.

Praz, M. 1964 [1939]. *Studies in Seventeenth Century Imagery*. Rome: Edizioni di Storia e Letteratura.

Quine, W. 1960. *Word and Object*. Cambridge: MIT Press.

————. 1973. *The Roots of Reference*. La Salle, Ill.: Open Court.

————. 1981. *Theories and Things*. Cambridge: Harvard University Press.

Rabinow, P. 1977. *Reflections on Fieldwork in Morocco*. Berkeley: University of California Press.

Radcliffe-Brown, A. R. 1948 [1922, 1933]. *The Andaman Islanders*. Glencoe, Ill.: Free Press.

————. 1952. *Structure and Function in Primitive Society*. London: Cohen & West.

————. 1957. *A Natural Science of Society*. Glencoe, Ill.: Free Press.

————. 1958. *Method in Social Anthropology*, ed. M. N. Srinivas. Chicago: University of Chicago Press.

Radhakrishnan, S., and C. A. Moore. 1957. *A Source Book in Indian Philosophy*. Princeton: Princeton University Press.

Raghavan, V. 1955. "Some Leading Ideas of Hindu Thought." *The Vedanta Kesari* (February 1955).

————. 1956. *The Indian Heritage: An Anthology of Sanskrit Literature*. UNESCO Collection of Representative Works. Bangalore: The Indian Institute of Culture.

————. 1966. *The Great Integrators: The Saint-Singers of India*. Delhi: Government of India Publications Division.

Redfield, J. 1975. *Nature and Culture in the Iliad: The Tragedy of Hector*. Chicago: University of Chicago Press.

Redfield, R. 1941. *The Folk Culture of Yucatan*. Chicago: University of Chicago Press.

————. 1954. "The Cultural Role of Cities" (with M. Singer). *Economic Development and Cultural Change* 3 (1): 53–77.

————. 1955a. *The Little Community*. Chicago: University of Chicago Press.

————. 1955b. "The Social Organization of Tradition." *Far Eastern Quarterly* 15:13–21.

————. 1956. *Peasant Society and Culture*. Chicago: University of Chicago Press.

————. 1962. *Human Nature and the Study of Society: The Papers of Robert Redfield*, ed.

Margaret Park Redfield. Chicago: University of Chicago Press.
———. 1963 [1953]. "Does America Need a Hearing Aid?" Reprinted in *The Social Uses of Social Science*. Chicago: University of Chicago Press.
Richards, I. A. 1967. "African Systems of Thought: An Anglo-French Dialogue." *Man, the Journal of the Royal Anthropological Institute*, n.s. 2:2.
Ricoeur, P. 1974. "The Question of the Subject." In *The Conflict of Interpretations: Essays in Hermeneutics*, ed. D. Ihde. Evanston: Northwestern University Press.
———. 1979 [1970]. "The Model of the Text: Meaningful Action Considered as a Text. In *Interpretive Social Science: A Reader*, ed. P. Rabinow and W. Sullivan. Berkeley: University of California Press.
Riesman, P. 1977. *Freedom in Fulani Social Life: An Introspective Ethnography*. Chicago: University of Chicago Press.
Rolland, R. 1924. *Mahatma Gandhi*. London: Allen & Unwin.
Rorty, R. 1979. *Philosophy and the Mirror of Nature*. Princeton: Princeton University Press.
Rosen, L. 1971. "Language, History, and the Logic of Inquiry in the Works of Lévi-Strauss and Sartre." In Rossi 1974.
Rossi, I., ed. 1974. *The Unconscious in Culture, The Structuralism of Claude Lévi-Strauss in Perspective*. New York: E. P. Dutton.
Royce, J. 1913. *The Problem of Christianity*, vol. II. New York: Macmillan.
———. 1970. *The Letters of Josiah Royce*. Ed. with an intro. by J. Clendenning. Chicago: University of Chicago Press.
Russell, B. 1948. *Human Knowledge: Its Scope and Limits*. New York: Simon & Schuster.
———. 1959. *My Philosophical Development*. New York: Simon & Schuster.
———. 1971 [1921]. *The Analysis of Mind*. London: Allen & Unwin.
———. 1980 [1940]. *An Inquiry into Meaning and Truth*. London: Unwin Paperbacks.
Sahlins, M. 1976. *Culture and Practical Reason*. Chicago: University of Chicago Press.
———. 1981. *Historical Metaphors and Mythical Realities*. Ann Arbor: University of Michigan Press.
Sapir, E. 1949a [1922]. *Language*. New York: Harcourt, Brace.
———. 1949b. *Selected Writings in Language, Culture, and Personality*, ed. D. Mandelbaum. Berkeley: University of California Press.
Saussure, F. 1966 [1915]. *Course in General Linguistics*. New York: McGraw-Hill.
Scheffler, H. W. 1966. "Structuralism in Anthropology." In *Structuralism*, ed. J. Ehrmann. *Yale French Studies* 66:80.
Schneider, D. M. 1965. "Some Muddles in the Models; Or, How the System Really Works." In *The Relevance of Models for Social Anthropology*, ed. M. Banton. New York: Praeger.
———. 1968a. *American Kinship: A Cultural Account*. Englewood Cliffs, N.J.: Prentice-Hall, 1968.
———. 1968b. "Rivers and Kroeber in the Study of Kinship." In Rivers, W. H. R., *Kinship and Social Organization*. Humanities Press.
———. 1969. "Kinship, Nationality and Religion in American Culture: Towards a Definition of Kinship." In *Forms of Symbolic Action*, ed. V. Turner. Proc. Amer. Ethnol. Soc.
———. 1976. "Notes Toward a Theory of Culture." In *Meaning in Anthropology*, ed. K. Basso and H. Selby. Albuquerque: University of New Mexico Press.

————. 1979. "Kinship, Community, and Locality in American Culture." In *Kin and Communities*, ed. A. J. Lichtman and J. R. Challinor. Washington, D.C.: Smithsonian.

Schneider, L., and C. Bonjean, eds. 1973. *The Idea of Culture in the Social Sciences*. Cambridge: Cambridge University Press.

Schoolcraft, H. 1851. *Historical and Statistical Information Respecting the History, Condition and Prospect of the Indian Tribes of the United States*. Philadelphia: Lippincott & Co.

Schutz, A. 1962. "The Problem of Social Reality." In *Collected Papers*, ed. I. M. Natanson. The Hague: Martinus Nijhoff.

Schwartz, T. 1975. "Cultural Totemism: Ethnic Identity, Primitive and Modern." In *Ethnic Identity, Cultural Continuities and Change*, ed. G. DeVos and L. Romanucci-Ross. Palo Alto: Mayfield Publishing Co.

Searle, J., ed. 1971. *The Philosophy of Language*. London: Oxford University Press.

Sebeok, T. A., ed. 1960. *Style in Language*. Cambridge, Mass.: MIT Press.

————. 1976. *Contributions to the Doctrine of Signs*. Bloomington: Research Center for Language and Semiotic Studies, Indiana University.

————. 1979. "The Semiotic Self." In *The Sign and Its Masters*. Appendix I. Austin: University of Texas Press.

————. 1981. *The Play of Musement*. Bloomington: Indiana University Press.

Sebeok, T. A., A. S. Hayes, and M. C. Bateson, eds. 1964. *Approaches to Semiotics*. The Hague: Mouton.

Sebeok, T. A., and J. Umiker-Sebeok. 1979. "You Know My Method: A Juxtaposition of Charles S. Peirce and Sherlock Holmes." *Semiotica* 26:203–50. Also in Sebeok 1981.

Segre, C. 1973. *Semiotics and Literary Criticism*. The Hague: Mouton.

Semeka-Pankratov, E. 1979. "A Semiotic Approach to the Polysemy of the Symbol *Nāga* in Indian Mythology." *Semiotica* 27:237–90.

Shands, H. C. 1978. "Verbal Patterns and Medical Disease: Prophylactic Implications of Learning." In *Sight, Sound, and Sense*, ed. T. A. Sebeok. Bloomington: Indiana University Press.

Sheean, V. 1949. *Lead Kindly Light*. New York: Random House.

Silverstein, M. 1972. "Linguistic Theory: Syntax, Semantics, Pragmatics." *Annual Review of Anthropology* 1:349–82.

————. 1975. "La Sémiotique Jakobsonienne et L'Anthropologie Sociale." *L'Arc* 60:45–49 (Paris).

————. 1976. "Shifters, Linguistic Categories, and Cultural Description." In *Meaning in Anthropology*, ed. K. Basso and H. Selby. Albuquerque: University of New Mexico Press.

————. 1979. "Language Structure and Linguistic Ideology." In *The Elements: A Parasession on Linguistic Units and Levels*, ed. P. R. Clyne et al., pp. 193–247. Chicago: Chicago Linguistic Society.

————. 1981. "Reinventing the Will: A Philosophy of the Elements of the Human Mind." *Reviews in Anthropology* 8:311–34.

Singer, M. 1955. "The Cultural Pattern of Indian Civilization." *The Far Eastern Quarterly* 15:23–36.

————. 1956. "Cultural Values in India's Economic Development." *The Annals* 305:81–91.

————, ed. 1958. *Traditional India: Structure and Change*. Philadelphia: American Folklore Society. Available through University of Texas Press.

————. 1961. "A Survey of Personality and Culture Theory and Research. In

Studying Personality Cross-Culturally, ed. B. Kaplan, Evanston, Ill.: Row, Peterson.

———. 1968a. "Culture." *International Encyclopedia of the Social Sciences* 3:527–43.

———, ed. 1968b [1966]. *Krishna: Myths, Rites and Attitudes*. Chicago: University of Chicago Press; Honolulu: University Press of Hawaii.

———. 1976. "Robert Redfield's Development of a Social Anthropology of Civilizations." In *American Anthropology: The Early Years*, ed. J. Murra. St. Paul: West Publishing Co. and American Ethnological Society.

———. 1977. "The Symbolic and Historic Structure of an American Identity." *Ethos* 5:428–54.

———. 1978. "For a Semiotic Anthropology." In *Sight, Sound, and Sense*, ed. T. A. Sebeok. Bloomington: Indiana University Press.

———. 1980a. "Signs of the Self: An Exploration in Semiotic Anthropology." *American Anthropologist* (September) 82:485–507.

———. 1980b [1972]. *When a Great Tradition Modernizes: An Anthropological Approach to Indian Civilization*. Chicago: University of Chicago Press.

———. 1981. "On the Semiotics of Indian Identity." *American Journal of Semiotics* 7:85–126.

———. 1982a. "Emblems of Identity: A Semiotic Exploration." In *Symbols in Anthropology*, ed. J. Maquet. Malibu: Undena Publishers.

———. 1982b. "Personal and Social Identity in Dialogue." In *Psychosocial Theories of the Self*, ed. B. Lee. New York: Plenum.

———. 1984. "A Neglected Source of Structuralism: Radcliffe-Brown, Russell and Whitehead." *Semiotica*. In press.

Spencer, R. F., ed. 1969. "Forms of Symbolic Action." *Proc. Amer. Ethnol. Soc.* Seattle: University of Washington Press.

Sperber, D. 1974. *Rethinking Symbolism*. Cambridge: Cambridge University Press.

Spiro, M. E. 1970. *Buddhism and Society: A Great Tradition and Its Burmese Vicissitudes*. New York: Harper & Row.

———. 1979. "Whatever Happened to the Id?" *American Anthropologist* 81:5–13.

Srinivas, M. N. 1952. *Religion and Society among the Coorgs of South India*. London and New York: Oxford University Press.

———. 1962. *Caste in Modern India and Other Essays*. Bombay: Asia Publishing House.

———. 1966. *Social Change in Modern India*. Berkeley: University of California Press.

———. 1973. "Itineraries of an Indian Social Anthropologist." *Int. Soc. Sci. J.* 25:129–48.

———. 1976. *The Remembered Village*. Berkeley: University of California Press.

Staal, J. F. 1966. "Indian Semantics, I." *Journal of the American Oriental Society* 86:304–11.

———. 1971. "What Was Left of Pragmatics in Jerusalem." *Language Sciences* 14:29–32.

———. 1979. "The Meaninglessness of Ritual." *Numen. International Journal of the History of Religions* 26:2–22.

Stanner, W. E. H. 1965. "Religion, Totemism and Symbolism." In *Aboriginal Man in Australia*, ed. R. M. Berndt and C. G. Berndt. Sydney: Angus & Robertson.

Stocking, G. W., Jr. 1968. "Matthew Arnold, E. B. Tylor, and the Uses of Invention," and "Franz Boas and the Culture Concept in Historical Perspective." Reprinted in Stocking, *Race, Culture, and Evolution*. New York: Free Press.

Sullivan, H. S. 1953. *The Interpersonal Theory of Psychiatry.* New York: Norton.
Tambiah, S. J. 1973. "Form and Meaning of Magical Acts: A Point of View." In *Modes of Thought: Essays on Thinking in Western and Non-Western Societies,* ed. R. Horton and R. Finnegan. London: Faber & Faber.
Tarn, N. 1976. "The Heraldic Vision: A Cognitive Model for Comparative Aesthetics." *Alcheringa: Ethnopoetics* 2, no. 2.
Tarski, A. 1956. "The Establishment of Scientific Semantics," and "The Concept of Truth in Formalized Languages." In *Logic, Semantics, and Metamathematics,* ed. A. Tarski. London: Oxford University Press.
Thernstrom, S. 1971 [1964]. *Poverty and Progress.* New York: Atheneum.
Thompson, M. 1953. *The Pragmatic Philosophy of C. S. Peirce.* Chicago: University of Chicago Press.
Turner, T. 1983. "Dual Opposition, Hierarchy, and Value: Moiety Structure and Symbolic Polarity in Central Brazil and Elsewhere."
Turner, V. 1967. *The Forest of Symbols: Aspects of Ndembu Ritual.* Ithaca: Cornell University Press.
———. 1968. "Myth and Symbol." *International Encyclopedia of Social Sciences* 10:576–82.
———. 1969. *The Ritual Process: Structure and Anti-Structure,* esp. chap. V. Chicago: Aldine.
———. 1974. *Dramas, Fields, and Metaphors.* Ithaca: Cornell University Press.
———. 1975. "Symbolic Studies." *Annual Review of Anthropology* 4:145–61.
———. 1982 [1974]. "Liminal to Liminoid, in Play, Flow, and Ritual." In *From Ritual to Theatre: The Human Seriousness of Play.* New York: Performing Arts Journal Publications.
Tyler, S. A., ed. 1969. *Cognitive Anthropology.* New York: Holt, Rinehart & Winston.
———. 1978. *The Said and the Unsaid: Mind, Meaning, and Culture.* New York: Academic Press.
Tylor, E. B. 1958 [1871]. *Primitive Culture.* 2 vols. Gloucester, Mass.: Peter Smith.
Umiker-Sebeok, D. J. 1977. "Semiotics of Culture: Great Britain and North America." *Annual Review of Anthropology* 6:121–35.
Umiker-Sebeok, D. J., and T. A. Sebeok, eds. 1976. *Aboriginal Sign Languages of the Americas and Australia.* New York: Plenum Press.
Uspensky, B. 1976. *The Semiotics of the Russian Icon,* ed. S. Rudy. Lisse: de Ridder Press.
van Buitenen, J. A. B., ed. and trans. 1956. *Ramanuja's Vedarthasamagraha.* Poona: Deccan College.
———. 1981. *The Bhagavadgītā in the Mahābhārata.* Chicago: University of Chicago Press.
Veblen, T. 1965 [1899]. *The Theory of the Leisure Class.* New York: Augustus M. Kelley.
Waddington, C. H. 1974. "Horse Brands of the Mongolians: A System of Signs in a Nomadic Culture." *American Ethnologist* I:471–78.
Wagner, A. 1978. *Heralds and Ancestors.* London: British Museum.
Wallis, M. 1975. *Arts and Signs.* Bloomington: Research Center for Language and Semiotic Studies, Indiana University.
Warner, W. L. 1958 [1937]. *A Black Civilization.* New York: Harper & Row.
———. 1959. *The Living and the Dead: A Study of the Symbolic Life of Americans.* New Haven: Yale University Press.
———. 1961. *The Family of God: A Symbolic Study of Christian Life in America.* New Haven: Yale University Press.

————. 1963. *Yankee City.* New Haven: Yale University Press.
Warner, W. L., and P. S. Lunt. 1941. *The Social Life of a Modern Community.* New Haven: Yale University Press.
Warner, W. L., and L. Srole. 1945. *The Social System of American Ethnic Groups.* New Haven: Yale University Press.
Weber, M. 1958 [1920–21]. *The Religion of India: The Sociology of Hinduism and Buddhism.* Trans. H. H. Gerth and D. Martindale. Glencoe, Ill.: Free Press.
Weiner, M. 1978. *Sons of the Soil: Migration and Ethnic Conflict in India.* Princeton: Princeton University Press.
Weinreich, U. 1968. "Semantics and Semiotics." *International Encyclopedia of Social Sciences* 14:164–69.
Welby, V. 1903. *What is Meaning?* London: Macmillan.
————. 1911 [1903]. *Significs and Language.* London: Macmillan.
————. 1931. *Other Dimensions.* London: Jonathan Cape.
Wells, R. 1967. "Distinctively Human Semiotic." *Social Science Information* 6:103–24.
White, L. A. 1962. "Symboling: A Kind of Behavior." *Journal of Psychology* 53:311–17.
White, L., and B. Dillingham 1973. *The Concept of Culture.* Minneapolis: Burgess.
White, T. H. 1978. *In Search of History: A Personal Adventure.* New York: Harper & Row.
Whitehead, A. N. 1898. *A Treatise of Universal Algebra with Applications.* Cambridge: Cambridge University Press.
————. 1959 [1927]. *Symbolism: Its Meaning and Effect.* New York: Putnam.
Whittier, D. H. 1970. "Language and the Self." In *Studies in Philosophy and in the History of Science: Essays in Honor of Max Fisch,* ed. R. Tursman. Lawrence, Kans.: Coronado Press.
Whorf, B. L. 1956. *Language, Thought, and Reality: Selected Writings of Benjamin Lee Whorf.* Ed. J. B. Carroll. Cambridge: MIT Press.
Wilson, E. O. 1978. *On Human Nature.* Cambridge: Harvard University Press.
Wittgenstein, L. 1958. *Philosophical Investigations.* New York: Macmillan Co.
Wolf, E. 1958. "The Virgin of Guadalupe: A Mexican National Symbol." *Journal of American Folklore* LXXI:34–39.
————. 1974 [1964]. *Anthropology.* New York: Norton.
Yalman, N. 1969. "De Tocqueville in India: An Essay on the Caste System." Review article, *Man,* n.s. 4:122–31.
Yengoyan, A. A. 1979. "Economy, Society and Myth in Aboriginal Australia." *Annual Review of Anthropology* 8:393–415.
Yngve, V. H. 1975. "Human Linguistics and Face-to-Face Interaction." In *Organization of Behavior in Face-to-Face Interaction,* ed. A. Kendon et al. The Hague: Mouton.
————. 1981. "The Struggle for a Theory of Native Speaker." In *A Festschrift for Native Speaker,* ed. F. Coulmas. The Hague: Mouton.
Zeman, J. J. 1977. "Peirce's Theory of Signs." In *A Perfusion of Signs,* ed. T. A. Sebeok. Bloomington: Indiana University Press.

INDEX

Social life, conceived in terms of symbols, 122

Social organization: of tradition, 17, 164; and Redfield's definition of civilization, 38

Social personality, Warner's model of, 104

Social psychology: and Peirce's theory of the self, 75; and G. H. Mead's theory of the self, 94–95

Social relations: as "total social fact," 20; empirical concept of, 20; psychology of in Bali, 100

Social structure: as element of social system, 13; Redfield's concept of, 17; and fallacy of substantialization, 19–20; abstract models of, 20; contrasting conceptions of in anthropology, 30; as "general structural form," 20

Social system: Radcliffe-Brown's concept of, 13; as relational structure, 19; distinguished from culture, 35; Warner's concept of, 103

Social usages, expressing social structure, 13, 20

Societal structure, and Redfield, 33

Society: concept of in British anthropology, 34, 38; distinguished from culture, 34, 35; Redfield's definition of, 37, 98; as "loosely compacted person," 64, 82; as a "vast symbolism," 150; traditional Indian, 161

Sociocultural identity, and personal identity, 71–72

Sociolinguistics, 24, 28, 70

Sociology, French tradition of, and anthropology, 35

Sperber, D., 34

Srinivas, M. N.: *Religion and Society Among the Coorgs of South India* (1952), 17–18; and Radcliffe-Brown, 17–18; "Sanskritic Hinduism" and "Sanskritization," 164, 196

Stanner, W. E. H.: critique of Durkheim's theory of totemism, 112–13; theory of totemism, 117–18; on proper names as classes, 152

Structural analysis: limitations of, 7–8; actor-oriented vs. message-oriented, 46; and objects of iconic signs, 117

Structural anthropology. *See* structuralism

Structural-functionalism: and symbolism, 11–14; and structuralism, 16–18. *See also* Radcliffe-Brown

Structuralism: and French symbolists, 6; and symbolism, 6–9; and mathematical concept of structure, 7–8; Lévi-Strauss's formulations of, 7, 20, 24, 30; and formalism, 8; as "concrete science," 8; and configurationism, 14–15; British vs. French, 16–18, 19, 33, 46; and psycho-

analysis, 61; and philosophy, 61; and analysis of infrastructures and superstructures, 116; and "concrete logic," 117; as anthropological generalization, 121–22

Structure: mathematical concept of, 17, 19; in relation to symbol and reality, 18–21

Subject: myth-making, 21; Eco's treatment of, 48; of semiotic systems, 57–62; and communication, 63

Subjectification, strategy of: and concept of identity, 156; and Peirce's theory of signs, 157–58

Surnames, as emblems of identity, 138

Symbolic anthropology: and semiotic theory of self, 32, 72; and theory of person, 53–54

Symbolic congruence, of emblem's meanings, 145–46

Symbolic icons, Jakobson's definition of, 108

Symbolic interactionism: Parson's theory of, 48; and semiotic theory of the self, 72; and semiotics of dialogue, 74; and personality development, 78; and interpersonal dialogue, 81; and corporate personality, 91

Symbolic logic: discoveries in, 25–26; criteria of completeness and consistency, 25

Symbolic representations: and Durkheim, 11; structural opposition in, 12; in cultural performances, 108–10, 136, 165; interpretation of, 182–83

Symbolism and structuralism, 6–9; and structural-functionalism, 11–14; dual character of in Yankee City cemeteries, 128–29; dichotomy of visual and verbal, 134–35

—theories of: in anthropology, 6–10; and Malinowski, 9–11; and Radcliffe-Brown, 13–14; and V. Turner, 16; general, 22, 24–25; in mathematical formalization, 25; Peirce's conversational model, 27–28; and Warner, 102, 123, 180

Symbolists, French, and structuralism, 6

Symbolization: and emblems, 11; and Peirce's theory of the self, 159

Symbols: as natural signs, 5, 167; referential and condensation, 14; in definitions of "culture," 14–17, 35–37; in relation to structure and reality, 18–21; and the "native's point of view," 22; meaning of, 25–26; and mathematical concept of structure, 27; Peirce's definition of, 44, 60, 105, 122; linguistic, 57; and dialogue, 80; pronouns as, 101; Warner's definition of, 104, 123; examples of, 105–106; emblems as, 110, 128; and representation of natural species, 111, 114, 120–21; personality as, 117–18; of life, 119; of social values, 120; sacred vs. secular, 129–34; historical in Yankee City,